The bleak midwinter
1947

Alex J. Robertson

The bleak midwinter 1947

In the bleak mid-winter
  Frosty wind made moan,
Earth stood hard as iron,
  Water like a stone;
Snow had fallen, snow on snow,
  Snow on snow,
In the bleak mid-winter,
  Long ago.

Christina Rossetti (1830–94)

Manchester University Press ⑭

Copyright © Alex J. Robertson 1987
First published in 1987 by
Manchester University Press
Oxford Road, Manchester M13 9PL, U.K.
27 South Main Street, Wolfeboro, N.H. 03894-2069, U.S.A.

British Library cataloguing in publication data

Robertson, Alex J.
  The bleak mid-winter : Britain and the
  fuel crisis of 1947.
  1. Great Britain—History—George VI,
  1936–1952   2. Nineteen forty-seven, A.D.
  I. Title
  941.085'4   DA588

  ISBN 0-7190-1902-8

Library of Congress cataloging in publication data
  applied for

Typeset by Williams Graphics, Abergele, Clwyd, North Wales
Printed in Great Britain
by Robert Hartnoll (1985) Ltd, Bodmin, Cornwall

Contents

List of illustrations

Preface

In the hour of their great electoral victory in July 1945 there could have been few members of the Labour Party who would have admitted the possibility that in only six years or so their triumph might have gone sour with the return to office of a Conservative government. Yet in 1951 just such a transformation in Labour's fortunes indeed came about. Writing about these events as the long period of Conservative ascendancy that had begun in 1951 was drawing to its close, the political commentator Anthony Howard observed that:

> Occasionally late at night at a Labour Party conference − or in the small hours of the morning at the more strenuous gatherings of the T.U.C. − the cry can still be heard, 'Where,' a plaintive, maudlin voice will ask, 'did it go wrong?'

In any ensuing discussion, no doubt many suggestions would have been forthcoming. But there might have been many fraternal delegates who would have felt no need to look any further for explanation than the winter of 1946−47 and the crisis in fuel and power supplies that lay at the heart of it. That period − only a few months of the Attlee government's term of office − was widely seen when Howard was writing as a turning point in the government's fortunes. This was the view, indeed, of no less an authority than Hugh Dalton, who had then been Chancellor of the Exchequer. His memoirs, published in 1962, described the fuel crisis as:

> certainly the first really heavy blow to confidence in the Government and in our post-war plans. This soon began to show itself in many different and unwelcome ways. Never glad, confident morning again!

The crisis officially lasted for three weeks, from 10th February to 3rd March 1947. But in fact its duration was much longer than the official chronology was prepared to allow, stretching for weeks, if not months, on either side of those dates. It is with this event that the book is primarily concerned. My chief intention has been to examine the fuel crisis in all its aspects, and I hope that readers will obtain a clear view of its duration, causes, character and ramifications from what follows. The weather during the early months of 1947 itself constituted a kind of crisis, being so bad as to make that winter a strong contender among meteorologists for the title of worst British winter on record. Indeed, the two events, fuel crisis and weather crisis, were so closely intertwined that they should perhaps be seen simply as two aspects of a single 'winter crisis'. Because of this, the weather too figures prominently in the book as a phenomenon that heightened enormously the hardships occasioned by the dearth of fuel.

There was no shortage of crises in Britain in early 1947, either present or imminent, and some of the others also pass across the stage in our story. Mention will be found, for example, of the crises in housing, in food supply and in the balance of payments. 'Crisis' was a much overworked word at that time. But these, as it were, subsidiary crises are dealt with only in so far as they relate to the two principal problems with which this book is concerned, the weather and the shortage of fuel and power.

Being an academic historian, it was inevitable that I should approach the writing of the book from an academic point of view, using the methods and materials proper to my profession. But although the book has a serious academic character and intent as a study of an episode of real significance in recent British history, I hope the contents and the way they are presented will appeal to more than simply an academic readership. While working on the book it became plain to me, as a result of many conversations with people who lived through the winter of 1946–47, either (like myself) as children or as adults, that many retained vivid personal memories of the experience and took a lively interest in what I was going to say about it. With their interest in mind, I have tried to ensure that the story of what happened is not obscured by the weight of formal academic analysis. I hope they will find in the book a satisfactory general context into which they can fit their own recollections.

One point about the sources and methods employed in the preparation of the book ought to be made at this early juncture. Despite what has just been said about the liveliness of people's recollections, the book is based almost exclusively on documentary evidence. I have not conducted interviews among the many participants in the events described who happily are still to the fore. This omission perhaps requires some explanation, especially in view of the present vogue for what is called oral history.

When I embarked on the project it was my intention to interview people like the late Lord Shinwell (who is the main character in the story in so far as there can be said to be one) and some of the other parliamentary and civil service survivors from the Attlee years. But the documentary record of the period, it rapidly became clear, was so extensive and detailed that there seemed to be no significant gaps of the kind which oral evidence can be so useful in bridging. My doubts about the necessity for oral evidence were then reinforced by misgivings about its reliability in this case. These arose partly from the fact that when a postgraduate student whose thesis on the Attlee government's economic policies I was supervising requested interviews with some of the surviving civil servants of that time, they generally referred him back to the documentary record as more reliable than personal recall of the events of nearly forty years ago. Then, when I read in quick succession four separate accounts of the Fuel Crisis published by Lord Shinwell over the space of some twenty-five years, my doubts grew stronger. To say that his accounts were not entirely consistent with one another would be to put it mildly. They provided an object lesson in the way in which perception of an event can alter with the passage of time, and brought vividly to mind the words of Shakespeare's Henry V on the eve of Agincourt:

> Old men forget: yet all shall be forgot,
> But he'll remember with advantages
> What feats he did that day.

On these grounds, I stand by the decision to rely essentially on the documentary evidence available to me.

I am deeply conscious of the debts I owe to a variety of individuals and institutions for the help they have given me in the preparation of this book. It is difficult to know where to begin in expressing my gratitude to them, and if anything even more difficult to know where to stop. If I might begin with the institutions, I must first of all express my thanks to the Nuffield Foundation for the research grant I was awarded in 1981 to enable me to undertake most of the basic research for the book in the libraries and record repositories of London. My own university supplemented this financial assistance with a generous provision of study leave. Without the time and the money these two august bodies made available, my progress would, to say the least, have been very much slower.

Every historian is massively in debt to those who preserve and make available the sources on which historical scholarship depends. My thanks in this connection are particularly due to the staff of the Public Record Office at Kew, but I am also under considerable obligations to those who work in several other libraries and archives. The Archive Department of the British Library of Political and Economic Science (London School of Economics) was extremely helpful, as were the British Library's newspaper department at Colindale and the Mass Observation Archive at the University of Sussex. Closer to home, the John Rylands University Library of Manchester and the City of Manchester Central Reference Library are equally deserving of my gratitude.

My colleagues in the Department of Economic History at Manchester University have all been most helpful, but I must thank in particular

Professor A. E. Musson for encouraging me to embark on this book in the first place. A brief conversation with Sir Alec Cairncross not only gave me a number of things to think about that I might otherwise have missed, but made me wonder about the wisdom of my decision as to the use of oral material. The intellectual stimulus provided by the undergraduates who have taken my Special Subject course, and the postgraduate students whose work I have supervised, over the past ten years or so has been extremely important in helping me to develop my ideas about the winter of crisis in 1947. My wife, Marie, and our two children have put up patiently with my preoccupation with the events of forty years ago and my frequent and prolonged withdrawals from normal family life as I tried to set my ideas down on paper. My gratitude to them knows no bounds.

1

The very dead of winter

The ways deep, the weather sharp, the days short, the sun
furthest off *in solstitio brumali*, the very dead of winter.

Bishop Lancelot Andrewes (1555–1626), *Of the Nativity*

By the onset of winter in 1946 enough had gone wrong with the readjustment to peacetime in Britain for people to take an increasingly jaundiced view of the high hopes and aspirations of the summer of 1945, when victory was fresh and peace an exciting novelty. There were, of course, many positive developments of a popular kind taking place under the direction of the new Labour government which had been returned with such an overwhelming majority — an advantage of 146 seats over all other parties combined in the House of Commons — in the previous summer's general election. Labour's programmes for the nationalisation of basic sectors of the economy and for far-reaching changes in the system of social welfare evidently enjoyed massive support in the country, and now seemed to be proceeding quickly, if not always smoothly, towards fruition. The Bank of England had already been brought under public ownership in the spring of 1946, as had the airlines, and plans were already well advanced for the railways, the coal, gas and electricity industries, and others to follow in the same path. The plans of the Minister of Health, Aneurin Bevan, to nationalise, in effect, the nation's health services had been unveiled in March 1946; and the Act of Parliament which embodied them received the royal assent on 6th November in spite of continuing opposition by the British Medical Association. The 1946 National Insurance Act marked the beginning of the final assault on the surviving vestiges of the detested Poor Law. All these things represented important planks in the platform that had carried the government to its great victory in 1945 and which was meant to usher in a new and better post-war world. In these areas, then, both the government and those who had backed it with their votes had every cause for satisfaction in hopes fulfilled.

In other respects this was not so clearly the case. In foreign affairs, things had begun to go sour very quickly after the end of the war, which proved to be a powerful solvent on the cement that held the wartime grand coalition of Britain, America and Russia together. In its election campaign the Labour Party had promoted the impression that it was uniquely well placed among the parties to deal with Russia on a basis of mutual respect and sympathy. 'Left understands Left,' Ernest Bevin had claimed in this connection at the party's 1945 conference. By 1946 Bevin's abortive effort to secure an extension to the Twenty-year Anglo-Soviet Treaty made it clear that in reality his party had few advantages over the others in handling the Soviet Union. Britain was in difficulties in Greece, where the continued presence of her troops was denounced by the Russians at the United Nations as a threat to world peace. She was in trouble in Palestine, caught in the crossfire between Zionism and Pan-Arabism. Indeed, there was quite a large body of British servicemen in various parts of the world (to say nothing of their next of kin) to whom the idea that 1946 was a year of peace must have seemed like a joke in poor taste.

Perhaps the most hurtful and puzzling aspect of post-war developments in foreign relations for the British lay in their dealings with the United States. The British had regarded themselves between 1941 and 1945 as equal partners with the Americans in the great enterprise of defeating fascist tyranny. But when the war was over it became evident that the Americans did not view the British connection in the same light. This was dramatically revealed in the events that followed from the abrupt and (for the British) unexpected American cancellation of Lend-Lease in September 1945. It left Britain with an immense balance-of-payments problem, as her export trade and her income from overseas investments, shipping services and so on had all been drastically run down in wartime, while her imports (supported by Lend-Lease) had not. It was reckoned that the balance of payments would continue to accumulate a deficit for several years after the war, to the tune of some £1,250 million, all told. How was the deficit to be covered? Our good and generous American allies would surely see to that with a loan on the easiest of terms. But the British negotiators in Washington at the end of 1945 found that the Anglo-American relationship in peacetime was not what it had been in war. There were many competing claims on American generosity, and Britain's was less eligible than quite a few others, from countries whose economic life and assets had been more severely disrupted than had Britain's, or whose case simply got more favourable publicity on Capitol Hill. The Chancellor of the Exchequer, Hugh Dalton, who was the Minister most closely involved in negotiations for American aid, described the progressive lowering of British expectations in the face of seeming American indifference, even hostility, to Britain's plight:

> So, as the talks went on, we retreated, slowly and with a bad grace and with increasing irritation, from a free gift to an interest-free loan, and from this to a loan bearing interest; from a larger to a smaller total of aid; and from the prospect of loose strings, some of which would be only general declarations of intention, to the most unwilling acceptance of strings so tight that they might strangle our trade and, indeed, our whole economic life.[1]

What emerged from the negotiations was an American 'line of credit' for $3,750 million (£930 million), on terms which − while admittedly far less favourable than the British had expected − were not in most respects as harsh as they were made out by commentators who were frustrated and bewildered by the attitude of their great wartime ally. When the matter came to be discussed in the House of Commons the Conservative MP Oliver Stanley observed that a visitor from Mars, entering the Chamber, might well be pardoned for thinking that he was listening to the representatives of a vanquished people discussing the economic penalties of defeat.[2]

He exaggerated, but clearly Britain's status in American eyes was not that to which the British thought their wartime efforts entitled them.

The balance-of-payments situation was indeed serious in 1945 and 1946, with a current account deficit in the latter year of £230 million or so. But there were also hopeful signs on the economic front: exports in 1946, for instance, were more than twice the 1945 figure, while imports had risen by only 18%. And among the former belligerents of Europe, Britain was unique in the fact that her industrial output in 1946 matched the pre-war level.[3] It was this kind of thing, indeed, that underlay the relatively low priority given by America to British claims: most other countries were a great deal worse off. But the British people themselves were not very impressed by calculations of aggregate industrial output and other such pieces of mathematical prestidigitation practised by economists. The ordinary Briton's appreciation of the economic situation was based on more down-to-earth considerations, and by such workaday standards of measurement things did not look good.

By November 1946 the inhabitants of these islands had undergone seven years of increasing constraints on the consumption of even the most commonplace commodities. The exigencies of war had brought restrictions on the supply of food and drink, tobacco, shoes, clothing, fuel, furniture, household utensils and so on. Rationing and price controls had ensured some measure at least of fairness in the distribution of such commodities as were available. There is no denying that British civilian consumers had been well served by comparison with most Europeans. But the restrictions on the supply of goods hd been irksome nevertheless, the more so since average earnings had gone up by more than a third between 1940 and 1945 while prices (according to the official retail index, at any rate) had gone up by only about 10%.[4] At the end of the war there was a growing reservoir of pent-up purchasing power in the economy, waiting to be released when the supply of goods became freer — as people confidently expected it would when hostilities came to an end. Not that anyone seriously expected all restrictions to be lifted right away to make room for an orgy of self-indulgence. The need to maintain many economic controls for some time was widely accepted as a means of ensuring an orderly transition of the economy from war to peace, avoiding the well remembered boom—slump cycle of 1918–1921. But there was a general expectation that peacetime would bring some easing of restrictions, allowing perhaps for the replacement of worn-out wartime wardrobes, a few more eggs and oranges, and maybe even the occasional bottle of whisky to celebrate the deliverance from war.

Material standards among the civil population after six years of war had deteriorated badly. When King George VI wrote to his brother, the Duke of Gloucester, in January 1946 that 'food, clothes and fuel are the main topics of conversation with us all' he was speaking not for his own intimate circle but for a very large proportion of his subjects. Shortly afterwards the King proposed to his Prime Minister that the government should adopt a more generous attitude to the provision of civilian clothing: 'I said we must all have new clothes & my family are down to the lowest ebb.'[5] The prevailing mood, however, was that things would indeed gradually and steadily improve. This feeling of cautious optimism was caught at the very beginning of 1946 by the *Daily Mirror* with a report that:

> Progress in the switch to peace production is showing itself in varying degree in the output of furniture, household goods, carpets, linoleum, wireless sets, motor-cars and cycles, cotton and rayon.
> And targets set by manufacturers for 1946 promise great strides.[6]

Returning to the theme the following day, the *Mirror* concluded that these developments:

> will mean a certain slackening of 'austerity' at home, but for the present it would be unwise to expect a large flow of goods for individual consumption in this country.[7]

In the event it was the last of the *Mirror*'s predictions that turned out to be the most justified: events were to prove that any expectation of an improved flow of consumer goods would have been exceedingly unwise, and far from becoming easier the lot of the consumer became steadily worse as 1946 wore on. Already, towards the end of 1945, the government had felt obliged to cut down on a whole range of imported goods for which payment had to be made in scarce American dollars, among them such basic items of consumption as bacon, cheese, dried egg powder and Virginia tobacco. But the continued balance-of-payments deficit of 1946 necessitated further restrictions on the supply of such commodities, and in July there came perhaps the most psychologically damaging event of this kind. Bread was to be rationed, something which had not been thought necessary even in the darkest days of the war.

During the war, when many other staple foods were in short supply, bread had become the essential stomach-filler, the necessary padding in an otherwise shrinking diet. Yet here in peacetime even that poor comfort was being threatened. The government could justify the measure in terms of safeguarding the balance of payments, and as a contribution to the alleviation of the world-wide scarcity of grain that had resulted from the combination of bad weather and wartime disruption of agriculture. But they had difficulty in getting this message across; to the ordinary Briton, bread rationing perhaps more than anything else brought home the fact that peacetime – far from bringing that 'certain slackening of "austerity"' which the *Mirror* had so blithely predicted – would mean yet more belt-tightening. What this meant in practice was set out for the Cabinet by a young scientist named Magnus Pyke, who worked in the Ministry of Food. Nutritional standards in 1945 and 1946, he reported, had fallen substantially enough to check and even reverse the improved physical state exhibited during the war by British children and adolescents.[8]

The situation with regard to other consumer goods was not so bad as that affecting food. In fact the position was improving at a fair pace. The London and Cambridge Economic Service – an academic body quite independent of government – was able to report that in the second quarter of 1946 the volume of retail trade in items other than foodstuffs was nearly one third greater than it had been in the preceding quarter, 'stimulated by increased supplies (especially of household goods), release of new clothing coupons and downpointing, purchase tax reductions, etc.'[9] But the statistical niceties of the situation were perhaps less appreciated by the ordinary consumer. What he or she saw instead were the advertisements appearing in all sections of the press, covering a whole range of goods from luxuries like whisky and motor cars to more mundane items like chocolate and soap powder, which – instead of exhorting the would-be consumer to rush out and buy – apologised instead for their continued non-availability. Thus, under the headline 'Courtauld's Rayons, for loveliness that lasts', the copy-writer lamented at the beginning of 1946 that 'It may be some little time yet before dresses and lingerie made from Courtauld's rayons are back in the shops in pre-1939 abundance'.[10]

And there, in a nutshell, was the consumer's problem: a 30% increase in the volume of retail sales from the first quarter of 1946 to the second still left the market place some way behind what people remembered fondly as *real* peacetime conditions, before the war. And the discipline which many had been willing to impose on their frustrated propensity to consume was not so easy to accept once the war was over. It was all very well for the government to explain the necessity for diverting many of the consumer goods that were being produced to export markets, to narrow the dreaded 'dollar gap'. Frustrated by six years of restraint and restriction, tantalised by the nostalgic tone of advertisements recalling pre-war plenty, and with money to spend as a result of the gap between wages rising steadily in conditions of full employment and prices for basic items like food, fuel and rent stabilised by the State — consumers were not readily impressed by rational explanations of continued austerity. If they could not satisfy their desires by legitimate means, then they would find others. Petty crime and its practitioners flourished, continuing a trend that had begun during the war itself. Indictable offences reported to the police of England, Scotland and Wales in 1946 were up by nearly two-thirds on 1938, with crimes against property (with or without violence) rather than crimes against persons as the main growth sector. Stolen goods, perhaps 'liberated' from an export consignment at or *en route* to the docks, were easily disposed of to an affluent public deprived of full opportunities for honest dealing. The 'spiv' — member of a new class of entrepreneur operating in a market that shaded from pale grey to deepest black — came into his own.[11]

All things considered, the ordinary Briton at the onset of winter in 1946 could be forgiven for finding little comfort in his or her situation. The ingratitude of allies was by now only too apparent. And the very real economic successes by way of rebuilding the export trade and securing an orderly change-over from wartime to peacetime production in industry made less impact upon ordinary life than the increased scale of deprivation as 'austerity' was screwed up to a new pitch. The Welfare State was certainly under construction, but still some way from being ready to go into operation. Even the weather was behaving strangely.[12]

In November 1946 it was chiefly determined by a series of deep depressions (as if to match the growing mood of the man in the street) moving in over western Europe and the British Isles from the Atlantic. The weather which these inflicted upon the British was wet: all parts of the United Kingdom experienced rainfall that was substantially higher than usual for November. A spectacular seven inches of rain fell in one day, 23rd November, at Princetown in the grim shadow of Dartmoor Prison, and England as a whole was afflicted with a monthly rainfall 78% higher than average for the time of year. As was only to be expected, the weather was also inordinately dull, with only about two-thirds the average November's sunshine. And, to crown it all, November 1946 was much warmer than usual, temperatures rising as high as 71°F (22°C). Dull, wet and muggy, the November weather was no morale-booster.

December began as November had left off, with further depressions moving in from the west and bringing rain on their coat tails. But towards the middle of the month conditions began to change, for the brighter if not for the better. An intense anti-cyclone or area of high barometric pressure from Russia moved westwards, bringing with it a dry, bright but very cold period from mid-December until about Christmas. Temperatures fell as low as 8°F (−13°C), though as some compensation there was a great deal more sunshine than usual for December. Some snow fell in south-east England on the 19th, but not enough to cause serious inconvenience.

Around the turn of the year the Russian anti-cyclone retreated to its lair in the Urals, and Britain's weather once again fell under the influence of the Atlantic depressions. The first half of January was generally stormy and wet, though punctuated by a brief but intense cold spell with heavy snow from the 5th to the 7th. In the middle of the month, however, the stormy conditions gave way to a period of unusual mildness, with temperatures rising as high as 57°F (14°C), which did nothing to prepare people for what was about to befall them. For 18th January 1947 was the last mild day most people were to experience for some time. The next seven or eight weeks would provide an ordeal by weather unequalled in the long time during which systematic meteorological records have been kept.

By the beginning of 1947 meteorology was a fairly well developed science, in Britain governed largely by the Air Ministry. Considerable strides in meteorology generally, and in weather forecasting in particular, had been made during the war. Weather conditions had been recognised as a crucial factor governing all kinds of military operations, especially large-scale air operations and perhaps above all the massive combined operations exemplified by the Allied landings in North Africa in 1942, in Italy in 1943 and in France in 1944. As is well known, this last in particular had hung on the word of the chief meteorologist at Eisenhower's headquarters on 5th June 1944, having been postponed for twenty-four hours because of bad weather.

The end of the war carried the study of the weather and the techniques of forecasting further still by making it possible to reactivate the institutions of international co-operation, such as the International Meteorological Organisation, that had fallen into abeyance during the war. But weather forecasting in 1947 — especially where the long-range outlook was concerned, but even with regard to the short-term picture — was still far from being an exact science. Nor is it nowadays, of course, despite the application of a technology vastly more sophisticated than anything available then. In any event, forecasts gave no inkling of what was about to happen between late January and mid-March. There was nothing in the pattern as it unfolded up to 22nd January to suggest that a prolonged hard spell was likely. Indeed, the winter had so far been remarkably mild, if rather wet, apart from the two short cold spells in mid-December and early January. The comparative warmth of mid-January had given way after the 18th to colder conditions, with some touches of night frost. But these conditions were nothing out of the ordinary for the time of year.

The published weather forecast on Thursday 23rd January predicted cold and mainly dry weather, with 'scattered wintry showers' in the south-east and the widespread prospect of 'keen frost'. The outlook was reckoned to be

Continuing cold and mainly dry, probably for several days.[13]

But before the day was out the weather god had begun to demonstrate that he had something else in store than what was being predicted by the inhabitants of the Air Ministry roof.

In the evening of 23rd January it began to snow. This was no slight spattering from 'scattered wintry showers' but a steady, silent downpour which enveloped London and the south-eastern counties. By the morning of Friday 24th the south-east was blanketed to a depth of as much as six inches, and other parts of the country, mainly to the east, had also had a share. To those who were thus afflicted it probably came as little comfort that they were not alone: it had also been snowing — even more unexpectedly — in the Azores.

This first taste of snow on the night of 23rd and 24th January, the weather forecasters now prophesied, would not be the last. More snow was forecast for the weekend, and duly arrived, accompanied by intense cold to the extent in some places of twenty Fahrenheit degrees of frost ($-11\,^{\circ}$C). The Saturday was not too bad; cold and with flurries of snow, but relieved by occasional intervals of sunshine. Sunday 26th January was something else: *The Times*, not usually given to over-dramatising the news, felt justified in describing it as 'one of the wildest days of the winter, with frost, snow, and a bitter wind that sometimes reached gale force'. Once again, the south-eastern region was hardest hit. By Saturday morning parts of Kent were already under nine inches of snow: by Monday 27th, what with gale-force winds and continuous snow falls over more than twenty-four hours, great snowdrifts up to ten feet deep had become common hazards over a large area of that country. Its neighbours — Sussex, Surrey and Essex — got off only a little more lightly.

Any unpleasantness visited upon the south of England tends to be viewed with a certain complacency by north-countrymen, Scots and Welshmen. On this occasion, however, they did not enjoy the discomfort of the supposedly effete south-east for long. In the course of Sunday 26th January the steady, continuous snowfall which had begun in the south-east the previous evening spread until it had covered virtually the entire face of Britain. The following morning *The Times* could report that 'Most of the country was last night covered with snow, which varied in depth from an inch to four feet'. There could have been few who would have imagined that it would stay that way for the next seven weeks or so.

The weather of the period from the weekend of 24th–26th January 1947 through February and into the middle of March established various records for unpleasantness, most of which still stand, despite some impressive attempts to surpass them in the early parts of 1963 and 1979, and between December 1981 and January 1982. None of these quite succeeded, though, in matching either the duration or the sheer comprehensiveness of the meteorological horrors of 1947. For a start, there was the unrelieved dullness: throughout most of the country – the west of Scotland being the only significant exception – people were denied even the most fleeting glimpse of the sun during almost the whole month of February. The observatory at Kew, for instance, recorded no sunshine at all from 2nd to 22nd February, the longest sunless period ever chronicled there. Then there was the constant cold, which descended into bouts of extreme frigidity lasting for days on end. Indeed, over a large part of the country the frost did not break at all between 11th and 23rd February, and the breaks that occurred at either end of that period were too brief to constitute serious relief. The mean maximum temperature recorded for February 1947 by the Greenwich observatory was the lowest registered for any month for well over a hundred years. Exceptionally keen frosts occurred at the two extremities of the period of bad weather, between 23rd and 25th January and again in the first eight days of March. Nor was the cold simply a matter of frost: the already freezing conditions were aggravated by a raw, penetrating wind from the east which blew without deviation for a solid month up to 22nd February – one of the longest such spells in the country's meteorological record. So to the freezing temperature was added a severe wind-chill factor.

To crown it all, of course, there was the snow. After the initial onslaught of 23rd–27th January almost the entire area of the United Kingdom experienced continuous snow cover until at least 13th March. On every single day between 22nd January and 17th March snow fell, not just on the hills where it would normally be expected at that time of year, but in low-lying areas as well. The result was that snow cover was not only prolonged and extensive, it was also very deep by normal standards. Leaving aside the spectacular instances of drifting to depths of ten feet or more (and by early March even these had become so commonplace as hardly to excite comment), snow cover to a level depth of as much as two feet was quite common. And the snow did not arrive in a gentle and picturesque manner. It came instead in a series of wild bursts, a sequence of furious blizzards no single one of which, perhaps, was unprecedented in its intensity but which, raging in from the east in steady succession, added up to a unique aggregation of climatic malevolence.

People were still trying to sort themselves out after the initial blizzard of 26th—28th January when the next blow fell on 3rd—4th February. This time it was the north and north midlands of England which were worst hit by a snow storm of great violence. The weather forecast had given warning only of snow on high ground, which did nothing to prepare people in places as far apart as Durham, Lincolnshire, the Lake District and the Derbyshire dales for a fall which continued non-stop for as much as thirty-six hours during which snow drifted to depths of ten or twelve feet. Hardly had those affected had a chance to dig themselves out when another blizzard struck on the following weekend, 8th—9th February. Its main target was London and the Home Counties, where up to ten inches of snow was experienced. This time people were given a little longer to recover: the weather remained bleak and raw, but in a relatively undramatic way which allowed the newspapers to devote their heaviest type briefly to other matters.

Some respite was undoubtedly needed, but the breathing space lasted less than two weeks. On Thursday 20th February heavy snow began to fall in the West Country and to spread north and east so as to cover more or less the whole of Britain during the next two days. A few days later, on the 26th, the north of England and Scotland experienced a short but quite spectacular blizzard on a day which, farther south, was noteworthy for being the first dry, bright, relatively mild one for some five weeks. To make up, perhaps, for this discrimination, the next storm a week later (4th—5th March) struck mainly at the south and midlands of England and was reckoned by some experts to be the worst of the entire winter. But with that the end of the ordeal by weather was almost in sight. The inhabitants of Northern Ireland, the south of Scotland and the north of England were the luckless recipients of one final blizzard on 12th and 13th March, the worst they had so far encountered. By that time, however, the south had begun to thaw out, and the thaw spread gradually northwards, to reach Scotland by 16th March. But the weather god had one final shot in his locker. The rain which had accompanied the thaw, coupled with the melting of the accumulated snow, brought serious flooding to no fewer than thirty-one counties. Rainwater and melting snow cascaded off the still frozen ground to overwhelm the river systems. Exceptionally high spring tides kept the melt water backed up in the rivers, forcing their levels up to record heights. The Thames, the Trent and the East Anglian river Ouse saw the worst flooding, but the Welland, the Medway, the Yorkshire Ouse and the Severn were also heavily affected, the last-named being at its highest level since 1770.

Constant cold induced by east winds and frost, the prolonged absence of sunshine, perpetual snow delivered by the dribble and by the ton —

any one of these conditions and the discomfort it could cause, expecially when prolonged over seven or eight weeks, would have been enough to test the sagging morale of the great British public. The combination of all three, topped off by the worst floods in fifty years, might have been expected to result in total demoralisation, especially in view of the other conditions that accompanied this worst winter on record.

The weather itself was an obvious cause of all sorts of disruption and deprivation, as well as calling forth many acts of personal heroism and even − though not very often − providing a source of amusement. Transport was perhaps the most obvious victim. Free passage on the roads was constantly bedevilled by the more or less continuous falls of snow. The storms bunched so close together that the precipitation from one piled up on the uncleared remains of its predecessors and the task of clearance became herculean. A full ten days after the blizzard of 8th−9th February had hit the south-east − bringing snow ploughs on to the streets of London for the first time in living memory − more than sixty trunk roads remained blocked, and another hundred or so were only partially cleared. After the earlier visitation of 3rd−4th February, the Automobile Association described England as:

> a country divided into two parts, one each side of a line from the Mersey through the Peak District to the Humber. Road communication between these two parts is well-nigh impossible as a result of snow drifts several feet deep.[14]

During the great storms, indeed, many roads all but disappeared under the drifts, leaving only the tops of the telegraph poles to mark the line of the right of way. When this happened on a grand scale, to every road whether major or minor within a highway authority's jurisdiction, it is hardly to be wondered at that clearance could take up to two weeks. No authority was equipped to handle that sort of problem.

During the great storms, road conditions could deteriorate so quickly that large numbers of vehicles became stranded and eventually snowed under. Quite apart from aggravating the problem of snow clearance through snowbound vehicles obstructing the snow ploughs, this situation contained the threat of tragedy as the drivers and passengers of trucks, cars and buses were unexpectedly trapped with their vehicles in some of the wildest weather recorded. On Monday 3rd February, for instance, there had seemed likely to be a break in the pattern of very cold weather as a slow thaw appeared gradually to be spreading throughout the country. In these comparatively clement conditions, several coach parties set out from various communities in East Yorkshire to attend the pantomimes then showing in the theatres of Leeds. By the time they were on their way home they faced blizzard conditions which led to over a hundred people being trapped in buses on the road between York and Hull. Their experience was shared by hundreds of others in different parts of the country between 23rd January and 16th March, but surprisingly few seem to have suffered any ill effects from such ordeals and there were very few fatalities.

Rail traffic was affected by the weather just as adversely as road transport, with the difference that the railway companies (for the system was not yet nationalised) were perhaps better equipped technically to deal with the snow than were the local authorities responsible for road clearance. Even so, lines became blocked by drifted snow in cuttings and similar places, and pictures of immobilised trains being dug laboriously out of drifts by gangs of men with shovels were part of the staple fare in the popular press throughout February. The weather brought about some bizarre accidents, as when on 29th January the fireman of the 6.23 a.m. Huddersfield–Bradford train leaned out of the cab as his locomotive passed under a bridge and was knocked out cold by an enormous icicle hanging from the underside. Later the same day, passengers on the 8.40 p.m. Penzance–Paddington sleeping-car express experienced the rigours of travel under such conditions. By the time it reached Exeter – just over a hundred miles from its starting point – the train was already nine hours behind schedule. Relays of railwaymen had to dig a path for it by hand in places through snow two feet deep and 'settling almost as fast as it was dug away', the *Railway Gazette* reported. The train being made up of sleeping cars, passengers were well equipped with blankets and other aids to warmth. But there was no dining car attached, so orders were telegraphed along the line through Westbury, Marlborough and Reading to London for station staff to man their buffets and provide hot drinks and sustenance for the intrepid travellers. Curiously, the *Gazette* failed to record the time of the train's arrival at Paddington after this epic journey.[15]

For the rail traveller, whether on long-distance or suburban lines, such experiences were confined to the immediate periods of particular storms. The railways were well supplied with snow ploughs, and clearing the main lines, both north-to-south and east-to-west, was a routine winter operation of which railwaymen had considerable experience. Lines could be reopened fairly quickly after a blizzard, and the only unusual feature of the early months of 1947 was perhaps the frequency with which the job had to be done. The storms caused a lot of disruption, however, in the short term, in the form of long delays, train cancellations and technical problems such as frozen points and electrical systems short-circuiting in damp snow.

After seven years of wartime train travel the British were inured to discomfort and uncertainty on the railways, but the wintry conditions of early 1947 added a new dimension of inconvenience.

Air travel too was severely disrupted, though no serious accidents seem to have been directly attributable to the blizzards. In any case, civil air transport was not a very significant element of transport facilities in 1947. Air freight and passenger loads in 1946 had been respectively 0·003% and 0·033% of the equivalent railway loadings. Sea communication, however, was much more important, and it too was subjected to serious difficulties. The east-coast ports of England were worst affected, the problems once again being most acute during the actual blizzards, as on 23rd January, when snow, hail and a powerful north-east wind kept most of the fishing fleet in port. This first storm also disrupted cross-Channel ferry services, not least because the sea in the habour at Folkestone froze, as did the Thames in its upper reaches and the river Medway. Particularly hard hit by conditions on the eastern coastal sea route was the still large-scale shipborne coal trade between Northumberland, Durham and the Port of London. On 6th February it was reported that fifty-seven loaded colliers were stormbound in north-eastern ports, and thirty more were marooned empty in the Thames, unable to sail north for fresh cargoes. This at a time when, thanks to the blizzard of 3rd—4th February, the movement of coal by rail had virtually stopped. This cessation of both sea and rail transport of coal had created, so the Ministry of Fuel and Power announced, a 'most serious situation ... in regard to the supply of coal throughout the country'.[16]

By 12th February the number of stormbound colliers in the Tyne had risen to 125, and it was not until three days later that the movement of coal coastwise to London was reported to have eased. With the prolonged period of very cold weather, aided and abetted by the protracted set of the wind from the east, ice was becoming a hazard to navigation off England's east coast, especially around East Anglia, on a scale that caused some concern. Not only were substantial bodies of ice a danger to small coasting vessels by their mere presence in the sealanes by late February; they were a greater hazard because they were sweeping away buoys and other aids to navigation which marked the safe channels through still unswept wartime minefields. On Friday 21st February sailings of the Dover—Ostende ferry were suspended because of icefloes on its route. Nor was it only seagoing shipping that was endangered: on 22nd February it was reported that boats taking part in the Oxford University Torpids event on the Thames were also threatened with the fate of the *Titanic*, and the races were suspended for two days.

Snowdrifts, storms, the disruption of transport and supplies all contributed to the undermining of normal conditions of everyday comfort for individuals and communities everywhere, but especially in the rural areas. Among the normal amenities of civilised life, the first casualty – apart from public transport – seems to have been household milk deliveries, suspended in some parts of the country on the first weekend of the great freeze-up. The state of civilian food supplies under an increasingly rigorous system of rationing was such that few people had very much in the way of accumulated reserves to tide them over even a brief suspension of normal deliveries. And within a few days of the first severe snowfall during the last week in January, many small isolated villages found that supplies of basic rationed foodstuffs were desperately low. From one such village – Beaumont in Essex, between Clacton and Harwich – two people struggled on foot for twelve miles through the deeply drifted snow to reach Dovercourt on the Harwich road to get food for the village, as the week's rations had not been delivered. Heavy snowfalls in the West Country a couple of days later cut off many of the moorland villages, among those affected being the inmates of Dartmoor Prison, as well as communities on the South Devon coast. The Salcombe lifeboat had to be called out to deliver bread to these coastal communities; but it could offer no assistance to the inland village of Simonsbath on Exmoor, 'some of whose inhabitants', *The Times* reported on 1st February, 'were yesterday down to their last loaf'. At Spurn Point it was the lifeboat station itself that was without bread. This was a situation that before very long was to threaten thousands of households in places normally much less prone to winter isolation than the villages of Exmoor. In the city of Sheffield, for instance, although bread supplies were not a real problem, 60% of households could get no milk on 6th February, as the Co-operative dairy which supplied them was cut off from its rural suppliers in Derbyshire.

Elsewhere in Yorkshire by that time the Royal Air Force was being called in to parachute basic food and fodder supplies to isolated farms and villages, and the following week the system of air-dropping had to be extended to more southerly communities. A squadron of four-engined Halifax heavy bombers was moved to the RAF airfield at Fairford in Gloucestershire to drop food and other supplies to villages in Staffordshire and other counties in the heart of England. The squadron's first mission, to supply the village of Butterton in Staffordshire, saw the death of its commander, his crew, and two journalists who had hitched a ride to report this rather unusual inaugural flight, when the Halifax crashed on its run over the village.[17]

It was not simply food supplies which had difficulty getting through. After the second great blizzard, in early February, it was reported that over large areas of northern England the weather had prevented the Royal Mail itself from being delivered. In several parishes the dead could not be buried because the ground was frozen too hard for the grave-diggers to penetrate. And at least one family, at Sheerness in Kent, found that the usual alternative method of taking the last leave of a departed relative was also temporarily closed to them: the hearse could not reach the crematorium because the roads were blocked by snow.

Less solemn occasions were also disrupted. Reporting the cancellations of the horse-racing at Plumpton and Wincanton on 22nd February, *The Times* recorded that it was now more than one month since the country's last race meeting had taken place, at Birmingham on 21st January. Most other forms of outdoor sport enjoyed similar records of cancellation and curtailment, to the undoubted frustration of those enthusiasts who, as players or spectators, were beginning to get accustomed again by 1947 to the resumption of normal peacetime programmes of events and fixtures in place of the confused and makeshift arrangements of wartime. But some sportsmen were made of sterner stuff. Plumpton and Wincanton race courses may have been unfit for use on 22nd February, and the grounds employed for the various species of football may for the most part have been declared unplayable due to snow and frost. But nothing like that was going to stop the English regional cross-country running championships − the Northern at Gosforth Park and the Southern at Ascot − from going ahead as planned.

Deprived of their more conventional Saturday pastimes, people turned to unusual alternatives. In London 'record crowds' were reported to have turned out on Hampstead Heath 'to watch winter sports', and extra police had to be drafted in to control the traffic. Curiously enough, only cricket lovers were able to rely on a regular diet of their favourite sport. Indeed, their diet was richer perhaps than they may have had any reason to expect, since, in the absence of much else to report by way of sport, the sports editors were giving great prominence to the activities of the MCC touring team in Australia. To preserve the balance, however, the news from that quarter on this particular Saturday was not good: MCC had only been able to amass 200 runs for seven wickets in response to the New South Wales first-innings total of 342.

Strenuous exercise may, by 22nd February, have become attractive to many people simply as a way of keeping warm. For among the commodities which were in increasingly short supply was coal, the basic source throughout the United Kingdom of heat, light and power. From the vantage point of the insecurely oil-dependent 1980s, the middle '40s may look superficially like some kind of golden age of energy supply, when more than 90% of the country's domestic and industrial heat and energy was derived from its own resources of coal.[18] In the face of the disruption of road, rail and coastal sea transport by blizzards and gale-force winds, however, the flow of coal from the pitheads to consumers had rapidly become impossible to maintain.

Estimates vary as to the amount of coal required by British industry around this time to maintain its normal levels of production. Leaving aside the needs of public utilities, railways, ships' bunkers and the like — that is to say, taking account only of the manufacturing industries — it averaged something of the order of a million tons per week. But actual deliveries to manufacturing concerns in the first two weeks of February 1947 averaged less than half a million tons. Domestic consumers were not quite so hard hit, on the face of it, as manufacturers: their coal deliveries in the first fortnight of February were about three-quarters of what had come to be regarded as normal in early post-war Britain. But 'normal' post-war household coal supplies were only about 70% of what they had been in 1938. A further reduction from this already perilously low level of some 20% to 25% during the worst winter of the century must have reduced standards of domestic comfort to a critically low ebb. Coal stocks at power stations and gasworks in the third week of February were also down to dangerously low levels, so to the shortage of coal itself was added the immediate threat of gas and electricity shortages.[19] Indeed, as early as 8th February *The Times* reported that 'a complete breakdown of electricity supplies can be avoided only by closing down some power stations and curtailing consumption for at least a week'. Small wonder, therefore, that the Ministry of Fuel and Power announced — somewhat gratuitously, it must have been thought — on 5th February that a most serious situation had arisen in regard to the supply of coal throughout the country. Collieries were actually ceasing production because their stockpiles were overflowing the space available. In some places transport difficulties made it impossible for miners to reach their work. The Ministry's announcement proclaimed that the highest priority was being given to the restoration of normal coal-traffic movements on the railways, even to the extent of prohibiting other forms of traffic. It ended by saying that:

> The position is particularly difficult in London, where the power stations normally draw the bulk of their supplies by sea from the north-east coast and south Wales.

On the day of the Ministry of Fuel and Power's announcement the Cabinet was considering proposals to reduce the consumption of coal, gas and electricity still further. On Friday 7th February, amid multiplying press reports about the mounting difficulties of maintaining fuel and power supplies — especially in the London area, the midlands and north-west of England — the government announced the imposition from the following Monday of a series of measures directed towards stretching available coal supplies as far as possible.[20] It was a draconian package, to say the least. It imposed the complete suspension of electricity supplies to industry in the London, Midland and North Western administrative regions. In the same regions all household electricity supplies were to be cut off for three hours from nine o'clock in the morning and for a further two hours from two in the afternoon each day until further notice. The government, however, rapidly came to the conclusion that these measures were not stringent enough, and that the restriction on household electricity consumption should be observed throughout the country. Within a week of the original restriction order being put into force, this extension was duly imposed, and every household was subject to power cuts totalling five hours a day. The nation was exhorted in addition to observe the greatest possible economy in its use of electricity and gas over and above the official restrictions, and to this end the government imposed further prohibitions. Various activities and amenities which used electricity, some of them only very recently restored after wartime proscription, were to be suppressed again. So, for example, the BBC's infant television service was once again suspended as it had been in 1939, and the corporation's minority-interest Third Programme radio channel was likewise closed down. All broadcasting by the BBC was to end at eleven o'clock at night. Newspapers were reduced in size, and large sections of the periodical press, including such august weeklies as *The Economist*, the *New Statesman* and the *Spectator*, were prevented from publishing — only for two weeks, as it turned out, but it was enough to bring down on the heads of Mr Attlee and his Cabinet some severe expressions of editorial disquiet. Street lighting, illuminated advertising signs and shop-window display lighting were banned, as was the use of electricity in connection with such frivolous pastimes as greyhound racing.

The imposition of these measures, together with the privations and restrictions imposed directly by the weather, inevitably invited comparison with the kind of conditions that most people had fondly imagined they were leaving behind for ever in August 1945. But there was more to the cheerlessness and discomfort of early 1947 than there had been to the domestic afflictions imposed by the war. The fuel supply position, particularly after the implementation of the government's economy package on 10th February, added to the situation an element that had not been present during the war — a steadily rising toll of unemployment which for a time was to reach levels that recalled the deepest days of the slump.

Simultaneously with their reports of the worsening weather and the dislocation of transport services, the press carried a growing volume of news, even before the cuts imposed on 10th February, of a steady and steep rundown in British industry. There were factory closures, short-time working, lay-offs — a pervasive disruption connected with the problems of coal, electricity and gas supplies. By the end of January it was threatening to put a stop to the activities of some of the biggest names in manufacturing. Among the concerns giving notice of imminent plant closures were the Dunlop Rubber Company, the General Electric Company, Imperial Chemical Industries, Morris and Austin Motors, the Rootes Group and Rover Cars, Rolls-Royce, and the paper makers John Dickinson. At Austin's alone 17,000 people were faced with the possibility of indefinite lay-off. The Lancashire cotton industry, which still used steam raised in coal-fired boilers as a source of power on a large scale, continued to be very hard hit. On 3rd February it was reported that

> Snow and ice have delayed so many [coal] deliveries that closed mills have been more easily reckoned in hundreds than in scores.[21]

The North West Divisional Office of the Ministry of Labour, within whose orbit most of the cotton industry came, reported an astonishing increase in the region's unemployment totals, from 14,000 on Wednesday 29th January to 20,000 the following day.

Nationally, the picture looked every bit as grim as it did in Lancashire. The government had assumed office in 1945 committed to the maintenance of 'a high and stable level of employment' as one of its primary objectives. There was to be no repetition after the second world war of the uncontrolled switch from boom to slump that had succeeded the first. There was to be no repetition in the 1940s of that demoralisingly constant elevated level of unemployment that had characterised the two preceding decades. It had been made plain to politicians of all persuasions both before and during the 1945 election campaign that this would simply be unacceptable to most people, and all the major parties adhered to the policy of full employment laid down in the 1944 White Paper, *Employment Policy*.[22] As constituents of the wartime coalition government under Churchill, they had all been parties to its formulation. In the immediate post-war period it looked as if the Attlee government might indeed have succeeded in taming the bogey of unemployment. Where even the most optimistic commentators of pre-war days had got into the habit of thinking of an 'irreducible million'

of unemployed workers, the actual number of people out of work in December 1946 had been about one-third of that.[23] Indeed, it was rapidly becoming apparent that a shortage of labour was more likely to be characteristic of the post-war period than a surplus: the 'irreducible million' was coming to be replaced in the minds of Ministers by 'the manpower problem'. As the government's review of the economic prospects for 1947 put it:

> The prospective labour force of 18,300,000 ... at December 1947 falls substantially short of what is needed to reach the national objectives.[24]

Yet no sooner had that prediction been made public at the beginning of 1947 than the number of people applying for unemployment relief began to rise rapidly and seemingly inexorably. In mid-January the overall United Kingdom register of unemployed had totalled just over 400,000. By 22nd February the number had climbed to over 1·75 million, with a further half-million described by the Ministry of Labour as 'stood off from employment' but continuing to receive wages under wage-guarantee agreements with employers. Such people were excluded from the official reckoning of unemployment.[25]

The greater part of the 'official' unemployed consisted of those described by the Ministry as 'temporarily stopped' — just less than 1·5 million on 22nd February. But as blizzard succeeded blizzard, and snowdrift piled up on snowdrift, there must have been many who began to wonder if the description was not perhaps a shade optimistic. Unemployment was also highly concentrated geographically, in the regions centred on England's three principal industrial conurbations, London, Birmingham and Manchester. Between them these three regions accounted for a shade more than two-thirds of the unemployed registered on 22nd February. This pattern was only to be expected, of course, given the way in which the Ministry of Fuel and Power had focused its restrictions on the industrial use of electricity primarily upon them.

As industrial activity declined and unemployment rose, and as the standards of household comfort and public amenity declined: as milk and mail deliveries became uncertain; as people actually passed out in the streets from the effects of the biting cold; as one by one the established certainties, large and small, from which people drew their sense of security evaporated in the face of the snow, ice and frost; as even Big Ben refused to mark the passage of time in due form because his works were iced up; as adversity piled upon hardship in a seemingly endless catalogue of misfortune, people began to look for somebody to blame. As is often the case in such situations, the government looked to many a likely target, and in the press and in

Parliament increasingly critical comment began to be heard, directed both against the government as a whole and against the Minister of Fuel and Power, Emanuel Shinwell, in particular.

Not surprisingly, the most prominent critics were Conservatives, for whom Anthony Eden — whose Warwick and Leamington constituency lay in one of the hardest-hit regions — succinctly summed the matter up in a Commons debate on industrial fuel supply on 7th February. 'In my judgment,' said Eden,

> the situation now confronting us is the gravest domestic industrial situation with which we have been confronted for the last 20 years,[26]

and he charged the Minister and the government with having

> completely misjudged the situation, by taking too optimistic a view of the gap which had to be bridged between the national industrial demand and the available supplies of coal.

Few of the government's supporters were willing, perhaps, to echo Eden's sentiments in their entirety, but in the same debate there was overt criticism from the Labour back benches of the government's lack of preparedness and its inflexibility in coping with the energy problem.[27] In private some of the government's supporters were very scathing indeed: the Chancellor of the Exchequer himself, in the privacy of his diary, described the performance of his Cabinet colleague, the Minister of Fuel and Power, in the most unflattering terms.[28]

The impact of factory closures, lay-offs, short-time working and industrial disruption was, in the short term at least, obviously severe. Activities which were vital to domestic reconstruction or to the revival of the export trade and the restoration of the balance of payments experienced in February 1947 falls in output of a quarter, a third or even a half from the levels they had attained in January, itself not a month usually noted for record levels of production.[29] The matter of making up for the severe February shortfall, and whether this could be achieved rapidly or only slowly (if at all), depended on whether the bad weather was responsible for the drop in output (which would therefore rapidly be made good when it changed for the better), or whether there was some more deep-seated weakness in the community which the weather had merely brought to a head and which would need more than a touch of the sun to make good. As the crisis reached its height in the third week of February, both views of its causes and character were widely canvassed.

2 A product of history

THE COAL PROBLEM BEFORE 1947

What is all knowledge too but recorded experience, and a
product of history?   Thomas Carlyle, *On History*

The line officially taken by the government in February 1947, as factory closures multiplied owing to cuts in electricity and gas supplies and the inadequacy of coal deliveries, and as the populace struggled to keep warm at home, was that the crisis was caused purely and simply by the exceptionally bad weather. In particular, the disruption of the transport of coal by road, rail and sea was portrayed in ministerial speeches and statements in Parliament and elsewhere as the fundamental problem. The tone of official pronouncements was set by the Ministry of Fuel and Power's declaration of 5th February which has already been quoted. Its view was echoed in a broadcast to the nation by Prime Minister Attlee himself five days later:

> So long as coal could be produced and moved we should have been able
> to get through the winter unless we had exceptionally bad weather,[1]

Attlee claimed, implying that the weather alone was responsible for the disruption of economic and domestic life which people were experiencing in such an acute form. His Attorney General, Sir Hartley Shawcross, had been more explicit in a speech at Prestwich in Lancashire the day before Attlee's broadcast, referring unambiguously to 'this weather-produced crisis'.[2] And Attlee and his colleagues were, for the most part, consistent long after the event in maintaining this view, which identified the crisis in production, employment and domestic comfort with the great freeze-up of the first quarter of 1947. Herbert Morrison's memoirs of 1960, for example, refer simply to 'the severe cold spell and the *resultant* fuel crisis of 1947'.[3] And Lord Attlee (as he had then become), on being questioned in 1967 as to the causes of the coal shortage, replied in his customarily terse fashion, 'Bad weather.'[4] In *Conflict without Malice* (1955), his first major excursion into autobiography, Lord Shinwell — as he was to become — observed that:

> The coal crisis, so far as the public was concerned, began with the great
> freeze-up which started in the latter part of January 1947.[5]

And indeed, extensive if not very systematic questioning of those who, as adults, actually experienced the event at first hand reveals that this is just how, nearly forty years on, the great majority remember it. Folk memory is a powerful ally on the government side.

But is it a reliable ally? For there were at the time those who took a different view, seeing the crisis as something which had been building up steadily over a period of years and which would have occurred more or less when it did and at a not significantly reduced level of severity even if the weather had not been so intemperate. Among this school, which embraced some members of the Labour Party, the 1947 fuel crisis was not seen as the result of an unpredictable meteorological act of God but as the all-too-foreseeable outcome of conditions which had been both evident and rectifiable for some time past. The editor of the *Economist*, smarting at the prohibition on publication which had been imposed on his paper and others in the interests of electricity conservation, was a powerful advocate of this case:

> Ministers put the blame on the severe weather, which has indeed made matters much worse than they would have been without it. But the weather is no more the cause of the crisis than the assassination of the Archduke Franz Ferdinand was the cause of the First World War. It would have happened in any case ... Never was there a clearer case of [ministerial] improvidence meeting its reward.[6]

In much the same vein the economist Lionel Robbins wrote at length to *The Times* on the crisis:

> I know of no competent person who, in the last six months, has not felt a crisis of this sort to be inevitable if the winter was at all severe ... that the Minister of Fuel and Power took an unjustifiable risk, and gave bad advice, seems to me to be incontestable.[7]

Lest it be thought that professional economists were uniformly in disagreement with the government's public stance, it should be said that Dr Robbins's letter was countered quickly by a defence of the government by the Oxford economist, Thomas Balogh.[8] Perhaps the most telling testimony, however, among those who dissented from the official government line came from Douglas Jay, who acted as Attlee's private secretary at 10 Downing Street between September 1945 and July 1946 before becoming Labour MP for Battersea North at a by-election. His memoirs record a belief, by no means confined to himself, as early as Christmas 1945 that:

> unless very vigorous action was taken at once, a breakdown [in coal supply] was highly probable in February and March 1947, and with very cold weather inevitable.

That such vigorous action was *not* taken, Jay conceded, was the result of the 'fatal obstruction' practised by the Minister of Fuel and Power himself, Emanuel Shinwell.[9]

Whether the imminence of a crisis, in the sense of an actual breakdown in coal supplies, was widely admitted or not, there can be no denying the widespread recognition on the part of the public at large as well as of their rulers of a chronic problem in coal supplies — and one, moreover, that was not something new and part of the unfamiliar circumstances of peacetime but one with which all had become familiar from quite early on in the war. For anyone who remembered the coal industry in its heyday, however, this increasing problem of shortage must have taken a great deal of getting used to.[10]

The British coal industry's greatest year had been 1913. The 287 million tons of coal it had then produced represented nearly half of Europe's entire output. This prodigious figure had been achieved by a labour force numbering more than a million men, relying almost entirely on their own physical vigour and manual dexterity: less than one-twelfth of the total was cut by machine. In this respect Britain lagged behind other substantial coal producers, whose geological conditions were more favourable to mechanisation and whose miners and owners were perhaps more willing to accept and invest in it. Nevertheless, in 1913 the British coal miner's productivity record could stand comparison with those of his European, if not his American, counterparts. And British coal was competitive in world markets as a result: 94 million tons of it were shipped abroad in 1913 for industrial and domestic consumption throughout the world, and as bunker fuel for the innumerable coal-burning merchant and naval steamships which dominated the world's sea lanes.[11]

Compared with 1913, the coal industry between the two world wars had been plagued with the most acute and chronic problems, but the possibility of *shortage* had not been among them. Indeed, the chief characteristic of coal supplies from 1920 to 1939 had been not dearth but glut. Competition from low-cost producers such as America, Germany and Poland, together with a growing tendency to utilise alternative sources of energy such as oil and hydro-electricity for domestic and industrial heat and power, progressively reduced overseas demand for British coal. The same tendencies operated, though perhaps less intensely, in the home market, where their impact was reinforced by the depressed state of traditional coal-burning industries such as iron and steel, heavy engineering and heavy chemicals. The problem faced by the coal industry between the wars, therefore, was not that of producing enough to meet demand but of finding a market for the great quantity it was capable of producing, and getting prices for its output that actually covered the cost of mining it. Among the methods that were tried to cope with this problem, the chief resort was to ways of reducing production costs to an extent which made it possible to retain some margin of profit, however small, at the low level of prices obtaining in British and world markets. These included greater mechanisation, schemes for 'rationalising' the structure of the industry by mergers and pit closures, and perhaps most notoriously attempts to reduce wage rates from the high levels of the wartime and post-war boom (1914–21) and to hold them at low levels in the long run. Since by far the biggest element in the cost of mining coal was labour, which accounted for some 70% of total production costs around 1926, the owners' seeming obsession with wage reductions was understandable. Equally understandable, however, was the resistance of the miners. Relations between capital and labour in the coal industry – never very affable even at the best of times – reached new depths of bitterness in the conflict surrounding the great dispute of 1925–26 which gave birth to the General Strike. The miners' defeat on that occasion ensured that the bitterness would endure for the remainder of the time during which coal mining remained under private enterprise. Indeed, the Attlee government was to discover that strong echoes of it remained even after the miners' desire for nationalisation had been gratified.

This is not the place to chronicle in all its particulars the plight of the coal industry between the wars, nor to portray in detail the vicissitudes that mining communities were forced to undergo.[12] On the eve of the second world war the industry's circumstances were manifestly much reduced from the heights of 1913: output in 1938 was a mere 227 million tons, less than four-fifths of the 1913 figure. Coal exports in 1938 were less than half the 1913 tonnage, and the 1938 labour force was not much more than two-thirds that of 1913.[12] In spite of much talk in Westminster and among the larger coal-owning concerns in the 1930s, and not a little legislation intended to improve the industry's technical and commercial efficiency, not much had actually been achieved by 1938 in the way of altering the industry's basic organisation and structure to enhance its competitiveness. Technological advance *had* taken place, and in 1938 nearly 60% of coal was machine-cut, compared with a mere 8% in 1913. But rather surprisingly, in the light of this substantial extension of mechanisation, output per worker was not remarkably higher in 1938 than it had been in 1913, having advanced only by some 13%.

For some years before 1938 the possibility of war with Germany came to be increasingly recognised, first by government and then in the country at large. From 1934 onwards the politicians, their military advisers, and industrialists became increasingly concerned to assess and develop the country's economic ability to fight such a war. It was clear that in many respects the potential was not high. The huge armaments industry which had sustained the war effort of 1918 had, within the space of a couple of years, all but disappeared, leaving as its most enduring monument in the communities that had served it restrictions on the hours during which alcoholic beverages could be purveyed. Serious deficiencies were recognised by 1935, when rearmament became the avowed policy of the National Government, in Britain's capacity to equip herself with the sinews of war. But despite the experience of the Great War, when declining coal supplies had seemed to threaten the economic war effort, no significant supply problems were anticipated in the event of renewed hostilities as far as coal was concerned.[14] From 1936, when the question of coal supply in wartime began again to be seriously considered by government and business, until after the actual outbreak of war in September 1939, it was evidently felt that the comfortable surplus of production and potential over peacetime demand offered an ample guarantee of wartime sufficiency.

Accordingly, no very special efforts were made, for instance, to discourage the recruitment of coal miners into the armed forces: the coal industry of the '30s notoriously operated under conditions of substantial labour surplus. And when, in the summer of 1940, the French and other European markets for coal exports were closed by German conquest, the relatively limited restrictions on recruitment of miners were significantly eased. Nobody seemed to appreciate that the intensification of economic mobilisation after May 1940, with all it entailed by way of expanding the energy-intensive heavy industries, was more than likely to offset the effects of the loss of export markets on the demand for coal. By the spring of 1941, as the war economy shifted into top gear, the hollow nature of previous assumptions about the abundance of supplies began to become apparent.

Almost from the beginning of the war coal output fell. Production in 1939, at 231 million tons, was slightly higher than in 1938, but in each succeeding year the output of the traditional coal-mining industry went down. In 1944, the last full year of hostilities, it stood at just over 184 million tons, and in 1945 at ten million tons less even than that.[15] Meanwhile, driven by the pressures of war, demand for coal from industry, transport and public utilities rose dramatically once the British woke up to the dangers of their position and the paucity of their resources for fighting a war with Germany single-handed. The growth of war production after the disasters of Dunkirk and the collapse of France was quite prodigious. Munitions output more than quadrupled between mid-1940 and the end of 1942. Tank production grew eightfold. Aircraft production more or less doubled.[16] And, with all this, home coal consumption grew steadily, from 186 million tons in 1939 to more than 197 million in 1942. In fact 1942 was a turning point in the coal supply position. Up to that point, annual consumption had customarily been comfortably surpassed by output. In 1942, and for the remainder of the war, Britain's requirements for coal steadily outpaced the production of her traditional coal-mining industry. By 1945 consumption at 188 million tons had come to exceed traditional deep-mined production by more than 13 million tons. From 1942 onwards the growing difficulty of obtaining coal in the quantities and of the qualities required threatened ever more seriously the expansion of war production, so much so indeed that the shortage has been described as the Churchill government's 'most serious problem on the home front'.[17]

In the face of this, coal could be provided for vital war industries only by developing alternatives to conventional deepmining, and by drawing on the stockpiles that had been accumulated in the pre-war years of glut. Open-cast production began to be developed on a significant scale from 1942 onwards. After two years 119 open-cast sites were operating, mostly in the north of England and the north midlands. As many additional open-cast sites were being surveyed. And thanks to the importation of heavy excavating equipment from America under Lend-Lease, open-cast production in 1944 came to exceed 8·5 million tons. Meanwhile the national stockpile of coal was run down from its peak at the end of 1940 of nearly 22 million tons to just over 15 million at the end of 1945.[18]

What could *not* readily be done was to expand production by conventional means. That it was falling was chiefly the result of problems among the labour force. In the first place, and crucial in an industry as labour-intensive as British coal mining, was the wartime decline in the number of miners, from 781,000 in 1938 to 709,000 in 1945.[19] Then there was the declining efficiency of a labour force whose most vigorous members had been inducted into the armed services or had taken themselves off to higher-paid and less dangerous work in munitions. The impact on productivity of the ageing of the labour force was reinforced by the dissatisfaction of many mineworkers with their pay and conditions and with restrictions imposed by government on their mobility under the Essential Work Order of May 1941. This device, intended to stem the outflow of labour from mining, effectively tied the miner to his pit in a manner reminiscent of the bonded servitude which had characterised the eighteenth-century coal industry. The declining physical fitness and increasing alienation of the miners found expression in a rising trend of 'absenteeism' − a term which in the official jargon of the industry could mean failure to turn up for work, either involuntarily (as from illness) or voluntarily (because of sheer disgruntlement, or indeed because thanks to government intervention to boost miners' wages a man no longer felt he needed to work all-out). In the public mind, however, it came to be associated more with the second definition than the first. Whatever the cause, the proportion of possible shifts lost as a result of failure to report for work rose steadily from under 7% in 1939 to more than 16% in 1945.[20] There were also several celebrated outbreaks of industrial militancy in the coalfields after 1941, with strike action on a substantial scale in defiance of emergency regulations prohibiting it. The strike at Betteshanger Colliery in Kent in 1942 is perhaps the best-remembered incident. For these reasons, and no doubt others too (such as the over-enthusiastic exploitation of the most productive seams early in the war so that they were increasingly exhausted by the later stages), output per man-shift − the conventional measure of coal-mining productivity − fell steadily from 1939 to 1945, by about 12% among the labour force as a whole and about 5% among those who worked at the coal face itself.

Once the government had woken up to the problem, as it did from the spring of 1941 to full-blown awareness of crisis by the spring of 1942, steps were taken to try to reverse these depressing and dangerous deep-mining trends. Pay and conditions were substantially improved following the Greene Committee's inquiry of 1942. State control over the mining industry was stepped up in an attempt to organise and manage it more efficiently and to reduce the unproductive and rising tension between the highly unionised miners and the private-capital coal owners. Attempts were also made to bring back experienced men from the armed forces, or other industries, and to persuade or even compel new labour to join the industry. They met with only limited success: it had to be recognised that the wholesale transfer of trained coalminers from the army would have all but destroyed formations within regiments like the Northumberland Fusiliers, the Durham Light Infantry and the Sherwood Foresters, whose traditional recruiting grounds lay in the coalfields. Conscript labour for the coal mines − the Bevin Boys, who took their name from the Minister of Labour and National Service responsible for their conscription − were frequently disaffected and generally inefficient.[21] Coal rationing was proposed in 1942 but rejected in the face of a threatened rebellion by hostile Conservative MPs and a well orchestrated campaign in the press to turn public opinion against it. The coalition government may have had doubts of its own: it was accepted that the imposition of rationing created an obligation for government to meet specified levels of supply, and by the summer of 1942 (when Parliament discussed coal rationing) it was increasingly evident that no firm commitment of that kind was possible. Instead, a new Ministry of Fuel and Power was created out of the Mines department of the Board of Trade, with enhanced powers of control over the production and distribution of *all* fuel supplies, which it exercised in conjunction with other departments of state such as its own parent, the Board of Trade, the Ministry of Transport, the Ministry of Supply, and so on. To make what coal there was go round, in the absence of a properly constituted rationing scheme, a system of priorities and supply allocations was developed. Deliveries were made on the basis of the customer's strategic significance and of other considerations such as known levels of consumption or estimations of need. An extensive network of local and regional representatives of interested Ministries, together with a substantial structure of committees to co-ordinate their activities, was created to implement coal allocations. Under this system the country's dwindling output of deep-mined coal, together with whatever supplies were available from stock or from open-cast sites, was manipulated to meet wartime requirements. American observers, who were seldom flattering about British industry, were most impressed by the thoroughness and flexibility of the arrangements, which they described in 1944 as 'the most complete form of distribution control obtainable'.[22] Strategically important sectors of the economy such as the railways and the engineering industry were assured of the increased coal supplies they needed as the war effort intensified. This was done by reducing supplies to low-priority sectors like the manufacture of civilian consumer goods and private households. Domestic coal supplies, indeed, were reduced by nearly a third between 1940 and 1945, even though the open fire remained the principal source of heat in most homes. Fortunately, subsequent wartime winters were more clement than that of 1940 itself.[23]

There were, however, alternative fuels to which those who found themselves on reduced coal allocations could turn, and which were less susceptible to control by the Ministry of Fuel and Power. Oil, of course, was ruled out by scarcity and dollar cost to a nation whose tanker tonnage had never been adequate and whose dollar resources had to be husbanded with the utmost rigour. But gas and electricity — neither, strictly speaking, an alternative to coal, since both were almost entirely derived from it —

could provide heat and power in home, office or factory. Consumption of both soared as the availability of coal declined, electricity by 41% and gas by 25% between 1939 and 1945. Household electricity consumption went up by no less than 48% as people switched on their electric heaters to make up for their inability to keep the home fires burning at anything like pre-war intensity.[23] The growing popularity of electricity and gas created problems of its own. At peak periods, demand threatened to overwhelm the capacity of both powerstations and gasworks. Admittedly, electricity generating capacity had undergone a substantial increase, on paper at least, during the war. in 1939 the Central Electricity Board had controlled 137 main generating stations — 'selected stations' in the Board's terminology — with an installed capacity of 8,660 megawatts. By the end of 1945 there were 142 'selected stations' with an installed capacity of 11,300 megawatts. But the amount of generating capacity actually available at any one time to was much less than the 'installed capacity'. Much of the plant was old — indeed, long overdue for replacement — and suffered frequent and prolonged shutdowns for maintenance and repair. The gas industry was not in a much better state. It had started the war with a substantial excess of capacity over demand, but gas plant had been knocked about during the bombing of 1940—41. Gasholders, by reason of their size and prominence, had been a favourite mark for German bomb aimers. As with power stations, gasworks were operated at full stretch during the war. Output increased by a quarter, but repairs, maintenance and the replacement of obsolete plant were all skimped or postponed for the duration. An official report of March 1947 described the industry as very run down as a result.[25]

What perhaps worried those who administered wartime fuel policy more than the physical state of the power stations and gasworks was their inability to subject the supply of gas and electricity to the same control in detail, the same elaborate fine tuning, as was possible with the allocation of coal. It must have been frustrating to the staff of the Ministry of Fuel and Power to know that in reducing household coal consumption by a third between 1939 and 1945 they had largely occasioned the need to increase coal supplies to power stations and gasworks by almost the same proportion over the same period. The victim of their attempts to rob the household Peter to pay the industrial Paul had found a way of limiting his liability which they were powerless to stop.

When the war in Europe ended and the British began to take serious stock of their position and their problems in a world in which the pursuit of victory no longer took precedence over all else, the energy base on which their hopes of post-war reconstruction fundamentally rested looked very precarious. The coal allocation system had effected considerable economies in the latter years of the war, so that internal coal consumption had fallen by about a tenth from 1942 to 1945. But, as the official history noted,[26] at the end of the war 'In almost every other respect, the coal situation was unsatisfactory and threatening ... The outlook for the coming year was very disquieting.' Gwilym Lloyd George, the Minister of Fuel in March 1945, thought that for the coming 'coal year' (a term devised under the wartime distribution scheme and running from 1 May one calendar year to 30 April the next), a total of 188 million tons might be available from all sources, current deep-mined and open-cast output plus drawings from stock. Against this, he estimated that demand from all sources would amount to 192 million tons.[27] Not all his Cabinet colleagues agreed with his precise calculations: the Paymaster General, Lord Cherwell (the former Professor Lindeman, Churchill's confidant), thought less would be available and more would be required, leaving a gap between supply and demand of 8 million tons rather than 4 million.[28] All, however, could agree with the general conclusion that the prospect was serious and that the possibility of a breakdown in supplies during the coming winter could not be discounted. The threat to activities which required the higher qualities of coal — for gas-making, steam-raising and coking — was reckoned especially severe. Urgent measures to build up the mining labour force, to utilise poor-quality coal in place of the scarce high qualities, and to improve transport facilities, especially by rail, were called for. Above all, perhaps, it was widely recognised that urgent steps had to be taken to improve the technical equipment and performance of the industry in accordance with the recommendations of the wartime Reid Committee.

The Coal Mining: Technical Advisory Committee, to give it its proper title, had been set up by the Minister of Fuel and Power in September 1944 under the chairmanship of Charles Carlow Reid, sometime manager of the Fife Coal Company and now Director of Production in the Ministry's Coal Division. Its members were, like Reid, production and engineering experts, of some eminence in the private coal industry, and their brief was:

> to examine the present technique of coal production from coal face to wagon, and to advise what technical changes are necessary to bring the industry to a state of full technical efficiency.

The committee's report (1944–45, Cmd 6610) was unequivocal in its conclusion that technical rehabilitation could not be effectively accomplished within the industry's existing structure, nor within the prevailing climate of labour–management relations. Effective technical reconstruction required a wholesale restructuring into larger and more efficient units of production under the direction of a strong central authority armed by the State with great powers to secure compliance with its strategic plans. A fundamental reappraisal of the rights, duties and interrelationships of colliery management and labour was also required, the committee believed, if labour relations were to be put on a footing that was favourable to technical progress in the industry, rather than the hostile and obstructive basis then current.

What the Reid Committee was proposing was not nationalisation: a reconstruction along the lines it recommended was theoretically possible within the framework of continued private enterpise, and both the Conservative Party and the coal owners (via the Mining Association of Great Britain) planned just such a course.[29] This was not an idea with wide popular appeal: the Reid report was widely (if not entirely fairly or accurately) interpreted as the authoritative condemnation of the private enterprise system in coal by some of its own leading acolytes, even among some sections of the Conservative Party. It may be doubted in any case whether the miners would have been willing to accept anything short of outright nationalisation after the second world war, having been (as they saw it) cheated of it after the first. Will Lawther, president of the Miners' Federation, had made their attitude abundantly clear in November 1944:

> under private ownership it is impossible for any permanent solution of
> the problems connected with the industry to be secured ... the miners' con-
> fidence in the industry will never be restored until it has been taken over
> by the State.[30]

If, as was widely predicted, the Conservatives under Churchill were to win the general election of June 1945, the stage might have been set for a confrontation between the government and the miners over the industry's post-war development, the consequences of which for post-war recovery would have made the wartime coal supply problem appear insignificant.

As events turned out the confrontation never occurred. The Labour Party − unexpectedly even to some of its own leaders − won handsomely, and the certainty of coal nationalisation was assured. In the euphoric atmosphere of that time, when the new government was settling in and its supporters were eagerly expecting the imminent construction of the new Jerusalem, the coal problem must have seemed to many to have, in effect, ceased to exist. Nevertheless, the new government appreciated that it would face great problems in organising the economic transition from war to peace, and to facilitate it retained many of the powers over industry, including coal, that had been accumulated by the wartime coalition. A Supplies and Services (Transitional Powers) Act was quickly passed to enable the government to continue to do many of the things that in war had been legitimised by the Emergency Powers (Defence) Acts of 1939 and 1940. In coalmining and other activities the wartime Essential Work Order and the Control of Engagement Order remained in force, and any 'Bevin Boy' who hoped for immediate discharge from the mines was doomed to disappointment. But the need to apply such coercive expedients seemed to be passing. With nationalisation guaranteed and good prospects of improved pay and conditions, the miners seemed to have undergone a transformation in morale that was bound to influence their commitment to the job, and hence also the production figures. The attitude in the pits is exemplified by a notice the Yorkshire Area of the National Union of Mineworkers issued to its local officers and members on 28th August:

> An extra output of at least 8 million tons is required to enable the Nation's immediate needs to be met ... We must show the Nation that whatever difficulties there may have been in the Coal Mining industry in the past, there is now a disposition for full co-operation between the Mineworkers, the Labour Government and the Labour Minister of Fuel and Power, and that we will spare no effort to bring to successful fruition the aims and purposes for which the Government has been elected.[31]

The basis of co-operation with the Minister of Fuel and Power seemed especially good. Emanuel Shinwell represented the mining constituency of Seaham, County Durham, having wrested it from Ramsay MacDonald in 1935. He enjoyed the firm confidence not only of the miners in his own bailiwick, who had helped him to a crushing victory in 1945, but of the miners in general. He also had experience of running the Mines Department of the Board of Trade, as a member of MacDonald's minority Labour governments of the 1920s.

The newly elected Attlee government was well aware of the dangers of the coal-supply position: many of its members, having been Ministers in the wartime coalition, were familiar with Lloyd George's gloomy prognostication. As early as 7th August Attlee asked Shinwell for 'a short appreciation of the situation with regard to the supply of coal in this country for the winter, as the matter must be dealt with urgently'.[32] Shinwell's reply was couched in almost precisely the same terms as Lloyd George's March memorandum.[33] And only a little over a week later, on 17th August, he was reporting to the Lord President's Committee − the Cabinet committee in charge of industrial reconstruction and development − that the deficit in the 'coal year' looked like being rather more than the 4 million tons predicted in March.[34]

But relations between the government and the miners seemed excellent, and the miners themselves seemed so thoroughly imbued with the desire not to let down this new government that they regarded as so peculiarly their own, that Shinwell (and perhaps many of his colleagues) may have been inclined to discount predictions that had been arrived at under a quite different atmosphere before the election. His inclination seems to have been more to back his instinctive trust in private assurances from the miners, and his belief in the efficacy of 'the new spirit' in the mines as a means of reviving Britain's faltering coal output. As he was later to record,

> I was told at meeting after meeting with the men and their representatives
> that I would get all the coal I wanted.[35]

It may have been his faith in such assurances which led him to announce in September 1945 that he envisaged bringing open-cast production to an end, on the expectation that deep-mined output would eventually be sufficient to meet both home and overseas demand.[36] This was a rather daring thought to give voice to at a time when, without open-cast production, the gap in the coal budget would have been three times greater than that predicted by Lloyd George in March and confirmed by Shinwell himself five months later.

It soon became apparent, however, that the miners' assurances of greater output were not readily to be translated into reality. The Lord President's Committee noted on 13th September that stocks of housecoal and gascoal had fallen to very low levels, and that, despite the co-operation promised by all parties in the industry, there was as yet no real sign of improvements in the position.[37] Indeed, it was if anything deteriorating, since open-cast production was falling because of the poor condition of plant and equipment and the problem of obtaining spare parts from the United States, whence much of the plant had originated. The Minister of Transport, Alfred Barnes, began to talk openly of the possibility of a crisis in the coming winter, and of the need to create an organisation to cope with it.

The crisis that Barnes envisaged was essentially a matter of coal transport and distribution. He was particularly concerned with the inadequacy of railway facilities for moving coal, above all to London and the south-east. As the official historian of the railways in the second world war recorded:

> The immediate post-war years found the railways with heavy arrears of
> replacement and repair of permanent way, locomotives and rolling stock
> to be made good. Indeed the ultimate consequences of overstraining the
> inland transport system during the war were only felt in 1946, 1947 and
> afterwards.[38]

There was a shortage of heavy freight locomotives of the type needed to move coal in bulk over long hauls. Wartime dilapidation among coal wagons had been severe, and as a result, at the beginning of October 1945, about 12% were out of service for repair, compared to the 3% or so that would have been regarded as normal before the war.[39] Labour to load and unload trains at railway mineral depots was in very short supply, and the supply of coal for locomotives was giving cause for concern. And it was on the London & North Eastern Railway, which provided the main inland link between the coalfields and the capital, that all these problems were most acutely concentrated. By early October, however, it became clear that the threat of crisis was by no means confined to the transport and distribution of coal; its production was also involved. Through August and September the government had been working on the assumption that the coal-budget deficit for the winter period between November 1945 and April 1946 would be more or less as predicted by Gwilym Lloyd George in March 1945 — something of the order of 4 million tons. The Minister of Fuel and Power, in memoranda to the Prime Minister and to the Lord President's Committee of the Cabinet in August, had simply quoted Lloyd George's estimate, with the vague rider that he expected the situation to be slightly worse than the March estimates suggested. But on 2nd October, at the Lord President's Committee, Shinwell made explicit his estimate of size of the margin: instead of an excess of consumption over supply of some 4 million tons, the likelihood of a deficit of *eight* million tons was revealed. It also became apparent that the stocks of coal held by vital sectors of the economy were already below what would normally be regarded as danger level. Coal stocks held by the railways, for instance, were less than half the amount — three weeks' normal consumption — they regarded as the absolute minimum required to guarantee secure operation of their services.[40]

Having made his colleagues' flesh creep with these appalling figures, however, Shinwell proceeded to take a fairly optimistic view of the prospects for coal production in the winter months, which he hoped (though without revealing on what grounds) would increase. The chief problems in his view were essentially those of transport and distribution, not the availability of coal itself. Herbert Morrison, the Lord President, closed the meeting with the observation that the coal problem would be, after housing, the most serious source of distress in the coming winter. Echoing Alfred Barnes's earlier plea for an organisation to handle the looming crisis, Morrison proposed a ministerial meeting, chaired by the Chancellor of the Exchequer, for 'further urgent study of the various aspects of the problem'. The meeting, first of a series held by what came to be called the Ministerial Coal Committee, was duly convened on 4th October 1945 in the Chancellor's office in the Treasury. The committee became the principal mechanism for monitoring the supply and distribution of coal through the winter of 1945–46, and the medium by which the activities of the various departments of state with an interest in the fuel question – the Treasury, Fuel and Power, Transport, Supply, Labour, and so on – were co-ordinated and governed in the ways that seemed best calculated to minimise the impact on industry and private households of the supply problems that existed. Much of the real work was transacted not in the Ministerial Committee (which was concerned more with matters of principle and grand strategy) but in its subordinate Official Coal Committee of senior civil servants, chaired by the Permanent Secretary of the Ministry of Fuel and Power, Sir Donald Fergusson. This official committee met much more frequently than its ministerial parent, and handled the tactical details of demobilising coal miners and railwaymen from the armed services, making arrangements for the repair of broken-down coal wagons, the repatriation of locomotives from the Continent, the use of military personnel and vehicles for moving coal, and so on.

Through the months of the 'coal winter' of 1945–46 (1st November–30th April) Ministers and officials kept a careful watch on all aspects of the coal supply. The complexity of the problem may be exemplified by the items discussed at the first ministerial meeting of 4th October, under Dr Dalton's benign chairmanship:[41] the release of experienced miners and railwaymen from the armed forces; the utilisation of military and prisoner-of-war labour to produce or shift coal; the possibilities of using timber as a substitute for coal; the allocation of the highest priority to coal traffic on the railways; the maximisation of the use of railway coalwagons; the repair of damaged wagons; the supply of coal for locomotives; construction of new wagons; the increased use of road and water transport to take pressure off the railways; a publicity campaign to reduce coal consumption. In each case a systematic process was applied: the relationship of the particular topic to the general coal problem was defined, and its potential to help analysed; then the action being taken, or which might be taken, to realise that potential by each department was set out in some detail for the benefit of the officials of the subordinate committee who would have to find ways of giving effect to the ministerial proposals.

To such effect did Ministers and officials labour that by late November the Minister of Fuel and Power felt able to present to his colleagues on the Ministerial Committee a progress report which professed optimism about the remainder of the winter, albeit of a guarded kind.[42] As far as coal production was concerned, he reported that recruitment to mining was beginning to overtake departures from it, that output per man-shift had improved, and that total output for the month of October was significantly up on that for September, while November's output seemed set to exceed October's. The picture in transport and distribution was less satisfactory, but was nevertheless improving in various respects: energetic action was being taken to improve the availability of railway wagons and the efficiency with which they were used; arrangements were in hand to increase substantially the coastwise shipment of coal, thereby relieving the railways; shipment of opencast coal by road had increased by nearly 50% compared with the previous November. As a result, he concluded:

> The general feeling of my Regional Controllers ... during the last week is that failing severe weather conditions and transport interruptions, we can see our way through the winter.

He qualified this sanguine view, however, by noting that stock margins were still narrow — as little as seventeen or eighteen days' consumption at gasworks in Scotland, for example, and less than two weeks' supply on the railways — and the house coal position would continue to be difficult.

By the latter part of March 1946, towards the end of the 'coal winter', it was clear that the crisis which Ministers had feared the previous autumn had fairly effectively been defeated. There had been problems: householders in particular had been hard hit in that their coal allocation, already substantially below pre-war levels, had been cut by about 8% from October 1945, and even then (as a Ministry of Fuel and Power internal memorandum put it) 'the domestic programme has been very heavily underdelivered', actual deliveries running at a mere nine-tenths of the already inadequate official allocation during the coldest months of the winter.[43] But there had been no crisis in the sense of a breakdown in supply such as to cause serious industrial disruption or domestic hardship. In January 1946 respondents to a Gallup poll had rated the coal problem a long way behind housing, food shortages and employment as the most urgent problem confronting the government at home. And the next month an overwhelming 65% of Gallup's respondents expressed themselves satisfied with the sufficiency of fuel supplies for household heating during the current winter.[44] At the Ministerial Coal Committee on 25th March 1946 Shinwell expressed his satisfaction that:

> generally speaking, the purpose for which the Committee had come into existence had been successfully fulfilled ... we had so far got through the winter without a serious interruption in coal supplies, despite the fact that production had been lower than in 1944–45 ... there was no longer a problem of transport for coal so much as one of coal for transport.

I must have SOME hot water, but...

I AM SAVING GAS and ELECTRICITY

SWITCH OFF

WATCH YOUR

TURN OFF

METERS

Coal production had increased slightly over the last two months, and, while the position was not yet satisfactory, production was now running rather above the danger point and ought to improve. In view of this, he suggested that, for the present at least, no further meetings either of the ministerial or of the inter-departmental committee were necessary.

His colleagues pointed to some sources of continuing concern – Alfred Barnes (Transport) noted the extremely low state of railway coal stocks, while George Isaacs (Labour and National Service) expressed concern about the disappointing response of demobilised servicemen from mining backgrounds to employment opportunities in the coal industry. But, by and large, Shinwell's colleagues agreed with him that they had successfully averted the threatened coal crisis by their effective management of both production and distribution, and could now afford to suspend their deliberations at least until the beginning of the next 'coal winter' in October 1946.[45]

The Prime Minister and the Cabinet concurred, and the Ministerial and Official Coal Committees were duly adjourned for the 'coal summer' of 1946 after the March meeting. All mention of a coal crisis was banished from the Cabinet's deliberations – many Ministers may have hoped for good, but at least, it was thought, until October. In the meantime, however, the coal industry itself remained in the forefront of parliamentary concern during the spring and early summer of 1946. For the Bill which was to bring in the nationalisation of the mines so long hoped for by the miners in particular and the labour movement in general had been introduced to the House of Commons in December 1945 and was making its progress through both Houses of Parliament in the early months of 1946. The coalowners and the Conservative Party had largely conceded the principle of nationalisation before the Bill was brought in: government supporters took particular delight in quoting a parliamentary speech by Winston Churchill from as far back as 1943, in which he had indicated acceptance of coal nationalisation provided the compensation paid to the owners was adequate.[46] And indeed debates on the Bill in 1946 tended to concentrate not on the act of nationalisation so much as on the terms on which it was to be implemented. Some Labour members voiced the opinion that confiscation rather than compensation would have been the coalowners' just deserts, and on the Labour side generally much play was made of the galvanising effect that nationalisation would have on the miners' efforts. A new spirit would enter into the industry: its character was summed up during the debate on the second reading by the member for Durham, an ex-miner named Grey.[47] 'I am convinced,' he said in his maiden speech:

41

that when the miners realise that they are working for their country, and
not for capitalist exploiters, the necessary tonnage will not only be reached
but vastly exceeded

By the time the Bill received the royal assent in August 1946, ensuring
the nationalisation of coalmining at the beginning of the new year, it was
becoming apparent that this much heralded 'new spirit' would be badly
needed. For, after an absence of three or four months, the term 'coal crisis'
was coming back into currency within the government and Cabinet. The
avoidance of a breakdown in coal supplies in 1945–46 had been, in the
Duke of Wellington's phrase, 'a damned near-run thing'. From June 1946
onwards there was growing concern within the government that the position
in the coming winter would be far too close, literally, for comfort.

3 O come, O come, Emanuel!

Everybody knows there is going to be a serious crisis in the coal industry except the Minister of Fuel and Power. I want to tell you there is not going to be a crisis in the coal industry, if by crisis you mean that industrial organisation is going to be seriously dislocated and that hundreds of factories are going to be closed down.

Emanuel Shinwell (Minister of Fuel and Power), Thursday 24th October 1946, as quoted in the *Daily Herald*, 25th October 1946

It is possible to detect in the attitude of Ministers when the Ministerial Coal Committee came to be adjourned at the end of March 1946 a note of complacency, a certain self-congratulation about what they had managed to achieve through their deliberations. Much play was made with the fact that there had been less industrial disruption due to inadequate fuel supplies than their predecessors of the wartime coalition had experienced in the winter of 1944−45, when both coal supplies and transport facilities had been better than they were in the winter just past.[1] Indeed, the committee was adjourned almost as if the coal problem had been solved, with the proposal that it be reconvened at the beginning of the next 'coal winter' (1st November 1946−30th April 1947), not as a matter of urgency, but merely 'to consider whether the machinery which has brought us through this winter would serve a useful purpose next year'.[2] At any rate, the immediate threat had been dealt with, and Ministers probably felt justified in putting the coal problem, if not entirely out of mind, then at least at the back of their minds while they turned their attention to matters that now seemed to be of more pressing concern. In the spring of 1946 there was certainly no shortage of problems waiting to supplant coal in the attention of Attlee and his colleagues: at home, housing and food supply were matters of acute concern, while the nationalisation programme was making heavy demands on government time; abroad, Palestine, the British zone of Germany, and India, together with overseas trade and the balance of payments, were all matters of urgency. In the circumstances any tendency to shrug off the coal problem in the spring and early summer of 1946, in the belief that all was well for the moment on that particular front, is perhaps understandable. With the adjournment of the Ministerial Coal Committee the problem certainly ceased to figure among the agenda at the highest level of the government's deliberations from April 1946 through May and into June.

But the threat posed by inadequate resources of fuel and power − which was to say essentially of coal − to the country's programmes of industrial reconversion, social advance and commercial and financial reconstruction was not being ignored during that time. Ministers at Cabinet level, concerned with the broad sweep of the State's affairs, might be able to relegate the matter to the back burner, but their subordinates − the Parliamentary Secretaries and senior civil servants with specific and well defined responsibilities, especially in those departments most directly concerned with economic matters − could not do so. Men like James Meade, head of the Cabinet Office's Ecoomic Section, and Max Nicholson, in the Lord President's office, which handled matters relating to economic planning and industrial reconversion; like Hugh Gaitskell, the Parliamentary

Secretary to the Minister of Fuel and Power appointed in April 1946, and the civil servants in his Ministry's statistical section — such men were well aware of the acute and continuing gravity of the situation.[3] They recognised the need for continuous monitoring of coal production and stocks throughout the 'coal summer', to ensure that stocks were rebuilt from the record low levels obtaining at the end of the 1945–46 'coal winter' to a point which could ensure that the anticipated demand, higher than ever before, of the coming winter might have a chance of being met. They recognised that the key to raising coal output and stocks lay with the coal industry's labour force, and the urgent necessity of taking measures which would increase the number of people in that labour force and at the same time improve their productive efficiency. They knew the time lags which occurred between the implementation of a policy and its coming to fruition: it was no good leaving consideration of the coal problem and the steps necessary to cope with it to a reconvened Ministerial Coal Committee meeting in October, on the eve of the start of the 'coal winter'. If the position for that winter was to be secured, the decisions that would influence it could not be delayed beyond the preceding spring. Indeed, some viewed leaving the decisions to that point as cutting things dangerously fine.

The problem for these men was to bring coal back to the forefront of affairs and to persuade the government to focus on it as a matter of urgency during the 'coal summer' and to take and put into effect the decisions that were necessary if massive disruption to Britain's post-war economic readjustment during the coming winter were to be avoided. For they were in no doubt about what would happen if, in the coming months of the coal summer, output and productivity in the industry were not substantially improved, and stocks were not built up by the end of October 1946 to something like at least double the 6·8 million tons that were available in April.[4] Such an increase would barely suffice to bring coal stocks at the start of the 1946–47 'coal winter' up to the level obtaining at the same point the previous 'coal year', and which had only just been sufficient to avoid industrial dislocation then. In their attempts to rekindle interest in the coal problem in the government's highest reaches, their greatest asset perhaps was the fact that among their number was the private secretary to the Prime Minister himself (until his nomination as a candidate in the Battersea by-election of June 1946) — Douglas Jay. Jay's position enabled him to act as a channel for communicating his friends' concern, and the disquieting data that gave it substance, together with their proposals for remedial action, direct to Attlee. This he did in a series of long, detailed, closely argued and essentially pessimistic minutes to the Prime Minister. They were intended to awaken Attlee as much as to the political as to the economic dangers of a coal crisis, and to persuade him to put pressure on his Cabinet colleagues – above all on the Minister of Fuel and Power – to act as quickly and decisively as necessary while there was yet time before the winter set in.

The essence of the case put forward by Jay and his friends was comprehensively set out in a minute which he wrote to the Prime Minister on 2nd April 1946,[5] little more than a week after the last meeting of the Ministerial and Official Coal Committees. It focused on the problem of recruiting more labour for coal mining: a net inflow of 4,300 men had indeed been achieved during the first three months of 1946, reversing the debilitating labour haemorrhages of the previous nine months or more, when over 20,000 more men left the mining industry than came into it.[6] The Minister of Fuel and Power, in his March report to the Ministerial Committee, had been inclined to see this as the start of a new and positive trend, but Jay disagreed:

> recruitment, which has been temporarily increased by the heavy rate of demobilization, is virtually certain to fall again after May when demobilization also falls. The Minister of Fuel and Power is, quite candidly, perhaps being rather misled by the temporary rise in recruitment into an excessively optimistic frame of mind about the longer term outlook. In fact, the outlook for next autumn and winter is very black; and the figures seem to me to show that the situation will certainly be worse then than now if something drastic is not done soon and stocks built up during the summer.

Jay's prediction, based on the extrapolation of existing trends of recruitment and the known rate of demobilisation from the armed forces of former miners, was that from May to December 1946 the coal-mining industry's labour force would fall from 699,000 to 675,000. In consequence, he reckoned, total production for the 'coal-year' 1946–47 would be 180 million tons rather than the 186 million for which the Ministry of Fuel and Power had allowed in its coal budget, against a level of demand running at 190 million to 195 million tons (a figure which was in line with the coal budget's estimate). This would produce a deficit, to be made good by drawing from stock, at least 60% higher than the Ministry of Fuel and Power was anticipating, and which at worst would substantially exceed the total stock of coal available to supplement current production at the start of the 'coal winter'. Were this to happen, Jay pointed out, 'at the outset of the National Coal Board's activities', the results:

> would be very damaging to the Government ... the generally serious effects of continous coal shortage on reconversion and the whole of our internal economic life really need little emphasis.

Jay's predictions that recruitment would decline after May turned out to be at least partly correct: there was a net outflow of nearly 10,000 men from the pits in the six months up to the end of December 1946, even if the decline in total numbers by that time was much smaller than he had foreseen.[7] This occurred despite growing pressure from the government to recruit men and boys for coal mining by means that were sometimes close to coercion. Labour exchanges, particularly in mining areas, were instructed that they should, as far as possible, direct men who were looking for work into the industry. But the government's powers of direction were not, in 1946, what they had been in wartime: pressure could be brought to bear by local officers of the Ministry of Labour in various ways on unemployed men seeking work, but outright coercion was no longer possible. And men who were, in one way or another, pressured into accepting employment in the mines could not be compelled to work willingly or efficiently, as experience with conscript Bevin Boys had amply demonstrated. On the whole, nobody in the industry wanted any more 'pressed men'. Indeed, they were anxious to get rid of those who were already there, either as Bevin Boys or as resentful victims of the wartime Essential Work Order, the revocation of which the government announced in July 1946, to become effective on 1st September. Such people, the Minister of Fuel and Power told the Cabinet, tended to be 'unwilling workers and contributed less than their fair share to the total output'.[8] They were a drag on productivity and contributed in undue measure to the problem of high absenteeism: the pits, it was widely agreed, would be well rid of them, if they could be replaced by willing volunteers whose commitment and efficiency would be greater. The problem, as the Ministry of Labour found in June and July 1946, was that such volunteers were hard to find. Ex-miners leaving the services showed a marked reluctance to return to their old employment: of the 23,000 demobilised by February 1946 nearly 40% had not gone back to the mines, to the disquiet of the Minister of Labour, George Isaacs.[9] In June it was reported that teams from the Ministries of Labour and Fuel and Power had interviewed over 5,000 unemployed men in coal-mining areas, of whom fewer than a thousand were willing to volunteer. Of 242 unemployed men interviewed in non-mining areas, only six were reported to be willing to take work in coal mining.[10] An intensive drive among the unemployed in South Wales to find recruits, undertaken by local officers of the Ministries of Labour and Fuel and Power from December 1945, resulted in the addition of no more than twenty-nine men to the underground work-force in the local coalfield, out of 357 originally thought suitable. Nearly two-thirds of those regarded as suitable flatly refused to consider pit work, whether underground or on the surface.[11]

As the Minister of Labour pointed out, in the absence of wartime powers to compel men to accept employment in coal mining and to keep them there once recruited, persuasion was in the final analysis the only way left to the government of bringing men into the industry.[12] And persuasion could succeed only if the work on offer was attractive in terms of pay, working conditions and social conditions in the communities in which the work was undertaken. Employment in coal mining was generally perceived as unattractive on all these counts, and any Minister or official who thought otherwise would be given ample grounds for modifying his views by the results of a survey undertaken by the government's own Social Survey organisation on behalf of the National Coal Board and the Ministry of Fuel and Power in autumn 1946.[13] The investigators sought to assess the attitudes in particular of boys and their parents, both in mining districts and elsewhere, towards coal mining as an occupation. They uncovered powerful negative attitudes with regard to pay, prospects, security of employment, working conditions, the social standing of miners, the level of amenity in mining villages, and so on. Only a tiny minority (3% or so) of boys and their parents, irrespective of family background in mining or the lack of it, showed any inclination towards mining as a career. In the face of such evidence the government and the Coal Board clearly faced a formidable task in trying to render the industry attractive enough to workers who could now, in general conditions of labour shortage, and with the dismantling of wartime controls, exercise considerable freedom in their choice of occupation.

The difficulties of recruiting for the coal mines in the new conditions of freedom in the labour market were recognised by all concerned with the problem. In the long term, of course, steps could be taken to improve those matters which discouraged men from taking employment in the mines. Indeed, even in the short term, it was felt, some things could be done to improve the occupational and social lot of the miners to a degree sufficient both to encourage new entrants to come into the industry and to improve the morale and commitment (and hence the productive efficiency) of the men who were already in it. Thus, in January 1946, Douglas Jay had suggested to the Prime Minister that the food rations of underground mineworkers should be increased, as 'the most practicable step to improve the disturbing coal situation'.[14] Attlee took the idea up with his colleagues. Shinwell, as Minister of Fuel and Power, was very much in favour: such a step, he argued, could have an important influence on production and might be of great assistance in encouraging recruitment. The Minister of Food, Sir Ben Smith, was, however, opposed to the idea as inequitable, impracticable and unacceptable to the Trades Union

Congress.[15] Discussion of the proposal – extended to include consideration of increased allocations of other consumer goods such as clothes, bedding and household utensils to mining communities, as well as more food – sputtered on through the spring and summer of 1946 without resolution. Eventually, in September 1946, the Board of Trade agreed to release to mining communities as an incentive to improved production extra supplies of household goods and utensils – bedding, wallpaper, galvanised iron baths and scrubbing brushes – together with the entire stock of men's clothing surplus to the requirements of the armed services' demobilisation scheme.[16] The actual effect on productivity among coal miners of the sudden availability of 29,000 'demob suits' with accessories was not, unfortunately, recorded. To secure agreement to the improvement of miners' food rations was not so easy: that matter continued to exercise the Cabinet's collective mind until the worst of the coal crisis was past.[17]

Proposals for incentives to increase recruitment and productivity were forthcoming too from quarters other than the government itself, not least from the National Union of Mineworkers. In what it described as 'The Miners' Charter'[18] the union put forward early in 1946 a package of proposals relating to pay, welfare provisions, and conditions of work – including such items as the introduction of a five-day working week and the granting of additional paid holidays – which, it was claimed, would bring the miners more into line with conditions in factory industry and in the process make mining more attractive to men seeking work while generating a better spirit among established mineworkers and so reducing absenteeism and departures from the industry. Again, Shinwell was enthusiastic, believing the effects on recruitment and productivity of the government's acceding to the main facets of the Miners' Charter to be potentially very beneficial. And, again, other Ministers voiced doubts about the utility of the charter's implementation. Several were worried about the effect that a reduction in the length of the miner's working week from five and a half to five days might have on output.[19] George Isaacs (Minister of Labour) was doubtful about the desirability of the government becoming directly involved with the NUM in negotiations regarding hours and conditions of work. These were matters for settlement between the union and the NCB: government involvement could weaken the NCB's position and created an unnecessary risk of making the government a direct party to industrial disputes when it ought to stand above them.[20] In Cabinet, Shinwell's optimistic view tended to prevail, to the extent at least that it was agreed that the major provisions of the charter, such as the five-day week, should be conceded. But the actual implementation of the concession was delayed until the beginning of the 'coal year' 1947–48, arguably minimising its impact at the time of greatest need during the preceding 'coal winter'.

It was the view of Douglas Jay and his friends that, as well as trying to improve the flow of indigenous labour into the coal industry, use should also be made of whatever foreign labour might be available. There were three sources which, in the summer of 1946, were regarded by some as capable of supplementing resources of British labour. The Irish Free State was one such source, not perhaps, strictly speaking, of foreign labour, since it retained until 1949 a residual formal allegiance to the Crown. High wages and excellent opportunities for employment compared with Ireland were exercising their customary attraction over Irishmen, who were making their way to Britain in some numbers in 1946. It was proposed that the Ministry of Labour should, as far as possible, direct this stream of Irish labour towards the coal mines.[21] A less palatable suggestion was that German prisoners of war − of whom nearly 400,000 remained in May 1946 − should be utilised, in effect, as forced labour: indeed, the Ministry of Fuel and Power was already employing a few hundred of them in May, though mostly on work connected with peat rather than coal.[22] Then, perhaps midway between the Irish and the Germans in terms of accept-ability to most people, there were the men of the Polish armed forces which were in the process of being disbanded in Britain in 1946. They numbered over 100,000, few of them anxious to return to a homeland dominated by Communists and the Red Army. When Poland had been divided up by Germany and the Soviet Union in September 1939 a large number of Polish soldiers had been taken into Soviet custody, from which a substan-tially smaller number had been released when the German attack on the Soviet Union in June 1941 brought General Sikorski's Polish government-in-exile into reluctant alliance with Stalin's Russia. They were not anxious to undergo a further bout of Soviet fraternalism, which for too many of their comrades had led in the past to the mass graves of the Katyn Forest. In recognition of their services alongside the British armed forces in Britain itself, at sea in the battle of the Atlantic, in Italy, Normandy and north-west Europe, those who did not wish to return to Poland were accorded the right to settle in Britain. The British and the exiled Polish authorities alike were anxious to find civilian occupations for those who decided to exercise that right, and there were many in Britain who saw in the men of the Polish Resettlement Corps (the medium through which Polish demobilisation was to be accomplished) the solution to the coal industry's labour problems.[23]

Unfortunately, there were equally many who were hostile to the employ-ment of foreign labour in general, and of the Polish exiles of General

Anders's army in particular, in mining or in any other industry. Foremost among them was the National Union of Mineworkers, with the General Secretary — the Communist Arthur Horner — as leader of the opposition. To a large extent the opposition was based on a fear of the effect on wages, conditions and security of employment if there should be a large-scale influx of foreign labour. This would, it was argued, tend to depress wages; foreigners would work for less, British miners would be thrown out of work to make room for them; and so on. Such objections in a way reflected the fear of a return to the bitter conditions of the 1920s and '30s. There were also, as it were, cultural and social fears: an uneasiness about the impact of foreigners on small, tightly knit mining communities, doubts about working in circumstances of ever-present danger alongside men whose command of English — or more especially of the local dialect of work — was suspect. And there was strong political suspicion of the Poles among men to whom the beneficence of socialism and the heroic stature of the Soviet Union were articles of faith.[24] If the Poles would not return home to help build a socialist Poland under the benign protection of the glorious Red Army, then was not their good faith towards socialist Britain suspect? Indeed, as the Minister of Fuel and Power himself was to report to his colleagues in government,

> there was very widespread dislike of the Poles among British miners who believed that because the Poles did not wish to return to Poland they must be fascists.[25]

If this was indeed a widespread belief, it can only be described — in view of what the Poles had suffered at the hands of the Nazis and the efforts they had made towards the destruction of Hitler and Mussolini — as grotesque. Nevertheless, the attitude in mining districts towards the introduction of Polish labour brought about a radical alteration in Shinwell's view of the question.[26] Having taken the initiative in February 1946 in raising the possibility in Cabinet of using the Poles in the mines, and in assessing their potential contribution to the solution of the industry's labour problems, he had become by the autumn actively opposed to their employment. The grounds of his opposition were essentially that only a few hundred of the Poles were suitable for employment in coal mining, and that the hostility of the miners and their union would negate any positive contribution that such small numbers could make to output. Rational considerations seem, however, to have been reinforced in Shinwell's case — as in, say, Arthur Horner's — by a more emotional, one might even say pathological dislike. Jay records, for instance, that at a meeting to consider the use of foreign labour in April 1946 Shinwell thumped the table and proclaimed, 'I will not have Poles in this industry, except over my dead body.'[27] This may, however, have reflected nothing more than exasperation with the way in which Jay, Meade and others had taken the issue up, making it almost the decisive test of Shinwell's determination to tackle the problem of coal supply. Caught between their pro-Polish fervour and the anti-Polish animus of the officials and members of the NUM (including his own constituents), he could perhaps be excused a certain impatience with matters Polish, certainly by the autumn of 1946. In any event, the wrangling within the government, and between the government and the NUM, dragged on through the autumn of 1946 and into the new year. Only in February 1947, when the fuel crisis was in full flood, were the obstacles set aside and the first of the Poles enrolled. By July 1947 more than 3,000 had completed their training, and by the end of the year twice that number were at work in the industry. Had such an accretion to the labour force taken place twelve months earlier, as it might well have done, it might have added an extra 1·5 million tons to that year's coal output.

The pressure brought to bear by Jay and his friends to put coal back on the agenda in Cabinet began to bear fruit in a substantial way in the high summer of 1946. Prompted by a minute from Jay, Attlee asked Shinwell early in June for a situation report. The response was a lengthy paper entitled *Output, Recruitment and Conditions of Employment in the Coal Mining Areas*, which was presented first to the Lord President's Committee and then to the full Cabinet.[29] In essence, Shinwell accepted that not all was well with the industry's recruitment, nor with the commitment and productivity of the labour force. Until such time as these matters improved, he admitted, 'we shall not secure the coal necessary to enable us to get through next winter without serious interruptions of industrial activity'. Rather surprisingly, his prescription for bringing about the necessary improvements was a *reduction* of the miner's working week from six shifts to five – the introduction, in other words, of the five-day week, which he recommended should be granted as soon as possible and preferably without loss of earnings. Consideration of the coal problem and the possibility of industrial disruption on a serious scale in the coming winter was thus decisively revived at the highest level of government. It went straight to the forefront among matters of urgent concern to the Cabinet when, on 24th June, Shinwell's paper, with supplementary papers by Herbert Morrison and George Isaacs, took up most of the agenda.[30] And at the forefront the coal problem was obstinately to stay up to and beyond the end of the year.

It would be fair to say that the coal problem and the threat it posed to the recovery of the economy were treated by Ministers as a matter of urgent concern during the later summer, autumn and early winter months of 1946 only in the sense of being extensively discussed and debated. The nature and seriousness of the problem and its likely impact were analysed at length and in detail. Expedients for dealing with it were canvassed almost *ad nauseam*, and their effectiveness or lack of it critically assessed. But there is about the records of meetings of the Cabinet and those of its subordinate committees where these matters were argued over, and in the minutes and memoranda from Ministers and civil servants which supported the arguments, something of the air of Nero fiddling while Rome burned. Because as June gave way to July, and summer to autumn, nearly to the point where autumn shaded into winter, out of all the talk and all the paper that Westminster and Whitehall devoted to the coal problem and its implications, few if any firm prescriptions for action emerged.

The main reason seems to have been a failure to secure agreement on the nature and severity of the threat the country faced in the winter of 1946−47. Analyses and assessments flowed from the pens of Ministers and their advisers, from Attlee down the hierarchy of the executive. All acknowledged the *potential* seriousness of the position, but there were differences of opinion about the likelihood of the potential being realised. Majority opinion, within and outside the Cabinet, was in varying degrees pessimistic, and as the autumn wore on became increasingly convinced that a crisis involving the large-scale disruption of industrial activity was unavoidable early in the new year. This majority view may be exemplified by one of Douglas Jay's memoranda to Attlee,[31] on 19th June 1946, just before its author ceased to be the Prime Minister's private secretary and entered the by-election contest in Battersea North. Current coal production, Jay wrote, was inadequate to build up stocks to more than 11 million tons by October − a level 20% below that of the previous October, which had itself been considered dangerously low. The winter run-down of stocks after October would reduce them to 'the impossible level of 3,000,000 or 4,000,000 tons', something around the level of one week's normal consumption. 'In fact', Jay concluded,

> as things are going at present, industry, transport and domestic consumption is bound to be dislocated on a wide and uncontrollable scale by December or a little later.

A little over a month later, James Meade − head of the Cabinet Office Economic Section − noted the general concern about the 'immediate and special' issue of coal in the committee charged with compiling the *Economic*

Survey for 1946–47, the basic document in the process of economic planning which the government was putting into effect. The outlook, Meade noted:

> is indeed grim ... we briefed the Lord President to the effect that he had better accept as inevitable a serious shortage next winter and turn all the heat on to considering the best means of ensuring that the available coal was allocated in proper proportions to the most essential uses.[32]

The impact of this prompting from Jay and his associates may be seen in a minute which went from Attlee to his Chancellor of the Exchequer, Hugh Dalton, on 24th July 1946. 'I have no doubt,' Attlee wrote:

> that coal is now the most urgent economic problem ... and that a disastrous failure can be averted only if it is most boldly and resolutely tackled.[33]

Morrison was equally convinced: his June paper for the Cabinet on the subject of output and recruitment might have been written by Jay.[34] The record of ministerial discussions in Cabinet and in the subordinate committees provides clear evidence of the influence of the views expressed by Meade, Jay and the latter's successor in Attlee's private office, Gorell Barnes. Their lobbying bore fruit in, among other things, the early recall of the Ministerial Coal Committee: instead of the tentatively scheduled reconvening in October, it began a new series of meetings on 1st August, under Dalton's chairmanship, in the hope at least of mitigating the crisis which most of its members were increasingly inclined to regard as inevitable.

There were, however, certain significant exceptions to the gloomy feelings prevalent in government during the summer and autumn of 1946. And the most significant of these was the Minister of Fuel and Power himself, Emanuel Shinwell. He did not dispute the basis of the prevailing pessimism – the statistics of output, stocks, productivity and recruitment which his own Ministry, after all, had supplied. But he disagreed completely with the gloomy interpretations that were being placed upon them by his ministerial colleagues at the urging of Jay and his friends. The gloss which Shinwell put upon the figures, and the attitude he took to the statistical calculation of the possibility of a fuel crisis, led him to far more optimistic conclusions.

In his memoirs[35] Shinwell defended himself against accusations of 'undue optimism' about the situation in the summer and autumn of 1946 by cataloguing the warnings he had given his colleagues, together with the measures he had proposed to increase output and reduce consumption, and by implying that his optimistic public statements were matched by a realistic appreciation of the true position which he expressed in private. There can certainly be no question of his public optimism, in speeches both inside Parliament and out. In a Commons debate on the coal situation called by the opposition, on 24th July, he admitted the danger that there might be 'some stoppages in industrial undertakings in the course of the winter'. But, he went on:

> I believe – and I think there is every reason for this belief – that as a result of the new dispensation and the new atmosphere in the industry resulting from the operation of the Coal Board, we shall get the output we want ... with the prospects of fuel efficiency, of conversion of coal to fuel oil, of open-cast production in excess of last year, the stepping up of manpower and ... a better atmosphere in the industry, I think we can get through.[36]

This, indeed, was typical of his parliamentary utterances on the subject in the run-up to the beginning of the 'coal winter' at the end of October: sober recognition at the start of the possibilities of disruption due to a shortage, but always ending on an upbeat note, giving the impression that the government, his Ministry, and above all he himself, had the matter well in hand.[37] His statements outside Parliament were even more sanguine, if anything, with the element of sober realism further subordinated to the element of confident reassurance. The most famous such extra-parliamentary pronouncement is probably that which furnishes the prologue to this chapter, though its fame owes something perhaps to the wisdom of hindsight on the part of Shinwell's critics, for it passed largely without comment when it was made at a luncheon for coke-oven managers on 24th October.[38] The sarcastic turn of phrase – 'Everybody knows there is going to be a serious crisis in the coal industry, except the Minister of Fuel and Power' – was only too readily turned against its originator as the crisis bit hard four months later.

Shinwell's defence, that his public expressions of sanguinity were matched by his private acknowledgement of the true position,[39] does not really seem to stand up in the face of the evidence provided by his statements in confidential meetings and papers, when presumably he was in a position to give voice to any private pessimism he may have felt. There is little indication that he availed himself of any such opportunity. In the Cabinet memorandum of 17th June which, in effect, signalled the return of the coal problem to a position high on the order of business, the same mixture is present as in his public pronouncements: recognition of present problems moderated by optimism about their future resolution.[40] With regard to recruitment, absenteeism and productivity, he maintained:

> there are signs that the worst is over ... we are entitled to conclude that ... the adverse factors introduced by the war are ceasing to operate and to look forward to further improvement.

A declaration by the government revealing its favourable attitude to the implementation of the Miners' Charter would:

> do much to improve the general atmosphere in the industry and will be sufficient to prevent a more serious situation from developing in the coal-fields.

To the Lord President's Committee on 19th July, a committee of the Cabinet itself whose proceedings were classified as secret, Shinwell reported that

> Generally, the atmosphere in the coal industry seemed to be improving rapidly and he hoped that in September, by which time it would be possible to see more clearly the prospects for the coming winter, the outlook would be reasonably good.[41]

At the Ministerial Coal Committee on 1st August he presented a revised 'coal budget' for the year to 30th April 1947.[42] In its details this made disquieting reading: recruitment had continued to decline, if not quite to the extent envisaged when the original budget had been drafted in March; absenteeism had declined somewhat, but so had productivity. In all, it was anticipated that an aggregate coal supply of 195·6 million tons would be available from all sources for that 'coal year'. But against this had to be set a total requirement – comprising inland consumption, exports and ships' bunkers, and the maintenance of essential stocks – of 205·1 million tons. But despite the yawning deficit of 9·5 million tons, Shinwell remained essentially optimistic. He and his officials had measures in hand, he assured the committee, to reduce consumption, chief among which was the programme of converting industrial plant from coal-firing to oil. On the output side, he proposed to make a personal visit to the coalfields 'to speed production', while making 'a special drive' to maximise open-cast output before November. As a result, he told his colleagues, he was:

> not unhopeful of being able to bridge the whole ... deficit ... A better atmosphere now prevailed in the industry and he felt sure that it would improve further. Besides improving output this would enhance the chances of recruiting large numbers.

On 17th October, just a week before his pronouncement to the assembled coke-oven managers, Shinwell produced a further update of the 'coal budget' for his colleagues on the Coal Committee and in the Cabinet.[43] In it he announced that his proposed economy measures 'are likely to produce rather larger economies than I forecast'. Meanwhile, as far as production was concerned, declining absenteeism and increasing productivity led him to expect a significant growth in the output of both deep-mined and open-cast coal compared with the estimates he had presented to the Coal Committee on 1st August. The gap between consumption and production, in consequence, had come down from the earlier estimate of 9·5 million tons to something between 2 million and 5 million. By Shinwell's reckoning, a gap of the order of 3·5 million tons seemed a realistic estimate. It could not, he pointed out, be bridged (as in the previous winter) by simply drawing on stocks: only increased output or reduced consumption could achieve that objective, and his Ministry was taking all possible measures to secure both.

Shinwell's attitude, therefore, in both public and confidential statements was quite consistent throughout the 'coal summer' from May to October 1946. He believed that, from the admittedly dangerous position with regard to output, productivity and stocks prevailing at the start of the summer, there would be a steady improvement which would take the country into the 'coal winter' on 1st November with a supply position that would enable any substantial degree of industrial disruption and domestic discomfort to be avoided. He discounted completely the predictions of disaster being put about by the likes of Jay and Meade and given credence by Attlee, Morrison and other senior Ministers. The nation's bacon would be saved, above all, by the 'new spirit in the pits', the 'new atmosphere in the industry', the great uplift in the morale of the mineworkers induced by the imminent prospect of nationalisation and the implementation of the Miners' Charter. This would alone be sufficient to improve recruitment and increase commitment among the miners, and so increase their output and productivity to a degree which, with reasonable care and economy on the part of consumers, would see the country through the winter more or less unscathed. If there was cause for concern on the fuel and power front, Shinwell believed, it lay not on the side of coal but rather on the side of electricity supplies. The demand for electricity was rising to unprecedented and unforeseen levels, and the programme of rehabilitating and enlarging Britain's battered wartime generating capacity had not yet got very far. Shinwell feared that capacity might well 'prove inadequate to meet the load during the coming winter'.[44] He also feared that, as in the previous winter, transport facilities for the movement of coal, especially by rail, would be hard pressed and might not be able to cope.[45] But as far as coal production was concerned, his faith that the miners would come through with the tonnage required was unbreakable during the 1946 'coal summer', even in the face of the most pessimistic prognostications of others.

Had this optimism any real basis? In fact there were a number of respects in which, during the summer months, things did seem to be going Shinwell's way. The coal-mining labour force remained fairly steady at 699,000–700,000 from May through August, instead of entering into the sharp decline predicted by the likes of Douglas Jay. Absenteeism was diminishing as well, both from the high winter levels of 1945–46 and even from the levels shown in the previous summer.[46] There was, therefore, some evidence (if slender) of greater commitment among the miners, though it cannot be seen as indicative of any dramatic enhancement of their morale. And coal output was running significantly ahead of the levels obtaining during the 1945 'coal summer', by about 7½%. Shinwell, it must be said, never assumed that production would come to meet or exceed consumption over the 'coal year' 1946–47, nor indeed in the 'coal winter' of that year. But his confidence was based on the expectation that matters would improve on the production side of the coal budget and that on the consumption side the requirement for coal would be significantly reduced, mainly through greater efficiency in gasworks and through the replacement of coal in both homes and industries by coke and, especially, heavy fuel oil, which had become more readily available since April 1946. His public and confidential statements through the 1946 'coal summer' always accepted that, at the moment of speaking or writing, consumption outweighed the supply provided by current production and stocks. But they always embodied the belief that, with a combination of energy on the production side and good housekeeping on the consumption side, the gap could, even in the short term, be reduced to insignificance or even abolished altogether. The changes required on both sides of the budget may have seemed to him slight, and readily capable of realisation. From his reports to the Ministerial Coal Committee in August and September 1946[47] it is clear that he saw salvation in terms of a saving through the substitution of coke and fuel oil of about five million tons (some 2½% of annual coal consumption) and of an increase in average weekly coal output of some 4% or 5%.

It became evident, however, that with the onset of the 'coal winter' on 1st November 1946 salvation even in those seemingly modest terms was nowhere near being achieved. Average weekly coal output did indeed rise in September and October to the level of 3·75 million tons at which, as Shinwell had reported to the Coal Committee in September, 'the general position would be reasonably satisfactory'. And this had been achieved despite an outflow during those two months of over 5,000 men from the pits. Productivity (output per man-shift) among those remaining had increased by more than enough to compensate for the loss.[48] On the other hand, consumption obstinately continued to grow along with production, and showed every prospect of continuing substantially to outstrip production during the winter. The expected savings on the consumption side, especially from the substitution of oil for coal, were not being achieved. The demand for coal gas and for electricity from the coal-fired power stations was rising to new heights, so that the demand levels of December 1945 had already been surpassed in October 1946. And perhaps most serious of all, the coal stocks with which the country faced the winter of 1946–47 were more than 20% (nearly 5 million tons) lower than those with which it had entered the previous winter – themselves recognised by the government to have been at crisis level.[49]

The buoyancy of Shinwell's pronouncements was not altogether sufficient to reassure his colleagues on the Coal Committee and in the Cabinet. Commenting to the Prime Minister on the Minister of Fuel and Power's report to the Coal Committee's September meeting, Hugh Dalton (the committee's chairman) remarked:

> These figures look reassuring, but it must be borne in mind that stocks of coal are everywhere dangerously low and that even small shortages may land us in great difficulties ... we are working on very fine margins, and, if and when it becomes clear that a substantial deficit is impending, it may be necessary to take emergency measures.[50]

Such measures, Dalton continued, needed to be prepared in advance, to be ready for implementation before the end of December. His warning to Attlee of the need to prepare for an emergency came not a moment too soon. Within a week, electricity and gas undertakings were issuing warnings that their coal supplies were not keeping pace with the growing demand for their products, and already small power cuts were being imposed on some electricity customers.[51]

Shinwell continued to pour cold water on such scaremongering: the electricity suppliers were denounced for making propaganda, their fears dismissed as 'a lot of nonsense'.[52] He did, indeed, issue an appeal early in October for a voluntary reduction in coal consumption all round of about 10%,[53] but an appeal to voluntarism was unlikely to cut much ice with people who had become accustomed over the previous seven or eight years to seeing *real* emergencies being dealt with by determined compulsion on the part of the State. And any response would be unlikely to survive in the face of such confident statements as the one Shinwell made shortly afterwards to the coke-oven managers.

It is clear, however, that by the beginning of the 'coal winter' on 1st November the Minister of Fuel and Power was beginning to wake up to the fact that, for all his cheerful prophecies, the supply of coal was indeed bascially unsatisfactory and likely to be a source of real danger to the fulfilment of the government's post-war industrial reconstruction pro-grammes in the winter months. He had come under considerable pressure from Cabinet colleagues, including Attlee himself, at the time of the Ministerial Coal Committee's meeting of 22nd October,[54] to consider the advisability of, and the administrative machinery for, the imposition of cuts in fuel deliveries to industrial consumers, who, in Attlee's words, 'had not yet taken voluntarily all possible steps for fuel economy'. And although in Shinwell's own opinion 'there was no call for the immediate imposition of cuts', and he was 'satisfied that a great deal can be done [to secure fuel economies] without bringing factories to a standstill', he nevertheless began to take the question of *imposing*, by means of the machinery for con-trolling coal distribution that his Ministry had retained from its wartime powers, restrictions on deliveries to industrial consumers to secure the economies that would be required to bridge the gap between demand and availability.[55]

But even the exercise of contemplating possibilities that he had recently denied would ever require contemplation seems not to have alerted Shinwell to the full seriousness of the position and the immediate imminence of significant disruption of basic industrial activity through a dearth of coal. Despite an exhortation from Attlee to come up with a plan to impose selective cuts in allocations to industrial consumers and to put it into immediate effect,[56] Shinwell showed little tendency to accept that speed was of the essence. Instead, he engaged in a solemn and elaborate *pavane* with his own departmental officials of proposal and counter-proposal, each ritually presented to the Coal Committee or the Cabinet for evaluation. As a result it was not until early December that the government's plan to restrict the consumption of coal, gas and electricity by industry was announced. And its implementation was not to take place for several more weeks, until 1st January 1947.

Shinwell's officials at the Ministry of Fuel and Power favoured the suspension of existing coal supply arrangements to industry. Based on the arrangements instituted in wartime and continued under the Supplies and Services (Transitional Powers) legislation of 1945, these were based on two criteria. First, there was the consumer's official allocation: a figure agreed at the beginning of the coal year and based on the consumer's re-quirements. Then there was the amount of coal available for distribution: this would not necessarily match the official allocation, but the system of allocations based on consumers' needs provided the local coal distri-bution officers of the Ministry of Fuel and Power with a basis for *pro rata* distribution to consumers, so that all received the same proportion of their requirements. What was proposed now, in November 1946, was that this set-up should be replaced by a system of weekly coal allocations to consumers based on a calculation combining their needs and the amount of coal available for distribution: deliveries would then be made up to the full amount of the allocation. Under the scheme now proposed, industrial consumers were to be divided into three categories of priority for coal deliveries. In the first were iron and steel, coke ovens and transport, supplies to which would not be cut. The second category embraced 'essential' industries – gas, electricity, building materials, dairy processing and flour-milling, textile spinning, shipbuilding, textile and electrical engineering being the chief ones – to which, it was proposed, coal deliveries should be cut by 5% from existing levels. Thirdly, there were the 'non-essential' industries, such as glass, cement, mechanical engineering and nearly all consumer goods, which would see their coal deliveries reduced by 12½%, though part of that cut would be used to create regional 'coal pools' to meet emergencies among consumers thus deprived. In addition, industrial users of gas and electricity would be directed to reduce their consumption by 10% from 'the amount which ... it would have been had it not been for the Direction'.[57]

Presenting his officials' scheme to the Cabinet, Shinwell made no secret of his dislike for it, and was given leave to devise his own, which he presented about a week later. What his officials had proposed was too complicated; it found little favour with either the Trades Union Congress or the Federation of British Industry; it would not in any case secure cuts in coal consumption on the scale required.[58] But his chief objection to the officials' scheme appears to have been that it would let the public know just how bad the position actually was. To abandon the existing system of annual allocations based on need for one of weekly allocations based on the availability of coal would require a public announcement, and, as Shinwell told the Cabinet, 'I am strongly opposed to such an announcement, since it ... would be calculated to have a severely depressing political effect.' He accordingly proposed leaving the existing allocation arrangements in place and simply cutting deliveries to essential industries by 5%, and to the 'non-essential' ones by 10%. Since the basis for calculating allocations would be unchanged, 'no public announcement need be made'. Shinwell was working on the same classification of essential and non-essential industry as his officials, but at the insistence of the FBI he proposed to extend 'non-essential' status (and the 10% cut in coal deliveries that went with it) to hotels and places of entertainment, which his officials had ignored. Both essential and non-essential industrial users of gas and electricity, he suggested, should be required to limit their consumption between December 1946 and March 1947 to an average weekly level not exceeding that of November 1946.[59]

Shinwell's plan was simpler than that of his officials; it was more in tune with the ideas of industry, as represented by the TUC and the FBI; its prescription for gas and electricity was more concrete and realistic. It was, accordingly, adopted by the government as the official economy scheme, to be put into effect at the new year. The belief that somehow the cuts in coal, electricity and gas consumption in industry could be put into effect without the public noticing and wondering about their implications, because the thing was done in such a way as not to require a formal public announcement, evidently cut no ice with the Cabinet. Indeed, it is remarkable that the Minister of Fuel and Power should have harboured the belief that it could, and should, be done in such a way as to hide the serious nature of the position from the public gaze. Even before the Cabinet had agreed on the scheme to be implemented, before indeed the abortive proposals of the Fuel and Power officials had been formulated, the public had been made well aware that something of the kind was in the wind. Rumour, as always, tended towards the apocalyptic, as when the *News Chronicle* reported on 4th November that:

> Drastic plans for saving fuel and power which may involve closing down hundreds of factories and workshops and throwing hundreds and thousands of men and women out of work in the less essential industries are now being prepared by the Board of Trade to meet the inevitable coal crisis this winter.[60]

The *Economist*, noting the wide circulation of such stories in the press, concluded that:

> On the fuel front ... the last illusions are vanishing and it is clear that the Government has no policy that is likely to affect the supply of coal this winter or next.[61]

The *Economist* also took note in the same article of the dire prediction made in the House of Commons by the Overseas Trade Secretary, Hilary Marquand, that the country would do well to prepare for a slump in the near future comparable to that of 1921, with the further possibility later on of something more akin to the 1929 depression.[62] Shinwell's worry that a public announcement of fuel economy measures would have 'a severely depressing effect' seems, in the face of such widespread public speculation on the subject, ill judged. To try to sneak in economies as he had suggested to the Cabinet on 19th November would have been much more likely to bring discredit on the government. So, probably sensibly, his suggestion was not followed and the new fuel economy plan for industry was announced on 4th December. On the whole, the press received it coolly. The *Economist* doubted whether the cuts in gas and electricity consumption could be enforced,[63] and there was general scepticism about whether the measures were stringent enough to make any real difference to the prospect of a fuel crisis in the months to come.

Some time before the new scheme was due to come into effect, on 1st January 1947, it was already becoming all too apparent that the measure was attempting to accomplish too little and that it was being applied too late. The stable door was already open when the scheme was announced on 4th December. By the time it actually came into operation the horse was well on its way out. The first signs of the industrial breakdown feared by the government were to be seen in the power cuts which some electricity undertakings had been obliged to apply in October and November 1946. These had been primarily due to the lack of generating capacity adequate for the level of demand prevailing. Despite the installed capacity of CEB 'selected stations' standing at 11,300 megawatts at the end of 1945, the Board had only been able to deliver a maximum of 8,906 megawatts against a peak winter demand of 9,210 in January 1946. Since then demand had continued to grow rapidly − to such an extent, indeed, that the peak of the previous winter was already being matched in November 1946. The CEB was putting in hand a large-scale programme of power-station construction to make good wartime deficiencies, but this had not so far had any effect on actual capacity, so the electricity supply industry was going into the winter of 1946−47 with plant which was acknowledged to be 'much below the capacity regarded as necessary to cater for the existing maximum demand'. But, as well as the inadequacy of generating plant, power engineers were also complaining that the poor quality of coal being delivered to many power stations forced them to operate below their maximum efficiency. The CEB also expressed concern about the parlous state of power-station coal stocks and deliveries. Nor was the position of the gas industry any better. Gasworks were not being given priority in the allocation of labour or materials, so even routine maintenance was difficult, while expansion and reconstruction were impossible. Meanwhile gas consumption was rising at such an alarming rate that 'the gas industry is in fact unable to cope with demand'. And once again, technical shortcomings were aggravated by problems with both the quantity and the quality of coal supplies.[64]

The power cuts of October and November provoked a flurry of correspondence from the Board of Trade's Regional Officers, the civil servants arguably most closely in touch with industry's cares and fears. They were critical of the fact (as it appeared to them) that sufficient efforts were not being made 'to provide the necessary mechanical equipment to increase the supply of solid fuel, electrical power and gas', and they called for a revival of the wartime sense of urgency in tackling production bottle-necks.[65] By late December the expected crisis in fuel and power supplies was beginning to become reality, particularly in the midland and north-western regions, centred respectively on Birmingham and Manchester, the one being the heartland of the engineering sector, the other of the cotton textile industry. Both industries were central to the government's, and indeed the entire country's, hopes of industrial recovery and the revival of the export trade.

The process began with the announcement on 19th December by the City of Birmingham Electricity Department that, at present rates of electricity consumption and coal supply, it would be able to meet only three-quarters of the demand likely to be placed upon it by its customers in January 1947, and that even then its coal stocks would be exhausted by the end of the month. It called for factories using electricity to shut down for one day each week, to prevent 'a national calamity'.[66] When the time came, however, for industrial undertakings to resume working after the Christmas holidays, it became only too obvious that many in the midlands and the north-west were unable to do so for lack of coal. The most notorious case was that of Austin Motors in Birmingham itself, with a labour force of 14,000 and a very substantial commitment to export sales. Government sympathisers hinted that the firm's announcement, on the eve of the holiday, that it would be unable to reopen because of a coal shortage was merely a political ploy designed by a leading representative of 'big business' to embarrass the government.[67] The Ministry of Fuel and Power in any case made a hasty emergency allocation of coal to Austin's, and the company duly went back to work.[68] But though it was saved by this timely intervention, others were less fortunate: *The Times* reported on 28th December that a number of Lancashire cotton mills remained closed for lack of coal. More seriously, letters and teleprinter messages were beginning to pour into the Board of Trade in London by the end of December from its Regional Officers and Boards for Industry about the extreme gravity of the fuel situation in various parts of the country. Summarising its Regional Officers' reports for that week, the Board of Trade noted that:

> Although total production of coal for both Christmas week and the preceding week were both well above the target figure, the shortage is now serious in most regions ... Deliveries to industry other than the top priorities (gas, electricity, iron and steel, etc.) ... are nowhere even approximately equal to present allocations.

Particularly unsatisfactory were deliveries in the midland region ('only about 55% of allocation') and the north-west ('only sufficient to meet the requirements of the "priority" industries ... and nothing left over for general industry').[69] Especially scathing was a message dated 1st January 1947 (the day the Shinwell economy scheme came into effect) from Miss Belson, Secretary to the Midland Regional Board for Industry. The economy measures now coming into operation, she claimed:

> would have been admirable if issued about 9 months ago as a means of building up stocks, but [were] quite inadequate as a means of coping with the present grave situation ... we have now reached the position I forecast last August ... that stocks are so low that *ad hoc* arrangements can no longer cope and the whole thing will start to disintegrate. I cannot see personally that we can get much beyond the next fortnight without some major breakdown.[70]

By that time conditions in the north-west of England had deteriorated to the point where local officials of the Regional Board for Industry talked openly of a fuel crisis, and the term was in routine use in the columns of the *Manchester Guardian*. Coal stocks and supplies in the heartland of the cotton industry — Bury, Blackburn, Burnley and Bolton — were close to exhaustion. Many factories, particularly in the weaving sector of the industry, had been forced to close down or were in imminent danger of doing so. The Regional Board called for cuts in street and shop lighting to save electricity, complained to Whitehall of spasmodic and unpredictable cuts in coal deliveries which were the cause of 'chaos ... much more harmful than an organised stoppage', and announced that its Fuel Allocation Committee would meet daily 'while the acute crisis existed'. The danger of large-scale factory closures in the Midlands persisted in spite of the rushing of emergency coal supplies to Austin Motors to enable it to resume work. And the problem was no longer confined to the midlands and the north-west. From the east and south on 3rd January came reports of the actual or threatened closure of cement and brick works, posing a serious threat to the already faltering housing reconstruction programme. From the north midlands, centred on Nottingham and at the heart of a major coalfield, the Board of Trade's Regional Controller reported the exhaustion of coal stocks with important firms in textiles, pottery and engineering, and threats of early closure. The South West Regional Board called for a Prime Ministerial broadcast, the ultimate rallying call to the nation in crisis, in view of the extreme gravity of the situation. As the *Economist* was to comment on 4th January 1947,

> the coal crisis, rather like an epidemic rash, has erupted in other areas and is now widely affecting industry.[71]

At the end of the first week of the new year there was a brief foretaste of things to come when snow fell throughout the country and temperatures plummeted. The bad weather only lasted for a couple of days before a thaw set in, but it was enough to disrupt transport by road and rail quite severely and to provoke a further rash of factory closures in the Leeds and Lancashire textile industies, together with the threatened curtailment of production at the great Dunlop Rubber Company's works at Birmingham, Manchester, Liverpool and Leicester. More ominous even than that was the imposition of nation-wide cuts in electricity supply, and the issuing of a warning by the Central Electricity Board of more to come unless consumers exercised the strictest economy. A similar warning was put out by the Gas Council: coal stocks at gasworks were a mere fraction of what was regarded as the safe level for the time of year, and many gasworks would soon find themselves with 'an unworkable margin' of stocks and would have to shut down. To avoid such a disaster, 'Strict and sustained economy by consumers was imperative'. The only bright spot on the scene was provided by the outcome of a visit by the Parliamentary Secretary to the Minister of Fuel and Power, Hugh Gaitskell, to Manchester to investigate the particularly acute situation in the north-west. He was able to provide temporary relief to the hard-pressed cotton industry by authorising it to draw, on a once-for-all basis, on the remnants of emergency stocks of house coal that the Ministry had laid down during the war.[72]

The mass of detailed evidence provided by the newspaper and periodical press and, perhaps more tellingly, by the correspondence of the government's own regional officials demonstrates beyond serious doubt that at the very beginning of January 1947 (if not indeed by Christmas 1946) the country was no longer merely moving towards a crisis in its fuel and power resources, but had gone over the brink. Coal and electrical power supplies were actually breaking down on a significant scale, and gas was threatened with the same fate. Industrial production was being interrupted across a range of basic activities, above all in the great manufacturing centres of midland and north-west England which then accounted for about half the entire industrial capacity of the country. The whole basis for the post-war rehabilitation of economic and social life was under acute threat: if output fell, with it went the hope of full employment, the rebuilding of the export trade, and ultimately the standard of living and the expectation of social security of the people themselves. By the time the major break in the weather occurred on 23rd January, the descent into the abyss was already well advanced.

If further proof of the existence of a crisis at the turn of the year is needed, it is provided by the evidence of what was going on in the inner-most councils of the government between 3rd and 7th January. The first significant development was the circulation of a long and detailed memorandum to the Cabinet by the Minister of Fuel and Power. Dated 3rd January, just two days after the ceremonies marking the transition from private ownership to nationalisation in the coal industry, it set out in full the disastrous state of affairs that the government and the country now faced. It revealed, as Attlee's private secretary observed, 'just the kind of position those of us who have been watching the coal position for a long time have been expecting to develop'. Deliveries to industry were running so far behind requirements that enforced factory closures were already occurring, and no measures could now prevent 'widespread in-dustrial stoppages'. Shinwell's memorandum was, in effect, an admission of defeat; an acknowledgement (to echo his speech to the coke-oven managers the previous October) that now *even* the Minister of Fuel and Power knew there was going to be a fuel crisis, indeed that it was already in full swing.[73]

This time Shinwell started on the up-beat, noting that coal output had been growing steadily since October. But the tone of his statement rapidly descended into extreme pessimism. Consumption of coal, and more especially of electricity from coal-fired power stations, had risen to such an extent that 'a critical situation has now arisen'. The key to this 'critical situation', he continued, lay in the fact that power station coal supplies were running down to the point of exhaustion. Such was the shortage of generating capacity that if a few power stations were forced to close down for lack of coal (as seemed likely) the remainder would be overwhelmed by the pressure of demand, and 'a complete failure of electricity supply over wide areas would be inevitable'. In an attempt to divert some of the blame from himself, he argued that some of the responsibility for the position could be laid at the door of his colleague, the Minister of Transport, and that of the Central Electricity Board. The shortage of railway wagons to move coal from the pitheads had aggravated the situation, as had the lack of reserve generating capacity. But he accepted that the fundamental problem was that not enough coal was being produced to meet demand and stave off the total depletion of stocks. 'It is clear,' Shinwell wrote:

that we cannot allow Power Stations to go out of production; the con-sequences of a complete failure of electricity supply over wide areas are far too serious. It would mean complete paralysis throughout those areas – loss of essential production, widespread unemployment, no lighting or means of cooking for many households, and stoppage of electric trains and trams, etc.[74]

To avert such consequences appeals for voluntary restraint were totally insufficient, and economy measures of the kind that had just come into force on New Year's Day — cutting industrial coal supplies by 5% or 10% and requiring industry to limit its use of gas and electricity for three months to the levels of November 1946 — pathetically inadequate. In their place Shinwell put two alternative courses of action before the Cabinet. The first was to divert coal at the rate of 50,000 tons per week from manufacturing industry to power stations, to forestall the complete exhaustion of their stocks. The second was to propose that electricity supply undertakings should be granted powers under the 1945 Supplies and Services Act to cut off specific industrial consumers with the object of securing an immediate overall reduction of 25% in the industrial use of electricity, or whatever reduction was thought necessary to conserve power station coal stocks at a minimum of two weeks' supply. In any event, voluntary savings were to be replaced by compulsory cuts; and while the Cabinet might be able to look upon Shinwell's proposals as alternatives, industry would find it less easy to see them that way. Either course represented a recipe for the collapse, in the short term at least, of an industrial effort which — as one hard-pressed manufacturer had put it a few days earlier — was living 'from shovelful to shovelful' of coal.[75] Nor did the Minister feel able to offer hope for the longer term. When he raised his eyes from the immediate crisis and tried to see further ahead, he felt constrained to warn the Cabinet that:

> for some considerable time there will not be sufficient fuel and power to meet the requirements put forward by Departments in view of the rising trend of consumption ... It is therefore for the Cabinet to decide which industries or sections of industries are to be refused raw materials including fuel and power for the purposes of production.

Viewed against the essential optimism of his statements the previous October, the memorandum is an abject document, the chastened account of a man who has had the wind taken abruptly from his sails. The impression is heightened by the fact that when the Cabinet met to consider the situation set out in the memorandum, on Tuesday 7th January, it was not Shinwell who made the running in promoting ways of handling the crisis, but rather his colleague, the President of the Board of Trade, Sir Stafford Cripps.

It may be unprofitable to attempt to assign blame for the fuel crisis that became so starkly apparent in the first days of 1947, but that has not stopped the attempt from being made. Shinwell's own successive excursions into autobiography between 1955 and 1981, for example, can be seen as increasingly peevish exercises in self-exculpation, loading the blame variously on the shoulders of his Cabinet colleagues (notably Barnes, Dalton and Cripps) or those of the National Union of Mineworkers. He cannot, though, dispose of the fact that as Minister of Fuel and Power it was he who carried the chief political responsibility for the maintenance of fuel supplies. There were certainly many in the early months of 1947, as there have been since, who regarded the blame for the crisis as primarily the Minister's. As early as December 1946 Hugh Dalton noted in his diary the currency of the slogan 'Starve with Strachey and Shiver with Shinwell' and made no bones about his agreement with this popular sentiment, at least as far as its second component was concerned.[76] Nor would several of Shinwell's colleagues — Jay and Gaitskell, for instance — necessarily have disagreed with the Editor of the *Economist* when he declared *à propos* the crisis that:

> The responsibility of the Government is collective; but the blame also falls specifically on Mr. Shinwell. It is known that the Micawber policy was peculiarly and personally his.[77]

Before saddling Emanuel Shinwell with this responsibility, however, it is pertinent to ask whether there was anything he might have done — during the 'coal summer' of 1946, for instance — that could have made any practical difference to the situation he and the country faced at the start of 1947. What, for example, of his failure to get Polish ex-servicemen into the coal mines in 1946, of which some of his critics made so much? It is undoubtedly true that negotiations with the NUM over the question dragged on for months into the winter of 1946–47 while the coal supply steadily deteriorated. But the fault was hardly Shinwell's. The chief sticking point was the hostility of the miners and their leaders, and even if Shinwell had been fired with the same zeal as Jay and others it seems extremely doubtful that he would have been able to get round this obstacle any more quickly. To have met the union's hostility head-on, and tried to bulldoze through the recruitment of the Poles — as Shinwell's critics appeared to wish in 1946 — was surely a counsel of frustration rather than a practical course of action. Retaliatory action by the NUM would certainly have followed, which would have worsened coal supplies in the short run at least. And in 1946 short-run considerations were paramount as far as coal was concerned. The union had to be cajoled and persuaded, patiently and tactfully, to accept the Poles, as eventually it did in January 1947. Admittedly this was too late to influence the crisis for the better, but at least in the meantime goodwill between the NUM and the government was preserved, together with the reductions in absenteeism and the increases in productivity that were its tangible manifestations.

Could Shinwell have done more to promote the exploitation of alternative fuels as a substitute for coal, particularly at power stations and in industrial processes? Dalton certainly thought so: in a minute of 28th June 1946 he accused Shinwell of having 'not really pressed' the possibilities of converting coal-fired industrial plant to oil firing as a means of economising in coal use in the coming winter. He asked Attlee to put pressure on Shinwell to promote a conversion programme that might save three to five million tons of coal by the end of 1946.[78] In fact Shinwell and his subordinates were exhibiting a great deal of interest in possible substitutes for coal. Most of their efforts were, indeed, devoted to fostering the use of heavy fuel oil in place of coal for industrial heating and steam-raising, as well as in railway locomotives and power stations. This coal-to-oil conversion programme is worthy of attention in some detail. Not only does its story give the lie to Dalton's accusation, it illustrates in graphic microcosm the formidable pressures and complex constraints within which the government's whole industrial reconstruction policy had to be implemented. It is also worth recording, however, that the Ministry of Fuel and Power was also engaged in a serious assessment of the large-scale use of peat. A survey of the country's peat resources was conducted by the Ministry's Regional Controllers in the summer of 1946, and feasibility studies were prepared later in the year. None, as it happened, seemed to offer any worthwhile possibility of relieving the immediate shortage of coal, and their longer-term development was seen to be uneconomic because of the problems of labour supply and transport posed by the remoteness of the main peat mosses and their difficult terrain. So the idea of perfuming the atmosphere of Britain's towns with the romantic reek of peat smoke came to nothing. But it showed the lengths to which Shinwell and his officers were prepared to go in pursuit of the possibility of saving coal.[79]

The substitution of oil for coal was always a stronger and more practical possibility. A small-scale programme had already been put into effect during the war with some success, but the high dollar cost of oil imports had been a serious obstacle to taking the matter further. However, in the spring of 1946 increased supplies of heavy fuel oil became available from Iran and Curaçao which could be paid for in sterling rather than in precious dollars. In consequence, Shinwell announced to the House of Commons on 8th April that his Ministry was anxious:

> to expedite a greater use of fuel oil for industrial purposes ... We hope there will be a greater expansion towards the end of this year, and manufacturers can rest assured that we shall render every possible assistance to them if they do convert ...[80]

The response from industry was enthusiastic, and Shinwell's officials quickly recognised the potential of coal-to-oil conversion for cutting the consumption of coal by something of the order of 3 million tons during the remaining months of 1946. There is little evidence that they lacked energy in pursuing their target, as Dalton was to suggest in June, and much that they did so with vigour. In July 1946, for instance, Shinwell's Ministry was involved in the promotion of nearly 600 conversion projects in manufacturing, transport and power generation with a potential coal saving in a full year of some 6 million tons.[81] The worry was that, if all the conversions in the pipeline were actually put into effect, the demand for oil thus generated 'would be likely to exceed the additional oil supplies in sight'.[82]

In the event, few of the projects were actually brought to fruition by the end of 1946. Of the 921 authorised by the Ministry of Fuel and Power only 184 (representing an annual oil consumption of some 300,000 tons, or a coal saving of roughly half a million tons) had actually been completed.[83] Shinwell was accordingly obliged to scale down drastically his estimate of the saving to be achieved through oil substitution in 1946 from the original 3 million tons.[84] This failure, however, reflected less on the commitment to coal-to-oil conversion of his Ministry and almost wholly on the chronic supply bottlenecks that bedevilled the provision of technical equipment for any substantial programme of industrial development. The quantity and variety of equipment required to convert boilers, furnaces and other industrial plant from coal burning to oil burning under the conversions authorised to mid-June 1946 were formidable: 12,000 tons of steel plate, 600 tons of steel tube of various kinds, thirty-five miles of electrical cable (some of types not made in Britain), 6,000 electric heaters to keep the extremely viscous fuel oil warm enough to flow, electric motors to pump it with, and so on.[85] It was never possible in 1946 to get hold of this equipment in the quantities required to put more than a fraction of the authorised conversions into effect. There were particular problems with the supply of electric motors, steel plates and tubes and lead-covered heating cable. The metal and engineering industries that had to provide them were already stretched to the limits of their capacity to cater for the requirements of other programmes that the government was pursuing as a matter of urgency. Although the requirements of the coal-to-oil conversion programme had been accorded the highest priority, they shared this status with so many other projects that, to the equipment manufacturers, the whole concept of priorities had ceased to have any practical meaning. The needs of the coal-to-oil programme simply took their place at the end of a long queue.[86] So, from the short-term perspective of the 1946–47 'coal winter', the oil substitution scheme was a flop. But Shinwell could hardly be blamed. He and his subordinates had recognised the opportunities for reducing pressure on coal supplies when oil became more freely available. They had pursued them with vigour. But they had been robbed of rapid success by the inadequacy of Britain's basic industrial resources to cope with the extreme pressures being placed upon them by the demands of forced-draught industrial reconstruction. It has to be said, however, that one of the main reasons why industry could not meet the needs of the oil substitution scheme was the limit placed on industry's productive capabilities by the chronic shortage of coal. The Minister of Supply, John Wilmot, who was in charge of steel production, reckoned that the coal shortage was costing the steel industry about half a million tons of lost output in 1946.[87] Shinwell, in a sense, was caught in a circular trap of a kind which was rather typical of its time: the problems in the coal section of his kingdom cut across developments in the oil section which might have offered some relief to the coal problems.

But if Shinwell could be absolved of blame for the failure of the coal-to-oil conversion scheme and the failure to get Polish ex-servicemen into the coal mines before the crisis struck, he is nevertheless open to criticism on other grounds. It could be argued, for instance, that he paid insufficient attention through the 1946 'coal summer' to the consumption side of the coal situation in his euphoria over gains on the supply side in terms of total output and productivity. By taking insufficient notice of the demand side he failed to give due weight to the inadequate build-up of stocks in preparation for the arrival of the 'coal winter' on 1st November, or to recognise in time the implications of the very low stock levels (even by the depressed standards of the previous year) for the winter supply position. Measures ought to have been taken in spring 1946 to restrict the growth of coal consumption, alongside those being taken to increase output and productivity. As Miss Belson of the Midland Regional Board remarked on 1st January 1947, the economy measures that Shinwell had promulgated three weeks before and which were only then going into operation would have been admirable had they been introduced nine months earlier as a means of building up stocks through the summer.[88] Applied as they were, when the crisis they were designed to prevent was really getting into its stride, they were irrelevant and useless.

In putting his faith entirely on the supply side through the 'coal summer', to the seeming exclusion of demand-side considerations, Shinwell was evidently motivated by his belief in the effect of the 'new spirit' that the promise of nationalisation was supposedly creating among the miners. It was a recurring theme of his in the spring and summer of 1946, and represented a king of mystic faith in the ability of his beloved miners to overcome what others — Attlee, Dalton, Jay, Meade and so on — regarded as the inexorable logic of the monthly statistics of coal production, consumption and stocks. As he remarked to Attlee in June, when the Prime Minister (at Jay's prompting) had once again tried to get him to recognise the statistical inevitability of a coal crisis in the new year if present trends continued, 'Prime Minister, you should not allow yourself to be led up the garden path by statistics. You should look at the imponderables.'[89]

It is noticeable that on the eve of the 'coal winter', in late October 1946, Shinwell's attitude underwent a quite dramatic change. Calm reassurance of worried colleagues by reference to 'imponderables' or 'the new spirit in the mines' gave way to increasingly nervous animadversion on the need to cut coal consumption. Two factors, perhaps, lay behind this change. In the first place, October was a time for taking stock in detail of the likely winter coal supply position, by drawing up an itemised account of supply and demand for notification to the Cabinet. In this process the continued rise of consumption in excess of the growth of supply and its implications for stocks became apparent in a form that brooked no easy dismissal. So did the failure of the coal-to-oil conversion programme. Secondly, Shinwell's faith in 'the new spirit' may have begun to wear thin as the NUM failed to live up to his expectations by way of gratitude and co-operation in return for what he was doing on its members' behalf.[90] In matters of pay and conditions, the union was just as tough and uncompromising with 'its' Labour government as it had been with the old coal owners. There was ample evidence in negotiations about the Poles, additional rations for miners, the implementation of the Miners' Charter, and the like, that the habits of a century's hard-nosed sublimation of class warfare in industrial negotiation died hard. As the *Daily Mirror* put it, reviewing the government's first year in office,

> Mr. Shinwell ... has completely failed to arouse in the miners that generosity he has some right to expect. There is no sign at all of a new spirit underground.[91]

It may have been a speech at the Trades Union Congress in October by Arthur Horner, the NUM General Secretary, that finally destroyed Shinwell's faith in 'the new spirit', which Horner dismissed as a basis for the expectation of more coal for the coming winter. The miners, Horner maintained, were already working as hard as they could, and their efforts alone could not prevent a crisis.[92]

Whatever the reasons for the Minister of Fuel and Power's increasingly realistic appreciation of the situation from late October onwards, his recognition of the dangers of the position probably came too late for effective preventative action. The time for that had been in the spring. But the possibility of action to minimise or mitigate the impact of the looming crisis still remained at the close of the 'coal summer'. It is hard to excuse Shinwell's failure to formulate a policy for that purpose until December, for implementation in January, when it had clearly been overtaken by the event it was intended to forestall.

4 The times that try men's souls

MANAGING THE CRISIS, JANUARY–FEBRUARY 1947

These are the times that try men's souls. The summer soldier
and the sunshine patriot will, in this crisis, shrink from the
service of their country; but he that stands it *now*, deserves the
love and thanks of men and women.

Tom Paine, *The Crisis* (1776), introduction

On Tuesday 7th January 1947, at eleven o'clock in the morning, the Cabinet met at 10 Downing Street to deliberate on the coal crisis. Coal and electricity supply was the sole subject before the Ministers. Four papers had been circulated to provide a basis for discussion. There was the Minister of Fuel and Power's memorandum of 3rd January drawing attention to the existence of the crisis, together with memoranda from the Minister of Transport, the Lord President of the Council and the President of the Board of Trade, all of which represented reactions to aspects of Shinwell's original paper. At the outset Shinwell in effect passed the initiative in dealing with the problem to Cripps by saying that 'He was in general agreement' with the proposals Cripps had put forward in his paper, CP(47)18: *Coal and Electricity*, for the revision of coal allocations to industry. Shinwell's own proposals, therefore, at no time figured prominently in the discussion, which tended to focus instead on Cripps's propositions. At the end of the day, therefore, it was the prescription of the President of the Board of Trade which was at the heart of the course of action adopted by the Cabinet to deal with the crisis, not that of the Minister with formal responsibility. Indeed, apart from an opening statement outlining the actual state of affairs with regard to fuel and power supplies, Shinwell appears to have taken no significant part in the proceedings. Given the subject under discussion and his departmental responsibilities, it seems an extraordinary abdication.[1]

Cripps's assessment of the situation was stark. Over the next couple of months, he pointed out, the Ministry of Fuel and Power's figures indicated that the supply of coal for industrial use and for generating gas and electricity for industry would fall short of the basic requirement of about 1·5 million tons a week by some 300,000 tons. Current arrangements were 'inappropriate to the circumstances now revealed',[2] so Cripps proposed that they be replaced with a set of restrictions on the industrial use of coal and electricity which can only be described as draconian. The only way of meeting the situation effectively and promptly, he maintained, was:

> that the allocations of solid fuel to all industrial firms outside iron and steel and coke ovens be cut by 40 per cent or if the Minister of Fuel and Power considers necessary 50 per cent. Similarly, directions should be served on firms that their consumption of gas and electricity per month must be reduced by 40 per cent from that of the month of November instead of the present 2½ per cent.

It was his intention that any reserves of industrial coal that might be created by these drastic reductions in allocation should be formed into regional emergency pools to be distributed by Regional Fuel Allocation Committees to meet special needs in their areas as these arose.

In the event the Cabinet adopted the more drastic of Cripps's suggestions by cutting industrial coal allocations by 50% rather than 40%. Even the sacred iron and steel allocation did not escape unscathed: it was cut by 20%, and only gasworks and electricity generating stations were exempt from the cuts. But when it came to Sir Stafford's recommendation that industrial use of gas and electricity should be cut propotionately, Ministers seem to have had cold feet. 'There was general agreement,' the Cabinet minutes recorded:

> that it would be undesirable for the present to impose any further restrictions on the consumption of electricity for industrial purposes or to limit the supply and installation of electrical machinery and appliances for industrial purposes.[3]

Considering that the Cabinet had been told at the start of its proceedings that even with ample supplies of coal it would be impossible to meet present levels of demand for electricity because of the lack of generating plant (demand exceeding capacity by an estimated 12%), this seems a strange decision, to say the least.[4] Almost as peculiar was the Cabinet's agreement that the cuts in industrial coal supply should be presented as 'a new system of allocations rather than a percentage cut in existing allocations'. Apart from the Cabinet itself, perhaps, it is hard to imagine who might actually be taken in by such a step. The Cabinet did, however, adopt a number of sensible and realistic measures to ease the problem of coal transport. Non-essential rail traffic, such as trains to sporting events and movements of surplus government stores, were to be suspended, for instance, in favour of extra coal trains.

Given the seriousness of the situation to which the Cabinet's deliberations of 7th January were addressed, together with the apparently urgent need for action, it is rather surprising to note that the imposition of the restrictions then agreed upon was delayed for nearly two weeks. Indeed, no public announcement of the proposed cuts seems to have been made for nearly a week. In the meantime the newspapers had got wind of the fact that large-scale cuts in coal allocations were imminent, and a number of speculative reports tending towards the worst possible scenarios that reporters could envisage had appeared. These caused great concern to Francis Williams, Attlee's Press Secretary and himself an experienced newspaper man, particularly when he discovered that the public relations staffs of Cripps's and Shinwell's Ministries had not been briefed on the Cabinet's decisions and were therefore in no position to answer Fleet Street's pessimistic conjectures. Williams warned the Prime Minister against the political consequences of letting the man in the street form his view of what was going on through 'complaints from industrialists sensationalised by Press critics':

> The public should be made to feel that it is being taken into the Government's confidence about the coal situation and that ... the Government is handling it with competence and efficiency.[5]

This did not, arguably, square very well with the attitude prevalent in the Cabinet, exemplified by its desire to emphasise that it was 'revising' rather than cutting coal allocations. But Attlee took the point, and the formal announcement of the cuts was duly, if belatedly, made on a suitably auspicious date − the 13th − to come into effect a week later.

The welcome accorded to the economy measures by the press was cautious and qualified. The *Economist*, for instance, noted that the coal situation 'remains desperate', and described the Cripps plan as 'largely a piece of statistical tidiness' the practical effects of which were almost impossible to foretell. Industry, it was reported, was confused about various detailed aspects of the scheme, not least the operation of the regional coal pools. And there were doubts in any case that the scheme would make any appreciable difference to industry's energy situation.[6]

But apart from these general expressions of concern about the workings of the new fuel plans, the two weeks or so following the Cabinet's meeting of 7th January seem to have been fairly quiet on the fuel supply front. The brief spell of snow and frost on 6th and 7th January had given way to some very mild weather, which at least reduced domestic demand for gas and electricity for heating purposes. *Ad hoc* emergency procedures like the one worked out by Gaitskell for the Lancashire cotton industry, together with the ingenuity of the regional Fuel Allocation Committees in distributing their remaining reserves of coal, took the pressure off for a while where industry was concerned. The press shifted its attention to other matters: the impending visit of the King and Queen to South Africa; the unrest in Palestine; the preparations for Indian independence; and, closer to home, a strike of road haulage workers. This last received extensive coverage, partly as an added threat to the economy but more, perhaps, because it threatened London's food supplies. The deployment of troops by a Labour government to break a strike, as happened in this case, was an event that delighted Fleet Street.

At any rate, the coal shortage ceased − for a little while at least − to be in the forefront of the news. What brought it back was the coming into operation on Monday 20th January of the Cripps measures, supposedly for a period of six weeks. The effects were immediate: the papers once again began to run stories of industrial shut-downs and short-time working due to the shortage of coal. The effect was most marked in the iron and steel industry, hitherto relatively sheltered from the impact of the fuel shortage. The industry responded to the 20% cut in its coal allocation by announcing the immediate contraction of activity in all its main locations from five days per week to four. As the Iron and Steel Federation explained, steelworks had long since exhausted their own coal reserves and could only react to cuts in coal supply with proportionate cuts in output.[7] The temporary alleviation of the Lancashire coal famine also came to an end: a fresh crop of cotton mill closures took place on 22nd January. On the same day a new round of cuts in electricity supply took place throughout the country, and cuts in beer production were announced from Burton-on-Trent as brewery coal allocations were cut by half.[8] It was into this rapidly deteriorating situation that the weather factor was precipitated on the night of 23rd January when the heavy fall of snow in London and the south-east initiated the meteorological reign of terror that was to endure for the next seven weeks.

Writing on the eve of his periodical's enforced suspension of publication by government decree in mid-February, and very definitely expressing himself more in anger than in sorrow, the editor of the *Economist* denounced the ministerial view that the weather was the cause of the fuel crisis. 'It would,' he maintained, 'have happened in any case.'[9] It is hard to disagree with this sentiment except on the grammatical grounds that the tense is inappropriate: the crisis was already unfolding significantly before the weather intervened. It is nevertheless relevant to inquire what the role of the weather actually was. As the editor of the *Economist* put it, the weather made things much worse than they would have been without it. But much worse in what particulars?

Arguably the most significant effect of the prolonged bout of severe weather following 23rd January, as far as the evolution of the crisis is concerned, was to create the chaos it did in London's fuel supplies. Until that point the fuel crisis had been essentially provincial in its impact, affecting above all the midlands and north-west England. Other regions had been affected too, albeit in a less substantial way, as the correspondence of the Board of Trade's regional staff indicates.[10] But some areas were hardly touched by the power problem before the weather closed in, most notably the coal-mining areas of north-eastern England, south Wales and central Scotland, but also the area immediately around London. Local coal distribution in the London area had been disrupted by the road haulage strike in the capital, but there had been no great concern about the availability of coal so long as the regular shipments into the Thames from

Northumberland and Durham and south Wales were able to get through. Even a brief, temporary interruption of London's supplies by sea and rail could be borne, since the Ministry of Fuel and Power had been building up stocks in the region for some time.[11] But the disruption of sea and land transport following 23rd January was neither brief nor small-scale, and after a couple of weeks of interrupted shipments and heavy reliance on stocks, the capital began to suffer acutely. By early February, Manchester and Birmingham no longer stood alone at the centre of the fuel crisis.

In the north west and the midlands, it is probably fair to argue, the impact of the weather on the evolution of the crisis was marginal, in the sense that the straw which proverbially broke the camel's back was marginal. Once more Miss Belson of the Midland Regional Board may be called in evidence. Reporting to the Board of Trade in London on 30th January, she gave notice that non-priority coal consumers in her region were unlikely to receive deliveries of more than 35% to 40% of their requirements, which would mean 'virtually ... an industrial closedown since in many firms this level will barely suffice to maintain space heating'. But just in case London harboured the illusion that this had been caused by the weather, she added emphatically that her appreciation 'is not repeat not taking into account present weather', which would only make worse a position that was already, in effect, impossible.[12] Much the same could be said of the north-west, where the incidence of cotton-mill closures, already serious before 23rd, steepened. North West Regional officers of the Ministry of Labour reported an overnight increase of 40% in the number of unemployed cotton workers on 31st January.[13] But still there were parts of the country that remained relatively unaffected, irrespective of the weather. Miss Belson's report on the plight of the Midland Region was closely followed, for instance, by one from her counterpart in the Scottish Regional Board, a Mr Grassick. It recorded that Scotland was so far faring quite well: coal deliveries were, as far as could be ascertained, more or less up to full allocation, even if some of the stockpiles were now so low that the coal being drawn from them had been found to date back as far as 1921! Mr Grassick expressed some apprehension for the future, but clearly had no present worries of the kind being experienced by his colleagues elsewhere.[14]

Having agreed on 7th January to implement at least in part Cripps's drastic prescription for economies in coal and electric power, the Cabinet seems to have turned its back on the fuel crisis for a month. Even without the problem of the weather, the implications of the Cripps measures — even in the bowdlerised version acceptable to the Cabinet — were serious. You could not cut the coal allocations of the greater part of industry by 50% and hope to avoid disruption in some degree, probably a substantial one, to employment, exports and domestic reconstruction. Yet no serious attempt seems to have been made in the higher reaches of government to monitor the position. And when the implications of the measures became clear on 20th January, with short-time working in steel and mill closures in cotton, there was no sign of a response at the government's higher levels. Even when the weather closed in, impairing the transport of coal and creating an upsurge in the demand for gas and electricity, there is no immediate evidence that Ministers took much cognisance of what was going on to begin with. Far from generating the impression called for by Francis Williams on 8th January — that the government was handling the situation 'with competence and efficiency' — one gets little sense from the official records of the four weeks following the Cabinet meeting of 7th January that the government was handling it at all. Having agreed to the Cripps measures after a fashion at that meeting, the Cabinet did not return to the subject of fuel and power until Tuesday 4th February, and even then the discussion exhibited little sense of urgency.[15] In the meantime no fewer than twelve meetings of the Cabinet had passed without the fuel situation being mentioned at all, despite the ominous reports emanating from the regions and the tales of factory closures and cuts in power supplies circulating in the press. On the face of it, this seems a quite extraordinary state of affairs. How is it to be explained?

In large part, the explanation probably lay in the sheer weight of problems that demanded the attention of Ministers. The twelve Cabinet meetings in question covered a wide range of grave matters both at home and abroad.[16] Bridging the fields of home and foreign affairs was the problem of defence. Here there was much discussion aimed at reconciling the government's concern to reduce defence spending and to free manpower from the armed services for civil employment in a labour-starved economy with the countervailing pressure of Britain's continuing worldwide military and naval commitments. The consideration of foreign affairs ranged from the state of the British Occupation Zone of Germany, through deliberations on relations with Spain and the USSR, on Britain's position in the Persian Gulf, the eastern Mediterranean, in India and in Burma, to the discussion of possible peace treaties and the shape of the post-war settlement in Europe. At home, there was the matter of the road haulage dispute and the agonising decision for a Labour government to use troops to break the strike; food supplies at home demanded attention, though less urgently than in the desperately deprived British zone of Germany;

there was economic planning, the criminal activities of deserters from the armed forces, leaks of Cabinet deliberations, and so on — all competing with the fuel crisis for the Cabinet's notice. Indeed, it is difficult to escape the conclusion that by the early weeks of 1947 the government was close to being overwhelmed by the sheer press of grave matters that compelled its attention. Inevitably, no single problem could be given systematic and sustained attention: Ministers devoted themselves to whatever seemed most urgent at any given time, shifting their focus from one problem to another in accordance with the immediate exigencies of the moment. The coal crisis itself, as a junior Minister remarked when it was at its height, provided:

> one more illustration of the fact that our governmental system in Britain never thinks ahead. All through the war, every Minister and every senior official was taken up with the crisis of the moment ... Just the same since the war; demobilisation, bricks, slates, baths, India, Palestine, Egypt, development areas, bread, timber, etc., etc. Always thinking hard about to-day, sometimes about to-morrow, never about next year.[17]

The apparent easing of the fuel crisis after 8th January allowed Ministers to switch their attention to other matters, of which there was no shortage demanding notice. To bring the crisis back on to the agenda to take precedence over India, Palestine or the disbandment of the Women's Land Army would require something dramatic by way of developments on the fuel front.

It is relevant to consider the physical and psychological state of Attlee and his colleagues at the beginning of 1947. Some, like Attlee himself, Bevin and Morrison, had carried demanding responsibilities in the wartime coalition government. All had been working under the most intense pressure since taking office in July 1945. By the beginning of 1947 many were simply exhausted, and their grip on affairs and capacity for rapid, effective action were slipping to a serious degree. In this connection Hugh Dalton's diary for January and February makes instructive reading. He records that Bevin was not well, that Ellen Wilkinson was dying, that even Attlee was 'slower, more timid and less decisive than he used to be'.[18] Morrison was in hospital with a thrombosis and pleurisy, and Dalton had been obliged to take on much of his work:

> I have been landed with the Chairmanship of several of his committees — Lord President's, Socialisation of Industry, Economic Planning — not to speak of a number of Committees over which I am already Chairman.[19]

This kind of load was impossible to reconcile with a close and competent control of affairs at a time of herculean effort in both national and international reconstruction. Small wonder, perhaps, that the fuel crisis seemed to get lost in the tangle of responsibilities.

Another factor in the postponement of further action on fuel and power in the wake of the Cabinet meeting of 7th January may have been that – having set the Cripps measures in train – Ministers were quite reasonably waiting to see what effect they might have. While it seems clear with hindsight that the effect was immediately deleterious, this may have been less apparent to those involved, particularly as the breakdown in the weather followed so closely. Some delay, perhaps, was bound to occur as Ministers and their officials tried to distinguish the impact of the Cripps plan from that of the weather. And this would probably have been compounded by a further delay until the realisation sank in that *this* visitation of bad weather was of a different order from the brief spells experienced before Christmas and in early January. Provincial cynics, of course, might further argue that it took the breakdown of fuel and power supplies in the metropolis to persuade the government of the full seriousness of the fuel crisis. And it is indeed remarkable how the sharp deterioration of conditions in London appeared to galvanise the government into adopting a more decisive approach and creating a more effective system of crisis management than anything that had been attempted while only the provinces seemed to be in serious jeopardy.[20]

On the last day of January, under the headline 'Heavy Cuts in Power: Many Factories Closed', *The Times* gave details of severe reductions in gas and electricity supply and of the increasingly serious dislocation of manufacturing industry in the midlands and the north-west.[21] Once again, the Austin Motor Company's works at Longbridge near Birmingham were at the centre of the stage, with the threat of indefinite lay-offs for the 17,000 people who worked there, because of a lack of coal. But it quickly became apparent that Austin's plight was by no means unique in the motor industry: most other firms were in a similar state. And, seeking emergency coal supplies from the regional pools created under the Cripps plan, they were informed that Sir Stafford had refused their industry any special priority.[22] Plant closures and short-time working spread rapidly, and extended into the rubber, metal and electrical engineering industries to reinforce the attrition already experienced by textiles. By Tuesday 4th February the state of fuel and power supplies and the plight of both industrial and household consumers struggling to cope with power cuts and inadequate or non-existent coal deliveries was felt by *The Times* to be sufficiently serious to merit pride of place on its leader page.[23] The first leader was very critical of the Minister of Fuel and Power for not having restricted fuel consumption in line with availability the previous year, though it was moderately favourable to the Cripps scheme. It also raised the question, not only of the immediate impact of the present crisis on exports and industry, but of the chances of avoiding a repetition next winter.

Perhaps responding to the prevalence of such alarming stories in the press, the Cabinet turned its attention to the fuel and power problem once again, and put it at the head of its order of business on 4th February.[24] The record of the meeting, however, does little to suggest that Ministers yet regarded the situation as critical. Certainly no prescriptions for immediate, drastic action emerged. There was a brief general discussion of the coal situation, which noted the plight of Austin Motors and suggested they should receive a special 'pool' allocation. It was noted that the weather was interfering with the transport of coal by road from open-cast workings. The public, it was agreed, should be informed that the gas and electricity cuts were due to the inadequacy of plant capacity to meet the current level of demand, not to lack of coal, and that everything was being done to expand capacity at gasworks and power stations. The Minister of Fuel and Power, however, did announce that he was thinking of imposing cuts in household use of electricity. It was felt that an early debate on fuel and power in the House of Commons was likely, and the Cabinet welcomed the prospect as 'useful in making the facts more widely known to the public'. The tone was quite calm, showing little sense of urgency or of impending disaster.

The following day, Emanuel Shinwell prepared two documents, one for private circulation and the other for publication. The first was a memorandum for the Cabinet in which he stated that because of the dislocation of transport by the weather 'a most serious situation' had arisen with regard to the supply of coal.[25] Immediately he had been informed of this, he claimed, he had taken action to alleviate the situation, which he now considered to be 'on the mend'. But he nevertheless passed on to the Cabinet the view of the Central Electricity Board (CEB) that, unless special action was taken immediately, power stations in London and the south-east, the midlands and the north-west would be forced to shut down by the weekend. The action recommended by the Board involved the complete cutting off of industrial power (with exemptions for a few special cases) in the regions in question, and the suspension of household supplies for three hours each morning and two each afternoon. Shinwell recommended that the situation should be reviewed daily, but hoped that such drastic measures might be avoided. The second document was the public announcement previously referred to, which repeated that 'a most serious situation' had arisen and explained that it was entirely the result of the 'far-reaching interruptions on the railways and coast line shipping' created by the exceptionally bad weather.[26] Details of some of the transport bottlenecks were given, and it was noted that the position of London's power stations was particularly difficult. But, beyond noting that the railways were giving the highest priority to coal movements, the announcement gave no inkling of remedial action and conveyed no threat of anything as drastic as widespread cuts in electricity supply.

At this point it is perhaps worth considering the role of transport, in view of the way in which the Ministry of Fuel and Power's announcement had laid on the transport system the whole responsibility for the sharp intensification of the fuel crisis that was then taking place. This was not the first time that Shinwell and his officers had blamed transport for the fuel problem, nor was it to be the last. The 'critical situation' whose emergence Shinwell had expounded to the Cabinet on 3rd January had also been laid partly at the door of deficiencies in the transport system. And long after the event, in his successive essays in autobiography, Shinwell preferred to present the fuel crisis as primarily the result of a failure on the part of the transport services in the task of moving coal. This served his own purpose of shifting responsibility for the affair from his own shoulders to someone else's. By focusing on the matter of transport he could transfer the onus to his colleague, the Minister of Transport, Alfred Barnes.[27]

The transport system certainly had its problems, especially when it came to the movement of a heavy, bulky commodity like coal. The difficulties were at their worst on the railways, where enemy action, overloading and under-resourcing during the war had produced the results referred to earlier – a high level of dilapidation among rolling stock and other equipment, an acute shortage of heavy freight locomotives, and a heavy incidence of equipment out of service for repairs. Calling attention to the critical state of fuel and power supplies at the beginning of January, Shinwell had made much of a build-up of coal stocks at pitheads and open-cast sites since October 1946 owing to the failure of the railways to keep coal movements up with production. Alfred Barnes had accepted that there might have been a slight build-up during December – owing to fog, holidays (and a measure of absenteeism) among the railwaymen, and the unusually high level of coal production in the miners' 'bull week' before Christmas. But he was able to produce figures to show that in the last quarter of 1946 average weekly coal movements by rail, road and sea had marginally exceeded coal output.[28] To a certain extent Barnes's case is supported by the official figures (emanating from the Ministry of Fuel and Power) for stocks of coal at pitheads and open-cast workings, which show a slight but steady decline from November 1946 through the following two months. It should be said in passing that by the end of 1946 such undistributed stocks of coal had been all but completely liquidated as sources of usable fuel.[29] Barnes may have been reluctant to accept Shinwell's strictures in detail in January, but he nevertheless co-operated by giving greater priority to railway coal movements. Passenger services were cancelled in large numbers to free locomotives to work coal trains, for example, and such trains were given precedence over all other traffic in clearing congested sections of the railway system. But what Barnes did was not enough for Shinwell, who — perhaps wrapped up in his own problems to a degree that blinded him to those of other people — gave scant recognition to his colleague's efforts to keep coal supplies moving.

In the face of the weather conditions that prevailed in the weeks following 23rd January it was inevitable that the movement of coal by rail, road and sea would be severely disrupted, with colliers stormbound in port, trains snowbound in colliery sidings, and access roads to open-cast sites feet deep in snow for most of their length. Coal, however, continued to be moved throughout the period of the blizzards, though for a time in quantities much lower than normal. Things were at their worst at the end of the first week of February, with eighty-seven ships of the east-coast coal trade immobilised in London river or in their north-eastern ports and with 20,000 loaded coal wagons stuck at colliery sidings. About 40% more coal than usual was in transit, and so unavailable for immediate consumption, at that point.[30] What is remarkable, in view of the continued ferocity of the weather in February and early March, was how quickly the bottlenecks were cleared. On 24th February Barnes could report to Attlee that the railways could now handle all traffic in coal and other goods, and that it was no longer necessary for coal to be accorded the absolute priority on the rail system that the Cabinet had given it earlier in the month. There was incredulity among Attlee's advisers about this claim, but investigation revealed its accuracy.[31] The way this was achieved will be dealt with later in this chapter: for the moment it will suffice to say that, by the third week of February, all coal movements were back to normal, and those by rail were being conducted with greater efficiency than was then accepted as normal. And no serious disruption by the weather was thereafter experienced.

While the disruption of coal movements in February lasted it undoubtedly had some bearing on the intensification of the fuel crisis that then occurred. But to characterise the fuel crisis as therefore essentially a crisis in the transport of coal seems to misrepresent the case. The essence of the fuel crisis did not lie in the failure of the transport system to move undistributed coal stocks, even if that might be regarded as a proximate cause of the breakdown in supplies in February. Underlying the transport problem, and far more fundamental as a factor in the fuel crisis — whether narrowly defined to restrict it to February or more broadly defined to include the acute difficulties that both preceded and followed the 'official crisis' — was the failure to control the growing divergence between coal production and consumption during the 'coal summer' of 1946, and the consequent rundown of *distributed* stocks. Without that fundamental difficulty the disruption of transport in February, brief as it was, would have made no significant impact. Indeed, one could almost argue that the transport difficulties of late 1946 and early 1947 were less a cause of the fuel crisis than a consequence of it. For it is clear that the shortage of coal was hampering the railways' operations in several ways, and so limiting their capacity to cope with the demands that were being made on them to transport coal and other things. For one thing, the railways, like all other coal users, were not receiving coal in the quantities they required: in the first six weeks of 1947, for example, deliveries had been 72,000 tons below allocation. As a result, locomotive coal stocks were declining steadily and had sunk, in England and Wales, to only about four days' supply by mid-February. In fact the failways were a good deal worse off for coal at that time than the power stations. So bad was their position that they had been obliged to commandeer 15,000 tons of house coal while it was in transit just to keep the system running.[32] For another thing, the railways were having great difficulty in making good the effects of war damage and arrears of maintenance, to say nothing of bringing in new developments, because of the dearth of materials and equipment — above all, of steel. To give but one specific example, it had been agreed by the railway companies and the Ministry of Fuel and Power in August 1946 that, in order to save coal, 1,279 locomotives should be converted to oil firing by 1st January 1947. It was not technically a difficult job, but by the end of February only twenty locomotives had actually been converted, owing to the scarcity of materials and equipment for doing the job. The chief obstacle to the provision of the necessary conversion equipment was, of course, the shortage of coal.[33]

Despite the fact that Shinwell's announcement of 5th February appeared in the press alongside reports of gas and electricity cuts and a spreading rash of industrial plant closures which had left sixty thousand people out of work in the city of Birmingham alone, the Cabinet — discussing the situation on the following day in the light of Shinwell's memorandum — did not appear to recognise any need for urgent or forceful action.

For this seemingly relaxed stance Shinwell's habit of stressing the up beat, his apparent inability to avoid putting an optimistic gloss on things, may have been responsible, lulling his colleagues into a false sense of security. He reported that coastwise coal shipments had resumed and that rail movements of coal were picking up. He did not consider that the measures proposed by the CEB needed to be imposed, but he would keep an eye on the way things were working out and arrange for 'detailed plans to be made ready to be put into force at once should a serious emergency arise early in the following week'. The Cabinet concurred, and apart from various small measures to facilitate the movement of coal, took no particular action. It did, however, reject the CEB's proposed electricity supply cuts.[34]

In the light of the Cabinet's deliberations on 6th February it is easy to comprehend the dismay felt by Ministers when *on the very next day* Shinwell brought before them the proposal that the CEB plan for cuts in electricity supply in the London and South Eastern, Midland and North Western regions should be implemented as soon as possible.[35] 'This,' Dalton recorded in his diary, 'is a complete thunderclap, following on the usual rather hopeful tales we have had from this man during the past week.'[36] The Cabinet indeed appeared stunned: it accepted Shinwell's recommendation, according to the official record, virtually without discussion.

Thus it was that, on the afternoon of Friday 7th February, the Minister of Fuel and Power announced in the Commons that, because the weather had made it impossible to maintain coal supplies to power stations in the three regions specified by the CEB, a number of them would have to be shut down. Accordingly, electricity supplies in these regions would be 'at a much reduced level', and to avoid a complete breakdown drastic cuts would have to be imposed on electricity consumption. For industrial concerns, apart from essential services like water, sewage disposal, transport, telephones and food processing, no electricity would be supplied. For households, supplies of electrical power would be cut off from nine o'clock in the morning till noon and from two o'clock till four in the afternoon. The restrictions would operate from Monday 10th February.[37]

Perhaps not surprisingly, a storm broke over Shinwell's head with this announcement, both in the press and in Parliament, where an immediate debate on the matter was held. Press comment was almost entirely hostile, to Shinwell at least, if not to the government as a whole, and increased in hostility when it was announced that the publication of general periodicals (including the most influential political weeklies) would be suspended for two issues from 15th February. There was much criticism of Shinwell's failure to act well ahead of time to control coal and power consumption in order to build up coal stocks for the winter, of his incompetence, his improvidence, and his undue optimism in the face of manifestly pessimistic facts, and so on. There were, inevitably, demands for his resignation, which he rejected in the strongest terms. He maintained that he had done enough to assure supplies of coal and argued, according to *The Times*, that

> Coal production has been increased, and, provided there had been some economy in consumption, we should have got through but for 'this blizzard'. The allocation scheme now working did not have a chance; it was 'knocked on the head by the blizzard'.[38]

In this view he was supported by some of his ministerial colleagues and by the Trades Union Congress, which issued a statement to similar effect.[39] Arthur Horner of the NUM condemned the exploitation of the crisis for political advantage by 'enemies of the government' and urged firm support for Shinwell.[40] But not all the hostile voices should be counted as 'enemies of the government'. Some would have counted themselves among its friends, like the Labour MPs Raymond Blackburn (Birmingham King's Norton) and Ellis Smith (Stoke), who made speeches critical of Shinwell and the government in the debate of 7th February.[41] And one especially bitter critic was actually a leading member of the government, as the vituperative entries in Dalton's diary for 7th–10th February testify. Dalton had no time for Shinwell's excuses about the weather and preferred the view that 'the root cause of all this trouble is the insufficient stocks with which we started the winter'.[42] It was a view which, in the public prints at least, was more commonly held than Shinwell's, and one that seems clearly to accord better with the facts of the case.

If Shinwell's precipitate announcement of what amounted (however it was euphemised) to a complete breakdown of fuel and power resources in England's three main manufacturing areas did nothing else, it seems to have jolted the government into taking fresh stock of the way it was handling the crisis. The initiative appears to have been taken by Gorell Barnes, who had replaced Jay as Attlee's private secretary in the previous June. In a minute to Attlee on 11th February he suggested that responsibility for dealing with the coal problem was too divided, and that it would be desirable for all aspects of the problem to be comprehensively dealt with by a single central committee. And since the handling of the fuel crisis would have repercussions for the reputation of the government as a whole, not just one or two of its members, he suggested that Attlee himself should play a leading part in the committee.[43]

The matter was hammered out with a speed and decision which hitherto, it can safely be said, had not characterised the government's actions in relation to the fuel crisis. Within not much more than twenty-four hours of Gorell Barnes's original suggestion, the new committee, with the Prime Minister himself in the chair, was holding its first meeting. Known as the Cabinet Fuel Committee, it was based on the kind of *ad hoc* Cabinet committee that had been set up in wartime to deal with especially serious emergencies. Indeed, a direct analogy was drawn by one of Gorell Barnes's colleagues in the secretariat in 10 Downing Street with the Battle of the Atlantic and Anti-U boat Committees of the war period.[44] The Cabinet Fuel Committee was a much more powerful body than the Ministerial Coal Committee which it superseded. As well as having the authority of the Premier in the chair, it was – unlike the old Coal Committee – an *executive* committee of the Cabinet, rather than merely deliberative. It took over, in effect, the individual authority of the Minister of Fuel and Power for energy production, the President of the Board of Trade for fuel allocations, the Minister of Transport for distribution, and so on, and became to all intents the supreme administrative organ for all questions involving fuel and power. It also had access to superior information compared with the Coal Committee. To enable it to monitor the fuel situation in detail, it was to be provided with daily situation reports setting out the particulars of energy production, consumption and distribution. These would be scrutinised each day by an executive sub-committee empowered to deal on its own initiative with matters of special urgency.[45] The main committee was to meet, always under Attlee's chairmanship, every two or three days during the most severe period of the crisis. It was seconded by the established Official Coal Committee under Sir Donald Fergusson of the Ministry of Fuel and Power, which continued to gather information and to work out ways of giving administrative effect to ministerial decisions just as it had done for the Coal Committee. Further back-up was provided by a working party of civil servants chaired by a junior Minister (Hugh Gaitskell), the function of which was to consider matters that might require legislation.[46]

With the establishment of the Fuel Committee, Emanuel Shinwell's responsibility for fuel and power for all practical purposes came to an end. Attlee was unwilling to drop him from office in mid-crisis, despite some pressure to do so from within the parliamentary party, so he remained Minister of Fuel and Power until October 1947. He was then moved to the War Office, which did not then carry with it a seat in the Cabinet, and replaced at Fuel and Power by Gaitskell. During all that time the Cabinet Fuel Committee continued to meet and to monitor in detail all matters of any significance relating to fuel and power. It was true, of course, that other Ministers were deprived of responsibilities by the creation of the Fuel Committee: Cripps and Barnes, for instance, have already been mentioned in that connection. But for them the deprivation was only of peripheral parts of their work. In Shinwell's case the committee took over virtually his entire sphere of responsibility. Gaitskell summed up the position with perfect accuracy in August 1947 when he remarked in his diary that by means of the Cabinet Fuel Committee 'the Office of Minister of F. & P. was virtually put in commission'.[47] We can only speculate about Attlee's views on Shinwell's conduct before the committee was established, but there is little doubt that he used the committee as a means of depriving of effective control of affairs a Minister he no longer trusted but whom, for the moment, he thought it impolitic to sack. Shinwell had a powerful constituency within the party, especially among the coal miners who were the most powerful trade union interest within the organisation at that time. He was the man who had delivered on nationalisation and on the Miners' Charter: no Prime Minister, during a crisis in which the goodwill of the miners was of peculiar importance, could risk the consequences of dumping such a man from office, however, unsatisfactory his performance. The best he could do was to deprive him of the chance to do any more damage by strictly limiting his practical sphere of action.

In some respects, under the Fuel Committee's management, the impact of the crisis became more rather than less acute. Almost the first decision the committee took, for example, was to extend the restrictions on the domestic use of electricity beyond the three original regions to the whole of Great Britain, with provision for some minor local variations in the timing of the five-hour cuts.[48] At its second meeting the committee heard that the coal-stock position at gasworks was critical enough for the Minister of Fuel and Power to have considered taking steps to restrict consumption of gas as well as that of electricity.[49] It was felt that for the moment such restrictions would not be justified, but the possibility remained a live one which raised its head again over the weekend of 22nd–23rd February and at the Fuel Committee meeting of the 28th.[50] In the event, however, gas supplies narrowly escaped the fate of electricity, but in the official view it had been touch and go, and gas consumers had been exhorted to practise the utmost economy.

It was only after the Fuel Committee assumed responsibility for managing the crisis, too, that the incidence of unemployment really embarked upon its positively stratospheric rise. At the first meeting on 12th February the Minister of Labour could account for some half a million people out of work because of the power restrictions, while admitting that the information he had was neither complete nor up-to-date. Two days later he was better informed, and could tell his colleagues that some 1·75 million people, or fully one third of the workers employed in manufacturing in the three 'black areas', were out of work. By 15th February the numbers had topped 2 million and were still rising to reach a peak, apparently, on 22nd February. On that date nearly 2·5 million people were unemployed, a figure that constituted 15½% of the insured labour force.[51] The incidence was rather uneven among the three regions principally affected, being worst in the midlands (with a rate of 32½% on 19th February compared with 25% in the north-west and a mere 15% in London and the southeast. It was explained that the London area's favourable position was the result of the high proportion of the exempted food processing industry that was to be found there, together with the larger number of small firms in the capital.[52]

The standard of civil amenity available to the population at large was also further reduced at the Fuel Committee's instigation. At its second meeting it decided to curtail severely the activities of the BBC, in effect shutting down the Third Programme and the infant Television Service and restricting the corporation to the use of one radio channel only for most of the day.[53] Travellers by rail had to contend not only with the periodic disruption of services by the weather in the middle two weeks of February, but also with the cancellation by the committee's decree of over 3,500 passenger train services so that their locomotives might be used to haul coal trains, to which the committee had insisted that the railways give absolute priority.[54] The intention of the organisers of the Ideal Home Exhibition at Olympia, to bring a little colour into the lives of an austerity-ridden populace, was threatened by the Fuel Committee on the grounds that not only did the exhibition itself consume electricity but it encouraged others to do so by prompting them to buy the electrical appliances that were on display. The committee at first wanted to cancel the exhibition altogether, but agreed that it could go on so long as it observed the 'restricted hours' and all electrical household appliances were removed from the stands.[55] Another pleasure of the ordinary man which came in for the committee's special attention was greyhound racing, of which some of Attlee's Ministers seem to have had a puritanical dislike. One of the committee's first actions was to accept a proposal from Shinwell that greyhound racing tracks be prohibited, by an order under the Defence

Regulations carrying severe penalties, from using any electricity, however generated, to pursue their disreputable activities.[56]

But to offset the deepening toll of restriction and deprivation, both petty and substantial, under the ministrations of the Fuel Committee after 12th February there was evidence of the underlying fuel and power situation gradually turning the corner and beginning to improve. It did not do so easily, and right to the end of February — and indeed for as long as the threat of further blizzards remained — there could be doubts about whether the improvement would be sustained so that further restrictions could be avoided and existing ones lifted. In fact, even at its first meeting, the Fuel Committee looked ahead to the easing of the restrictions it was then imposing, albeit in a hypothetical way, by discussing the particular circumstances in which some relaxation might be possible. The CEB thought that when power-station coal stocks had been built up to the equivalent of two weeks' consumption the controls might be relaxed. The Ministry of Fuel and Power, ever sanguine in spite of recent experience, thought supplies for a week and a half would suffice. But nobody could foretell when even the lower of the two targets might be attained.[57]

The rebuilding of distributed coal stocks, above all at power stations and gasworks, but also for direct consumption by industrial, commercial and domestic consumers, was the key to recovery. The whole object of the restrictions was to promote this build-up, primarily by sharply reducing the current consumption of coal and enabling the coal thus saved to be transferred to stock. The Fuel Committee, however, did not just concern itself with savings from current consumption. It sought strenuously to augment what could be achieved in that way by improvements in overall coal output, in the productivity of miners, and in the efficiency with which coal was transported from the pitheads to the final consumers or stockholders. Reductions in current coal consumption and consequent transfers to stock, however, offered the most immediate and striking evidence that the committee's objectives were being achieved. These were initially quite striking. The Fuel Committee's estimates indicated that by the end of the first week of restrictions power-station coal consumption had been reduced by over 35% in the country as a whole. In the so-called 'black areas' the saving was over 45%. There was some falling off in the savings achieved in the second week, though, with the national average coal consumption at power stations on Friday 21st February only 28% below that of the control date of 7th February. Nevertheless the official reckoning for that two-week period as a whole was that more than 350,000 tons of coal had been added to power-station stocks instead of being burned. One result was that by the 21st all three 'black areas' were in the relatively secure position of having power-station coal stocks that comfortably exceeded, on average, the target of two weeks' consumption, even though individual power stations occasionally remained well below that desirable level. Particular difficulty was experienced in building up stocks at the important London stations at Barking and Fulham. Gas-coal stocks proved much less resilient, presumably because gas consumption was not subject to formal control. In London, for instance, gasworks stocks hovered around the ten days' consumption mark throughout the two weeks after 7th February. Nevertheless the Fuel Committee had reason to be pleased with the way coal stocks for electricity generating had responded to the restrictions.[58]

The situation with regard to industrial coal stocks was less of a source of satisfaction. Inevitably the priority accorded to power stations and gasworks meant the diversion on a large scale of industrial coal to these undertakings. Meanwhile, though deprived of the electricity to maintain production, manufacturing industry still needed to heat its buildings and plant to avoid frost damage, so coal continued to be burned for space heating. Reports from the Board of Trade's regional officers suggested that, as a result, coal stocks available to industrial concerns were declining. The Ministry of Fuel and Power's information, on the other hand, suggested that they were increasing. There was something of a wrangle over the true state of things at the Fuel Committee on 18th February, which was resolved three days later by an admission from the Minister of Fuel and Power that closer investigation had tended to confirm the Board of Trade's pessimistic impressions.[59] The figures that had been gathered to resolve the dispute showed only too clearly how desperate the condition of industry was. On 15th February coal stocks held by firms in the iron, steel and engineering industries amounted to $1 \cdot 2$ weeks' supply and those held by the rest of the manufacturing sector to $1 \cdot 3$ weeks' supply.[60] These figures, if anything, overstated the case, since the concept of supply was calculated not on the basis of what industry required to maintain full production, but on the basis of official allocations which were notoriously less than the full industrial requirement. Coal deliveries to industry during the first half of February had, in fact, fallen quite substantially below the already inadequate level of official allocations. This led Cripps to remark dryly — as the Fuel Committee discussed the restoration of electricity to industry — that:

> It would be unfortunate if industry started up, on the basis of the restoration of electricity supply, only to find that coal supplies were not forthcoming in sufficient quantities to keep them going.[61]

During the third week of the month, however, coal deliveries to industry were pushed up to a level significantly above the official weekly allocation, and the committee felt able to assure industrialists that they could expect current levels of delivery to be maintained and even, in time, increased.[62]

One method of boosting coal stocks quickly was deliberately eschewed. When the coal crisis entered into its most acute phase President Truman had offered to divert to Britain shipments of American coal destined for Europe that were already on the high seas. It must have been extremely tempting to accept, but Attlee was well aware that the fuel situation on the Continent was even worse. At the beginning of the year he had received a dramatic plea from his French counterpart, Léon Blum, begging for one or two million tons of British coal per month. On such a trifling amount, Blum averred, hung the question of 'our economic reconstruction or our political destruction'; indeed, it would determine the fate of democracy and socialism in France and in Europe as a whole.[63] Moved by this kind of consideration, Attlee thanked Truman for his offer but declined it on the grounds that Europe's need was just as acute as Britain's. In the circumstances it was a not ignoble gesture on Attlee's part.

The actual production of coal during the period of bad weather was affected adversely in a number of ways that were faithfully recorded region by region in the Fuel Committee's papers and discussions. Snowdrifts on roads made mines in many areas inaccessible to those who worked in them, sometimes for days on end. Pithead stockpiles froze solid and could not be loaded for transport. Surface machinery for screening and washing coal also froze up. In both cases production often had to be suspended, as there was nowhere to store fresh output until the blockages had been cleared. Snow on the tracks and frozen points prevented the clearance of loaded coal trains from pithead sidings: and again production often had to be stopped until they could be moved and empty wagons brought in. Opencast coal workings, which were more dependent on road transport, were even more vulnerable to this kind of problem than traditional deep mines. Among the miners, absenteeism (generally of the 'involuntary' sort resulting from the effects of the weather on the journey to and from work) underwent a noticeable rise in January and February, though it remained substantially below the levels of the same months in the previous year. There was also a slight tendency for the size of the mining labour force to grow through the first two months of 1947, after a period of stagnation in the previous three. And output per man-shift, the classic measurement of productive efficiency in the coal industry, was as high at the height of the disruption in January and February as it had been in any of the preceding twelve months.[64] The result was that, despite the problems the industry faced, production held up remarkably well. Indeed, Attlee was able to congratulate the miners on achieving an output of over 4 million tons in the week ending 22nd February.[65] It was calculated by the statisticians at the Ministry of Fuel and Power that the loss of production resulting from all causes in February 1947 amounted to only three per cent or so of the output that might have been expected in that month.[66]

The problem, once the coal had been mined, was to move it to the stockyards of the public utilities, industrial concerns and house-coal merchants. To achieve this in the face of the obstacles put in its way by frost, snow and storms at sea after 23rd January seemed initially beyond the powers of the transport system, both by sea and by land. One of the most important tasks facing the Fuel Committee on its establishment was to find ways of beating the transport bottlenecks threatening both the production of coal and its availability to consumers. Reviewing the position at its first meeting, the committee found that nearly 96,000 railway wagons loaded with coal were either immobilised by the snow or in transit between collieries and consumers, instead of the 65,000 or so that was considered normal at any one time. This meant that nearly half as much coal again than usual was, as it were, strung out inaccessibly along the railway system. The seaborne coal trade was to all intents and purposes at a complete stand-still. More than a hundred colliers were normally engaged in running a shuttle service up and down the east coast to keep the capital supplied. These were now confined to port, along with many of their sister ships in the South Wales trade. Open-cast coal was piling up at the production sites because the road vehicles used to distribute it could not get through the blocked country roads that served the workings.[67]

Gradually the transport bottlenecks began to respond to efforts to unblock them and to keep them open despite renewed onslaughts from the weather. On 12th and 13th February alone fifty-three of the storm-bound colliers put to sea with more than a hundred thousand tons of coal for London's power stations, gasworks and domestic hearths, despite the continued severity of the weather and sea conditions.[68] By the third week in February, seaborne shipments to London were running at more or less the level that had obtained before the weather broke, at a daily average of around 45,000 tons. These were still subject to interruption by bad weather: the blizzard of 27th February reduced the volume for that day to only 15,000 tons. But this was offset by the shipment on the following day of over 75,000 tons.[69] Similarly, on the railways, the number of loaded wagons at colliery sidings or in transit or waiting to be unloaded was reduced from nearly 96,000 on 7th February to only 54,000 two weeks later, the latter figure being 20% below what was considered normal for that time of year. It was not low enough to satisfy the Fuel Committee entirely; it had been aiming to reduce the number to less than 50,000 in that time. But it was a good enough result for Ministers to agree to the lifting of the absolute priority that had been accorded on the railways to coal trains.[70] By the end of the month the number of loaded wagons in transit had risen again to around the normal seasonal level of about 64,000 at any one time, and the Fuel Committee felt able to pronounce this 'satisfactory'.[71] The committee was able to make a direct contribution to solving the problems of moving coal by road, chiefly from open-cast sites, by making available large numbers of military vehicles and personnel for the purpose. It was hoped thereby to clear the stockpiles at open-cast workings within four weeks. In fact the job was done in not much more than one, and by the end of the third week of February the military resources involved could be returned to their bases.[72]

So in spite of the worst winter weather for at least fifty years, and from a point in time very shortly after the Cabinet Fuel Committee had been set up, coal was being produced in record quantities and transported in volumes, if anything, rather larger than in the months preceding the breakdown in the weather. The disruption, while it had lasted, had been severe. But this high pitch of severity had not lasted long – not much above a fortnight. The Fuel Committee was able, from a remarkably early date, to think in terms of restoring electricity supplies to industry, and even to give most of its time and attention to the state of fuel supplies in the longer term, as required by the second aspect of its brief. As early as 18th February specific dates for the resumption of electricity supplies to industry in the 'black areas' were being considered. On the basis that in each region power-station coal stocks should be at the minimum of two weeks' supply recommended by the CEB, and that a flow of coal deliveries sufficient to keep stocks at that level could be established, Sir Donald Fergusson of the Ministry of Fuel and Power reported that it would be safe to restore industrial power in the midlands on 24th February and in the north-west on 3rd March. But he thought that London and the south-east might have to wait until a week after the resumption in the north-west. The committee was prepared to agree at least as far as the midlands were concerned, and accordingly announced the date of the resumption in that region as suggested by Sir Donald. The decision to restore industrial power in the north-west from 3rd March was approved on 21st February. But the case of the south-east proved more intractable. Coal stocks at two of London's main power stations remained obstinately below the requisite two-week level, and the decision to resume electricity supplies to industry in London and its hinterland was deferred until the last day of February. The committee then agreed, however, to restore the supply on the same day as in the north-west, rather than a week later, as had once seemed likely. In all areas the restrictions on the non-industrial use of power remained in force.[73]

So rapidly did the short-term situation seem to be changing for the better that in the second week of its existence the Fuel Committee began to turn its attention to matters of the longer term, such as the accumulation of coal stocks for the winter of 1947–48 and the relief of pressure on electricity generating capacity in the coming year by staggering hours of work in industry.[74] By its third week its meetings were concerned primarily with long-term considerations, above all with the means that might be employed to bring the demand for coal, gas and electricity into more satisfactory equilibrium with supply during and beyond the coming 'coal year' of 1947–48.[75] In what must surely have been a rare, if not entirely unprecedented, moment in the history of the Cabinet and its committees, the meeting of 27th February was attended by the leaders of the National Union of Mineworkers, to discuss with Ministers the ways and means of securing a minimum output in the coming 'coal year' of 200 million tons. The union's recipe for success was to increase manpower while improving productivity with a combination of better capital equipment and better wages and social conditions for miners and their communities. The ministerial reaction was to defend what the government had already done in these respects while remaining noncommittal about the future. The meeting had about it the air of an industrial negotiation, with Ministers cast as the cagey representatives of capital refusing to be drawn by an extravagant set of demands from representatives of labour who were confident of their power, despite the expressions of mutual esteem with which the proceedings opened and closed.[76]

By the time this fraternal gathering took place it was clear that the worst was over. The supply of industrial power for the midlands was restored, as the committee had said it would be, on Monday 24th February, when it was announced that industry in the north-west would restart the Monday following. The next day the Deputy Secretary of the Ministry of Fuel and Power announced that the country was 'drawing out of extreme crisis conditions'. The most visible and damaging manifestation of these 'extreme crisis conditions' from the government's point of view was unemployment, which fell by more than 600,000 in the week after 22nd February. The government's announcement of this reassuring statistic coincided on 1st March with its notice that industrial power would be restored in London and the south-east in two days' time, simultaneously with the north-west.[77] And so, indeed, it was.

What part did the Fuel Committee, as the government's chief crisis management agency, play in the attainment of this happy outcome? The easing of the fuel and power situation after the committee took over the burden of dealing with the crisis was rapid and substantial, though it was far from complete (as non-industrial consumers of electricity, for instance, appreciated only too well as they continued to cope with their daily five hours of withdrawal). But to what extent could this easing be credited to the committee? Did its members, standing fast in the face of crisis, indeed deserve (in the words of Tom Paine) 'the love and thanks of men and women'?

Inevitably the committee had to feel its way into its work and had to deal with problems, both as to policy and as to practice, that it had not been able to foresee. On both counts, responses had to be improvised as the problems arose. It quickly became plain, for example, that the distinction between 'essential' industries and services, which *had* to be kept supplied with power, and 'non-essential' activities that could be made to shut down was not as easy to define as had been thought when the restrictions were first introduced. 'Essential' services were often dependent on a day-to-day basis on the 'non-essential' sector for materials and components, and sometimes found their operations threatened by the dearth of such supplies as their sources closed down for lack of power. Every day, Sir Donald Fergusson informed the Fuel Committee, 'brought to light further ancillary industries which had to be allowed to use electricity, if essential industry was to continue in operation'.[78] Fortunately the institutional arrangements within the committee and *its* ancillaries, together with the attitudes of the Ministers and officials who served on them, were well adapted to solving such problems. The whole set-up favoured flexibility and enabled speedy decisions to be reached. There were problems of communication between London and the provinces that had to be ironed out, along with inconsistencies in the local application of general policy. One such came to light when the MP for Oldham complained that all the cotton mills in his constituency had been shut down, while many of those in neighbouring Bolton had been allowed to keep going. It turned out that the Oldham mills had asked for a ruling on their position from the local office of the Ministry of Fuel and Power, while those in Bolton had applied to their local Board of Trade office. There were no standardised criteria on which the local officers could base a ruling, so each had ruled differently.[79] Local officers complained that they were having to rely on newspaper reports of official policy and their own common sense and experience in order to deal with decisions like these. Small wonder they gave rise to inconsistent results.[80] The solution was to set up a kind of 'hot line' service between the Ministry of Fuel and Power's head office at Millbank and its Senior Regional Fuel Officers in the main provincial centres, through which national policy could be communicated and explained to those who had to apply it at local level. Equally, local queries could swiftly and authoritatively be sorted out by national officials. The system was in operation by 19th February, to the obvious relief of officials in the regions.[81]

Only to a limited extent did the Fuel Committee exercise direct control over resources which enabled it to act by itself to improve coal production and distribution or to influence its consumption, in the short term at any rate. It could, and did, direct the resources of the armed services to facilitate coal movements. Service leave trains were cancelled by its order so that their locomotives might haul coal; servicemen and their vehicles could be allocated by it to clear roads and move open-cast coal; and naval assistance could be given to the movement of coastwise shipments. The committee could promulgate regulations with the force of law to prohibit the use of electricity by householders during the 'restricted hours'. And it did so under Defence Regulations 55 and 92, which prescribed for those who breached them the alternatives of fines up to £500 or imprisonment up to two months.[82] These regulations also applied to the organisers of greyhound race meetings, which the committee could, in effect, ban outright. But the chief functions of the Fuel Committee were not coercive but rather supervisory, exhortatory and analytical − the last, perhaps, above all. It was charged with analysing the very detailed information about transport conditions, coal production and distribution, and the production of electricity and gas which it received from officials of various departments through the Ministry of Fuel and Power, in the form of daily situation reports. This analysis made it possible to define specific problems, to decide on the best means of dealing with them, and to exhort, cajole or (in the last resort) compel those who might be able to give practical effect to the solutions to do so. Not the least important of the committee's functions was to keep people informed about what was going on. The Cabinet seems to have got over its earlier desire to keep things to itself and instead decided to grant the wish expressed by Francis Williams early in January that it should take the people into its confidence about the fuel crisis. At its meeting of 10th February the Cabinet had agreed that:

> Special care should be taken to ensure that the public were kept fully informed of the facts of the situation, and measures which the Government were taking to meet it, and the need for all sections of the community to co-operate in overcoming it. Though the Government would have to meet political criticism, it was desirable that a factual and objective statement should first be made and that political controversy should if possible be reserved for subsequent Parliamentary debate.[83]

These principles the Fuel Committe also seemed to take to heart. Every meeting was followed by at least a press statement during the high point of the crisis from 10th February to 3rd March, generally issued by Attlee himself. These statements conveyed in a straightforwardly factual way the main aspects of the committee's deliberations and decisions. They were fully reported in the press, with occasional broadcast reinforcement, and comparison between the reports and the committee's proceedings shows a high degree of candour on Attlee's part. The fact that the public was now being kept so fully informed of what was going on, in contrast to its previous ignorance, may have been an important factor in mobilising compliance and co-operation with the economy measures. All in all, as an agency for collecting and analysing data about the crisis, for identifying areas in which action was required, for prescribing action appropriate to the problem, and for monitoring the effectiveness of action as it was implemented, the Fuel Committee must be recognised as a very successful *ad hoc* crisis management agency. It might be argued that with its inception it was not just the public which for the first time was adequately informed about what was happening but the government as well.

When it came to puttings its prescriptions into effect the committee, of course, enjoyed formidable powers in theory under the Supplies and Services (Transitional Powers) Act of 1945, the peacetime successor to the even more sweeping wartime Emergency Powers Acts. But it was equally recognised that in practice these immense powers could be used only to a limited extent. For example, undertakings which were allowed to continue to use electricity during the restricted periods – hospitals, public utilities, food-processing plants and so on – were so intermingled with places that had to observe the restrictions that it was technically all but impossible to cut off supplies to one group while maintaining them for the other.[84] So in practice the government had to rely on electricity consumers, particularly private households, voluntarily observing the hours of restriction. It did not have the means to secure compliance on any other basis. The Fuel Committee seems to have been aware of this problem from the start, and recognised that the chief purpose of the orders it made to prohibit the use of electricity was that of 'impressing on the public the gravity of the situation and the need to economise in the use of electricity'.[85] And on later occasions when the use of its powers to restrict fuel and power consumption by order was being considered, the committee proved reluctant to apply them. The difficulties of enforcement were given great weight, as were considerations of equity as between those who were to be restricted and those who were not.[86] On the whole, the committee favoured the voluntary principle over coercion – save in the case of greyhounds.

This applied to the supply of coal, gas and electricity as well as to their consumption. The coal miners, dockers, power-station and gas workers, railwaymen and lorry drivers whose job it was to produce and distribute fuel and power could no longer be compelled to work overtime or at week-ends. The government's powers to make them do so had ended with the war. If fuel and power workers were to make special efforts to overcome the crisis they had to be persuaded to do so. Fortunately the Labour government could draw upon its special relationship with the trade unions, whose leaders appealed to their members to put in the extra shifts required to maximise coal output and speed up the loading, despatch and discharging of coal trains and ships.[87] It was these voluntary efforts that were crucial to the fulfilment of the Fuel Committee's efforts to keep the lines of com-munication open and to build up fuel stocks so that industrial power sup-plies could be restored and restrictions on gas consumption avoided. The manpower and vehicles controlled by the government itself which were deployed on these tasks were of real but essentially subsidiary importance. What the government, through the Fuel Committee, could and did do, beyond appealing to the unions for co-operation, was to see that voluntary efforts were effectively co-ordinated. The committee kept the transport unions and the 'production' unions informed of each other's activities, so that when coal miners volunteered to work an extra Sunday shift, for instance, there would be railwaymen available to move the coal they pro-duced and powerstation workers to unload the wagons when they reached their destination.[88]

With the resumption of industrial activity in the north-west of England and in the London area on 3rd March, the most acute phase of the fuel crisis may be regarded as over. The government had shown that it had the capacity to handle the emergency with energy and decision. It was just a pity that it had waited until almost mid-February to do it. The same candour, vigour and administrative skill exercised, say, the previous September or October – or better yet in May or June – might have enabled the disruption and hardship of January and February 1947 to be largely avoided. So the government could not, perhaps, take too much pride in its achievements. Nor could it yet afford to be complacent: difficulties remained both for in-dustrial energy users and the still restricted non-industrial consumers. The weather still had some unpleasant tricks up its sleeve too, as the south and midlands of England discovered on 4th and 5th March and the north of England and Scotland a week or so later, when the final two ferocious blizzards hit them. But the worst, though people probably did not quite realise it, was past. They had weathered the storms, both literal and meta-phorical – but in what sort of shape had they emerged from the experience?

5 Overdoing the joke

EVERYDAY EXPERIENCE, JANUARY–MARCH 1947

The frosts, snows and fogs ... continue unabated, and whoever is trying to be funny in arranging all this is rather over doing the joke ... The most satisfactory place, these days, is in bed!

Hugh Dalton, *Diary*, vol. 35, 24th February 1947

Like those who governed them, the British public had perhaps become so punch-drunk as a result of the succession of critical problems they had had to face since their supposed victory in 1945 and in the six years before it that they had some difficulty in recognising the immediacy and severity of the fuel problem. The way the Minister of Fuel and Power insisted on playing down the seriousness of the situation up to 3rd January 1947, and the way thereafter that the Cabinet as a whole remained unwilling to take the people fully into its confidence, cannot have helped them to reach an informed view of the nature and gravity of the crisis. They had so many other crises on their plates that it was difficult to gauge the significance of the fuel crisis relative to the others.

Yet it is possible to trace, in the findings of the Gallup polls for instance, a growing public awareness of the seriousness of the fuel and power shortage. In January 1946, despite the difficulty the government was then going through to balance its fuel budget (a difficulty that had called the Ministerial Coal Committee into being), Gallup found that only 2% of those interviewed rated 'the coal crisis' as the most urgent domestic problem facing the government. Housing was regarded as by far a more urgent issue, nearly two-thirds of Gallup's respondents placing it at the top of the list of items requiring the government's attention. And food shortages and employment were regarded by many people − 10% and 7% respectively of the Gallup sample − as problems of greater moment than coal. In the high summer of 1946 more people were inclined to see 'the coal crisis' as the government's most pressing domestic problem. Six per cent of those polled by Gallup in June put it in that category. But their numbers were dwarfed by the 42% and the 31% who opted respectively for food shortages and housing instead.[1]

By the beginning of January 1947, as we have seen, the fuel crisis was making its presence felt in an acute way, and the government was contemplating the desperate measures proposed by Cripps to deal with it. The gravity of the situation was being widely proclaimed by the press and was already impinging directly, through the periodic disruption of employment and of the household power supply, on the lives of a substantial number of people. Yet a poll conducted that month still showed that housing was taken more seriously than 'coal: fuel situation', though the latter had at least moved up to second place in the order of urgency, with 19% of respondents putting it at the top of their list as against 33% for housing.[2] It may be that this result reflected to a degree the reluctance of the government to place the facts of the fuel crisis fully before the public, in contrast to the publicity that was given to the housing shortage and to the government's determination to end it.

For the ordinary citizen the acute shortage of fuel and power which manifested itself with growing severity after Christmas 1946 made its presence felt through the impact it had on industry — and so on the security of the citizen's livelihood — and through its impact on the comforts and amenities of home and family life. The latter effect, in the early weeks of January, was the one most commonly experienced. Long before the weather broke down at the end of January, the growing prevalence of voltage reductions in the electricity supply, or of what the power engineers described euphemistically as 'load shedding' (which usually meant local shut-downs in power supply for limited periods as the demand for current outstripped generating capacity), together with periodic drops in gas supply pressures, made life difficult for housewives in particular. These things interfered with domestic arrangements in various ways, most commonly during the peak hours of industrial demand for gas and electricity. But as yet, before the blizzard of 23rd January, such problems were perhaps more irritating than seriously damaging to routine domestic arrangements for heating, cooking or illumination: sporadic, unpredictable, but not yet too frequent; a nuisance while they lasted, which was seldom for very long. House coal to fuel the still predominant open household hearth and even — for example, in the tenement buildings of central Scotland — to provide heat for cooking on the kitchen range, was in acutely short supply. The official allocation nation-wide before the introduction of the Cripps measures had been 620,000 tons per week, but officials of the Ministry of Fuel and Power admitted in private (and the public were doubtless generally aware) that this was no more than a polite fiction. Actual deliveries of house coal fell behind the allocation by substantial amounts, varying somewhat from one part of the country to another, between 10% and 30%. The allocation was itself some 30% below pre-war house coal consumption.[3] But as long as gas and electricity continued to be available without restriction, beyond the occasional voltage reduction or pressure loss, people would continue to switch to their gas or electrical heating appliances to remedy the shortfall in their coal supplies. Household consumption of electricity in 1946 had been almost a third higher than in 1945: in January 1947 it rose sharply to still greater heights.[4]

From Christmas 1946 to the implementation of the Cripps measures on 20th January 1947 the effects of industrial disruption were experienced largely by fairly localised and specific groups of workers, like the Lancashire millhands whose mills were closed down by coal shortages in the last days of the old year and the first of the new, or the cement workers of Sussex who suffered a similar fate in the first week of January. The localised nature of the unemployment, however, could have been of small comfort to those who experienced it. The new National Insurance Act of August 1946 had done much to improve and render more humane the system of unemployment relief, but it had not done as much as many would have wished to bring the levels of benefit up to the point where they might offer more than fractional compensation for the loss of a regular wage. The basic rate of benefit for a single unemployed man was 26s per week (£1·30): the average earnings of male manual workers in manufacturing during 1946 had been 120s 9d (£6·03) per week.[5] There was also the matter of the qualifying period: no benefit was payable until the claimant had been out of work for three consecutive working days.[6] Since, before the ban on non-essential industrial activity imposed on 10th February, industrial stoppages had tended to follow no organised pattern with regard to frequency or duration, this qualifying period could cause problems for people whose factories might be stopped for only a day or two at a time while awaiting a coal delivery. However, a curious anomaly took some of the sting at least out of the three-day wait for some workers. Despite the fact that the five-day working week had become the norm in much of British industry since the war, the administrative conventions under which unemployment benefit was assessed (which dated back to 1932) assumed a normal working week of six days. As a result, workers who finished their normal five-day week on a Friday and then found their place of work closed through lack of fuel on Monday and Tuesday the following week were allowed to count the intervening Saturday, when they would not have been working anyway, as one of the three 'waiting days' that qualified them for benefit.[7]

For many factory workers in the afflicted regions before the enforced closure of industry the problem was not unemployment for days at a time but the loss of work for periods of less than a day. For some, at least, the impact of this problem on earnings was moderated by the arrangement — operated by many Lancashire cotton mills, for instance — known as the 'guaranteed week'. If normal work was possible for at least four hours in the day, the worker received wages at the full rate for the period so worked, plus about three-quarters of the normal rate for the hours in which normal work was not possible.[8] Probably all employers who operated such a system would find it costly to keep going in the conditions obtaining in January 1947. Many must have felt inclined to sympathise with the Dunlop Rubber Company when it announced on the 7th that, in these uncertain times, the 'guaranteed week' was likely to be suspended at its large Birmingham, Liverpool, Manchester and Leicester plants.[9]

With the Cripps cuts in coal allocations coming into effect on 20th January, the number of people affected by industrial stoppages and short-time working increased by a substantial margin. Reports of these phenomena became a daily feature, for instance, of the Manchester newspapers in the week before the first blizzard hit the north-west on 26th January, and the number of people affected climbed steadily into five figures in the city and surrounding cotton towns.[10] From the textile and engineering industries of the north-west and midlands the blight spread with the Cripps measures to the steel towns of south Yorkshire and elsewhere. The breakdown of the weather after 23rd January diffused the experience of lay-offs and short time to the south-east, as well as exacerbating the difficulties of the areas previously affected. But of course all this was as nothing compared with what was to happen after 10th February. Until then, while a large number of workers in certain localities were affected by short periods of unemployment or short time as their factories – having run out of coal – awaited fresh deliveries that usually arrived within forty-eight hours, the number of people affected seriously enough to warrant claiming unemployment benefit remained quite small in aggregate.

As work became less secure and regular, especially as the impact of the fuel crisis was aggravated by the weather, so the inconveniences and discomforts of home life also grew. Particularly hard hit were those whose homes exemplified the recent trend towards absolute reliance upon electricity for heat and cooking as well as light. The 'all-electric house' had a prominent place in the post-war housing programme; in particular, large numbers of prefabricated dwellings of this description were being produced. But even before the war many people had been seduced by the promotional campaigns of the electricity undertakings, which stressed the cleanliness, convenience and controllability of electricity over the other domestic energy sources, above all coal. They paid a high price for their attachment to modernity as the power engineers reached for their 'load-shedding' switches with increasing frequency, while the snow piled up and the temperatures plummeted. The *Manchester Evening News* of 29th January gave some insight into the conditions being endured by its readers. The temperature in Manchester at nine in the morning had been less than 22°F: with a certain air of civic pride the *News* noted that this was lower than the temperatures then being recorded by an American navy expedition in Antarctica. Electric power almost throughout the city had been cut off between 7.55 and 9.30 a.m., so 'People who relied on electricity shivered over cold breakfasts'. Nor were those who relied on gas much better served, as the city gasworks could only maintain a supply at about a quarter of the normal pressure, a level 'so poor as to be almost useless'. Housewives lamented that it took half an hour to boil the water for a cup of tea 'over the flickering gas flame'. Eating out was no answer, either: the hotels, restaurants and cafés reported great difficulty in preparing hot food, with potatoes put on the gas at eight in the morning still not boiling three and a half hours later. Reading such a report in centrally heated comfort forty years after the event, it seems at first a mildly amusing curiosity. But life under the threat of the regular repetition of these conditions, unable to heat the house and prepare hot food or drinks in the coldest winter of the century, went, as the Chancellor remarked, far beyond a joke.

In a way, the restrictions on the use of power imposed on 10th February may actually have made life a little easier, if only in the sense that from then on the power cuts were regular and predictable, and so made some domestic organisation possible to meet them. For industrial workers the impact of the restrictions varied. Throughout the country, those whose activities were defined as essential could look forward, more or less, to uninterrupted full-time effort. For those in 'non-essential' industries in the three so-called Black Areas, apart from the works maintenance crews, the cuts meant mass lay-offs. Some were fortunate, and continued to be paid by their employers under 'guaranteed week' or similar provisions. For the rest, after the first three days, it was a matter of applying for State unemployment relief and hoping that the stoppage did not last. Many were left in a state of uncertainty, like the bewildered Cricklewood die-caster interviewed by Mass Observation who told his interviewer:[11]

> We've been stopped indefinitely and told to go back to work when the wireless tells us to go back … I don't know what the position is and who is going to pay us − if it's just dole money or not.

Outside the Black Areas non-essential industry continued to struggle on from hand to mouth with uncertain and inadequate coal supplies, but at least the industrial supply of electricity in the White Areas was put on a safer footing by the restrictions on domestic consumption, and to that extent the workers concerned found their position more secure.

1947 has become the yardstick by which we in Britain measure the severity of our winters, which compete for the media accolade of 'coldest since 1947' or some variation of it. None of the close contenders for the title, in 1963, 1979, 1981−82 or 1986 contained the special ingredient of the fuel and power shortage which made the hardships of 1947 so uniquely unpleasant. It is hard to see how people who were, on the whole, adequately employed and paid, relatively well fed, housed, clothed and heated can compare their lot to that of the people of 1947, above all to the plight of the industrial communities of the north-west, the midlands and the south-east. Cold that can be readily avoided or counteracted is a very different thing from cold that cannot be escaped. The difference is one of kind, not of degree.

The most serious hardship, probably, ws being thrown out of work and on to unemployment relief at very low rates. The Fuel Committee wanted to ease matters for people in this position by abolishing at least for the time being the three-day 'qualifying period', but this turned out not to be possible without new legislation to alter the recently passed National Insurance Act. So the three-day wait remained in force, the committee comforting itself with the reflection that some of the leeway would be made up by the repayment of income tax to which those who were out of work were entitled.[12] Meanwhile the unemployed − bored, cold and short of money − sought solace and warmth where they could. A north London librarian reported the return of that phenomenon so characteristic of the 1930s, the public reading room crowded on weekdays with out-of-work men desultorily picking over its newspapers and magazines. The public libraries also reported a substantial rise in the borrowing of books. Others resorted to more materially rewarding if also more dangerous activities: London shopkeepers reports a rise in the incidence of petty theft, which they regarded as an inevitable concomitant of the fact that people were short of money.[13]

Unemployment was strictly the plight of industrial manual workers. Offices, shops, warehouses, cinemas and other commercial premises were not forced to close. They were, however, obliged to observe the same restrictions as householders with respect to the use of electricity in the three hours before mid-day and the two before 4.00 p.m. For some concerns, such as cinemas, this provision had the effect of severely restricting their hours of business. An exception, as arbitrary in its way as the outright prohibition on greyhound racing, was made for hairdressers, who *were* permitted to use electrical equipment other than permanent-waving machines during the restricted hours. A directive to this effect went out from the Ministry of Fuel and Power to its regional officers on 17th February, in response to representations by the hairdressers' trade association.[14] Other people muddled through in various ways. One of Mass Observation's correspondents reported that in her office there was no light:

> but work continues as usual. People have moved their desks to near windows where possible. Some candles and a storm lantern in use in the darkest spots.

Mass Observation's surveys suggest that these expedients were fairly typical of the methods used by office staff to carry on in the face of the restrictions. But they did not do so without great difficulty and not a little risk to themselves. A note circulated to the members of the Fuel Committee commented that 'The restrictions are now causing ... real hardship to some of the employees', in the form of severe eyestrain and higher sickness rates — to say nothing of much discontent.[15]

Many shopkeepers found that although they were able to stay open for business, the volume of that business declined sharply, especially in areas where industrial closures were prevalent. Some reported a drop of as much as 80% in their takings. As the owner of a Camden Town clothiers, which had experienced a 25% drop in its trade, explained to Mass Observation, his customers lived precariously at the best of times, so:

> As soon as the cuts came into force people immediately stopped spending because they didn't know where their next lot of money was coming from.

Small newsagents, tobacconists and confectioners in factory districts, whose trade depended on workers making casual purchases on the way to or from work, were especially hard hit. On the other hand, the shops serving more affluent suburbs felt little effect: as a chemist in one of the more prosperous parts of Surrey remarked, 'It will be a long time before it touches Richmond.' Sales of some commodities actually increased markedly during, and indeed because of, the emergency. An obvious case in point was paraffin for domestic heating, which afforded hardware shops some compensation for the decline of their other sales. Perhaps equally predictable was the increased sale of hard liquor as the populace resorted to whisky, gin and rum as a source of internal warmth. It was an expedient of decreasing availability, as the bottling plants for spirits — and for that matter beer too — were not on the list of essential industries permitted to use electricity in the Black Areas. So, in artificial defiance of Say's law, the supply of spirits declined as their consumption rose.[16]

At home, apart from resorting to strong drink as an aid to warmth with more than their usual enthusiasm, people tried to keep warm as best they could. Like industry, the domestic consumer of coal had been living from hand to mouth for some time. Deliveries had lagged behind requirements for so long that few had coal stocks of their own to fall back on. As the cold intensified and snow disrupted the distribution of house coal as of other varieties, many households found themselves without coal at all, often for days, sometimes for weeks on end. When that happened, they burned whatever else they could lay hands on to keep their homes warm. Timber traders in Manchester were reported to be overwhelmed with orders for wood to burn.[17] Timber in any form, however, was in short supply, and was therefore always expensive and frequently unobtainable. A Mass Observation investigator, visiting Sanderstead Woods, south of Croydon, observed what appeared to be the wholesale plunder by local residents of trees that had been felled the previous summer:

> Approaching the woods via Addington Hill Investigator saw two school boys aged about 15, hauling a sleigh laden with three large pine logs; an elderly gentleman pushing a wheelbarrow filled with sawn logs; and a middle-aged man and a boy, pulling along a pile of logs lashed together with ropes. In the woods a number of people were busy at work, some selecting and removing the large logs, others cutting logs, filling sacks, boxes, wheelbarrows, and in one case a small handcart.

One man questioned by the investigator claimed to have been 'without a bit of a fire for over a week', and to have travelled five or six miles for the logs he was now taking away.[18] For others, especially in the large towns where access to wood was difficult, coke was the favourite substitute for coal. One of the commonest recollections that people have of this period is of queues outside their local gasworks of men, women and children with old prams, sacks, boxes, handcarts — anything that might hold and transport a few pounds of coke from the retorts. Old railway sleepers — solid timber impregnated with creosote which burned readily — were much in demand, though sawing them into pieces of manageable size must have been hard, if warming, work. Anything that would burn, however, briefly or unwillingly, was put to the flame. One family tried burning worn-out shoes. Another, using instructions from a leaflet published by the Ministry of Fuel and Power, mixed the coal dust from their cellar with cement to produce briquettes. As Mass Observation remarked, 'With some ingenuity it seems that many managed to avoid the worst effects of the crisis.'[19] Few, however, probably considered going to the extremes to which one Manchester man resorted when he demanded a supply of coal at pistol point from a coal yard at Greenheys. The magistrates, moved perhaps by a certain fellow feeling, merely fined him £1 and confiscated his revolver.[20]

Household warmth was a particular problem, as always, for the old, especially for those who lived alone and whose means did not extend much beyond the basic old-age pension, which, in spite of a hastily introduced rise in October 1946, still stood at less than £1 a week. 'Hypothermia' was not then a word that was in general use, but it was nevertheless apparent that the extremely cold weather, coupled with the problems of keeping a house heated in the face of coal shortages and electricity restrictions, was taking a heavy toll among the old. A letter writer to *The Times* on

15th April noted that the number of death notices appearing in the paper each week in respect of people aged eighty or over had shot up after the first three weeks of January. Having numbered sixty or seventy per week in that period, they reached a peak weekly average of 115 in the three weeks up to 1st March, when the fuel and power restrictions were at their height. Only towards the end of March did they fall back to the level of early January. Another letter on 24th April noted a similar upsurge in mortality among the older inhabitants of the village of Hever in Kent during the same period. That these rather random observations represented a general national trend was officially confirmed two years after the event by the publication of the Registrar General's analysis of mortality in 1946 and 1947. His returns indicated that overall mortality in the first three months of 1947 had been 18% higher than in the corresponding period of 1946. Deaths from diseases such as bronchitis, pneumonia and asthma were higher in the first quarter of 1947 than in the same part of 1946 by a margin of no less than 22%. And mortality from these causes, the Registrar General's statistics clearly showed, was particularly severe among those aged sixty-five and over. Normally the first three months of the year exhibited a death rate about 30% higher than the rate for the year as a whole: but in 1947 the margin of difference was 43%.[21]

Heating was not the only problem people faced in their homes as a result of the fuel crisis. The compulsory restriction on the use of electric power between nine in the morning and noon and between two and four in the afternoon was geared rather to the needs of industry during these hours than to the requirements of housewives. Again, the Mass Observation surveys testify that housewives had a lot to contend with as a result. Those with small children or aged or infirm relatives to look after found the business of coping with power cuts, cuts in gas pressure and the house-coal famine especially trying. The restricted hours took little account of their charges' needs for heat, light, hot drinks, hot food and hot water. Some managed to improvise solutions to the problems, like the Mass Observation respondent who described herself as being acutely affected by the restrictions in her:

> ... all-electric house with one decorative but extremely inefficient coal fire. I have found it extremely difficult to deal with the baby's daily washing.
> Everything else, cooking, ironing, washing, cleaning, bathing, has either to be arranged for other times or improvised — hay box for cooking, tin kettle in fire for small quantities of hot water, flask kept for hot drinks, etc.[22]

The crisis would almost seem to have taxed the powers of household management of Mrs Beeton herself.

The women's situation was not always viewed very sympathetically by their menfolk. The same survey recorded one man's view that:

> ... the women complain a damn sight more than the men – they're always on it. My wife complains bitterly that almost all her time goes in scrounging around for food and now with the cold weather she complains more than ever.

But men complained bitterly too, and none more so than the young ex-serviceman, now a student, whose feelings were also recorded by Mass Observation. The survey report characterised his attitude as 'definitely a minority one', which may well have been true to the extent that the strength of his feelings and the force with which he expressed them may not have been typical. But the general gist of what he had to say must have been felt in some degree by many of his compatriots. He lived in a student hostel, he had flu, and he was extremely fed up.

> What the crisis means to me is: 1.30–3.30: lie without lights; my bedroom is rather dark so this means I cannot read. I cannot listen to the radio. I cannot sit up in bed and do anything since the power is off and I cannot use my electric fire. The place is almost unliveable in from the point of view of heating, from early morning to six at night. I hate cold. I wish I were back in Egypt. I wish I were anywhere but in this goddamned country where there is nothing but queues and restrictions and forms and shortages and no food and cold. Flu and the fuel crisis is the last straw ...

Here was one man at least who evidently did not share the Chancellor of the Exchequer's view that, these days, the most satisfactory place was in bed.[23]

Getting out of 'this goddamned country' to somewhere warmer and more congenial was not so easy, though thousands of Britons – nay, *hundreds* of thousands – shared the young man's wish to do so. Strict exchange controls made foreign currency even for short holidays in sunnier climes difficult to obtain. As for emigration, arrangements for settling British migrants in large numbers in the colonies and the dominions had not yet been reinstated after their wartime interruption. Nor, it was suspected, was the government particularly keen to see them fully revived at a time when economic growth seemed likely to be hindered by a serious shortage of labour, even though Canada, Australia, South Africa and New Zealand were more than happy to accept new immigrants from Britain. The Australian government especially wished to build up its country's population as quickly as possible, having been made painfully aware between 1941 and 1945 of the scarcity of manpower to defend such a large area of territory against attack from Asia. Not that the British government overtly restricted emigration. It did not have to. It simply, and not unreasonably, proclaimed that there were more urgent calls on acutely scarce shipping than the mass transit of potentially very productive workers from the United Kingdom to the dominions. When, on 31st March 1947 — in the immediate aftermath of the fuel crisis — a new Anglo-Australian emigration agreement came into operation, the response was enormous. Arthur Calwell, the Australian Federal Minister for Immigration, announced at a press conference at the beginning of July that 400,000 UK residents altogether had signed up to take advantage of it. But, because of the shipping famine, the actual movement of would-be migrants from Britain to Australia in the coming year was unlikely to exceed 15,000. In all, during the first nine months of 1947 only 46,502 people succeeded in leaving Britain to settle in the dominions — less than a tenth of all those who were thought to want to go.[24]

Among women, a particular plunge in morale was chronicled by the journalist Anne Scott-James. Writing in *Picture Post* a few weeks after the crisis reached its peak about the experience of a supposedly typical working-class housewife,[25] she suggested that:

> the fuel shortage, which burst on her in its full intensity in February ... is the worst thing that ever happened to her. Food is difficult, but it can just be managed; and she could always provide enough for the children by going short herself. But to see them looking pinched with cold was a misery — and her own spirits fell to zero after hours spent between a frozen outdoors and a chilly house. Add to this the gloomy news of permanent fuel cuts, to disorganise her whole closely planned day.

And when the cold let up, it often served simply to compound domestic difficulties. Thus, in Manchester, one of the most notable accompaniments of the brief thaw of 31st January and 1st February was a bumper crop of burst water pipes. About twenty water mains were fractured, and the Town Hall was reported, appropriately, to have been inundated by calls from council tenants whose homes were flooding. A chronic shortage of lead pipe made the work of repair very difficult.[26]

Yet, however vehemently people complained about their situation — bereft of many of the normal comforts of home during the bleakest winter in memory, with their hopes of post-war amelioration frustrated by the seemingly unrelenting pressure of austerity — there was nevertheless a strong disposition, initially at least, to co-operate with the government's fuel economy measures. The restrictions that came into force on 10th February were of a kind which people with six years of wartime regulation behind them could understand and accept. At last they were being told that the situation was really serious, and what they had to do about it. The Mass Observation survey reports of the high crisis period in February indicate a kind of rallying round, reminiscent of the war, even on the part of Conservative voters who saw the crisis as being of the government's own making. Acceptance and observance of the restrictions during the most acute phase of the emergency, from 10th to about 21st February, seem to have been general, if not enthusiastic. Something like the sort of communal self-discipline that had made the wartime black-out and rationing schemes work so well seems to have reasserted itself, for a time at least. From the government's point of view this was just as well, for − as we have seen − the regulations were not backed up by the technical capacity to switch off all electric power during the restricted hours, even in non-industrial districts. Nor was it practicable for local officials of the Ministry of Fuel and Power, or for that matter the police, to enforce the restrictions on every household, office, shop, cinema, hotel and hairdressing salon in the land. Some policemen, indeed, expressed an unwillingness to enforce the regulations.[27] Observance, for the most part, depended on the co-operation of the individual citizen, backed up most immediately by neighbourhood disapproval of those who broke the regulations. State power was a very distant long-stop indeed.

There were, of course, some people who for one reason or another did not observe the restrictions at all; and others who − while observing them in the letter − did not go along with the spirit. At the start of the period of restriction there was inevitably some confusion and uncertainty. People expected the power to be physically cut off, and when they discovered that it was not, they tended to assume that they could go on using it. This, probably, was what lay behind the Dartford incident on the very first day of the restrictions. *The Times*, noting that on the whole the public response had been good, reported that in Dartford, Kent:

> all power was cut off for a large part of the day because domestic con-
> sumers used the electricity when it was left on to supply essential
> services.[28]

Mass Observation recorded that at first many people did not take the restrictions seriously, feeling that the whole thing was 'just a scare' which would not last more than a few days. But, the report went on, they quickly came to appreciate the seriousness of the position and to co-operate scrupulously with the restrictions.[29] The same survey, however, reported a number of instances of calculated defiance by individuals. In some cases this was politically motivated: a few people saw non-compliance with the restrictions as their personal contribution to bringing down a government they opposed. In others the motives were more personal, as in the case of the personnel at a Royal Air Force base in Lincolnshire who believed that 'The more light, etc., we burn the more chance we shall have of getting three weeks' leave', through the base being shut down as an economy measure. The Mass Observers seem to have had some sympathy for those who broke the regulations out of concern for the welfare and comfort of the infirm, the old and the very young. Generally, they tended towards the view that deliberate, systematic flouting of the restrictions was exceptional, though many people – perhaps a majority – were guilty of occasional lapses through momentary thoughtlessness. To its question 'Who are the fuel wasters?' Mass Observation returned the answer 'Most of us have been guilty at times' but appeared to believe that most people were disposed to co-operate most of the time.[30]

The evidence of official sources seems broadly to confirm, as far as the first couple of weeks of restriction are concerned, that people conformed fairly conscientiously with the restrictions both at home and at work. Reports coming into the Ministry of Fuel and Power from its chief regional officers around 20th February attested to the public's willing co-operation with official attempts at enforcement.[31] The Fuel Committee received reports of the saving to power-station coal supplies achieved by the restrictions, based on a comparison between the amount of coal used weekly after the introduction of the cuts and the level of consumption in the week ending 9th February, immediately before the cuts were imposed. These indicated a uniformly high level of economy in the first two weeks of the emergency, between 10th and 23rd February. The rate of saving in the first week was 29%, and in the second 28%.[32] Thereafter, however, the savings tended to decline. By the fourth week of the restrictions they had fallen to a mere 15% and in succeeding weeks they diminished still further.[33]

To a certain extent the diminution of the savings was the result of government decisions to ease the cuts. The most notable of these, of course, were the successive removals of the bans on the industrial use of electricity in the so-called Black Areas, on 25th February and 3rd March. Some minor restrictions were also eased about the same time, like the prohibition on the publication of certain periodicals. On 8th March it was announced that electricity might once again be used during the restricted hours in certain 'commercial and non-industrial premises', provided consumers reduced their overall use of electricity by one third compared with the corresponding months of 1946.[34] Households, however, remained subject to the full rigour of the February restrictions until the end of April, when a revised programme was introduced for the summer months which eased the lot of the domestic consumer to a small extent.

At quite an early stage in the emergency there had been official doubts about the public's patience in conforming to restrictions that caused such inconvenience, not to say hardship. On 22nd February the Central Electricity Board warned the Fuel Committee that:

> in the white area domestic consumption during the prohibited hours was increasing and it seemed that the admonitions to the public not to use electricity were losing their effect.[35]

A few days later the Fuel Committee was informed that cuts in domestic and non-industrial consumption of electricity in London and the south-east – the most intractable of the Black Areas – were falling off as well.[36] By the end of the month the general opinion in the committee was that the restrictions on domestic electricity consumption in their present form 'could not be maintained in force for any length of time and were in fact already breaking down'.[37] The committee responded by trying to find alternative ways of controlling domestic and non-industrial fuel and power consumption with which the public could be persuaded or obliged to comply more reliably over a longer period of time. The increasing unwillingness of the public to continue to observe the existing, essentially voluntary, restrictions seemed to point clearly to the need for the government to take sterner powers of compulsion. As Attlee's private secretary observed, whatever was substituted for the existing arrangements, 'it should be compulsory. It is a fallacy to believe that the British people prefer voluntary appeals'.[38] It might be argued, however, that the government could have secured a more prolonged observance of its February restrictions if it had made more determined use of the legal provisions and sanctions on which they rested. Only one person ever appears to have been prosecuted for beaches of the restrictions on the domestic use of electricity imposed in February, and even that prosecution was not pursued in any exemplary fashion. Eight weeks were allowed to elapse before it was brought to court, and the case came up on the same day as it was reported that the lifting of the February restrictions was imminent.[39] Perhaps if a few more recalcitrant householders had been haled before the magistrates with suitable despatch and publicity, *pour encourager les autres*, the decline in compliance with the restrictions might have been less rapid. As things were, however, electricity consumption among domestic and other non-industrial consumers crept steadily and stealthily upwards after23rd February, to the extent that coal stocks at power stations and gasworks – so painfully built up over the previous two weeks – began to run down again and to cause the Fuel Committee fresh concern.[40] On 3rd March the CEB reported that some unscheduled 'load shedding' had been necessary in the midlands and the south. Power-station coal consumption in the first two weeks of March exceeded the Fuel Committee's target figure by 6% as the last burst of snow and frost caused people to reach once more for the 'on' switches of their electric heaters in defiance of the regulations.[41]

The weather may have presented some hardy souls with the opportunity to indulge in winter sports on Hampstead Heath, and provided the more intrepid university oarsmen and cross-country runners with an additional challenge in their chosen sports. But it made routine outdoor tasks like getting to work (for those whose workplace had not been shut down) and shopping considerably more difficult, even dangerous. Public transport was disrupted, conditions underfoot were treacherous because of packed snow and frozen slush, and there was the constant, unremitting cold. Activities like long-distance travel were rendered at times downright impossible. The government's attempts to deal with the fuel crisis in February compounded the problems of life outside the home. The cancellation of railway passenger services to clear the tracks and free locomotives for coal trains; the withdrawal of the only recently restored street lighting; increased shortages of goods in the shops because of the closure of the places that produced them; lack of money; the dismal and unwelcoming state of the shops themselves, unheated and unlit − external conditions conspired to discourage people from leaving their homes. Many schools were forced to close because of the lack of fuel for heating, burst water pipes and frozen lavatories. The very ink froze in the inkwells, and in some parts of the country the public examinations had to be postponed.[42]

Recreationally, there was not much to leave the house for, either. Dance halls, cinemas, theatres and music halls had their hours of opening restricted, though when they were actually open their box offices were doing quite good business. Their warmth, as well as the opportunities they offered for temporary escape from reality, may well have exercised an important attraction.[43] The disruption of the regular sporting programme had already been remarked upon, as has the government's prohibition of greyhound racing. Official antipathy to that particular sport, as the National Greyhound Racing Society perceived, was based on more than just a desire to save electricity. As the Society remarked, the ban applied even to tracks at which no electricity was used. Indeed, the NGRS claimed that dog racing actually promoted economy, since the tracks used less power than their patrons would do were they to stay at home, a claim they asserted was supported by the electricity undertakings.[44]

The government was unmoved: the ban on greyhound racing remained in force until the middle of March. Even then it was not completely removed: the Cabinet merely agreed that electricity could be used at greyhound tracks on Saturdays only.[45] The NGRS was right in thinking that there was more to the government's attitude than saving electricity. Ministers took a dim view of any activity that held out the possibility of high financial returns without honest toil, especially if it involved betting. Some of the large urban dog tracks had rather unsavoury reputations (however undeserved) as the meeting place of spivs, black marketeers, petty criminals and other drones. But, in truth, official dislike of greyhound racing represented the extreme form of a general disapproval among Ministers and civil servants of sport as a diversion from productive activity. The government was concerting measures in the spring of 1947 to limit the extent to which sport might deflect the energies and attention of workers from their proper role in life — namely work. There was perceived to be a direct connection between sport and the fuel crisis: the Lord President's Committee had noted the previous September that the St Leger had cost the country some sixty or seventy thousand tons of coal as large numbers of Yorkshire miners had absented themselves from work to attend the race meeting at Doncaster.[46] With this kind of thing in mind, the Official Steering Committee was briefed to report to the Fuel Committee on 'measures that might be taken to limit the interference with production arising from mid-week sporting events'. The Fuel Committee in turn recommended to the Cabinet that, as well as confining greyhound racing to Saturdays (a day on which meetings did not normally take place in many areas), the number of mid-week horse-racing meetings should be substantially reduced, mid-week football matches should cease to be held for the rest of the season, and motor-cycle speedway racing should also be limited to Saturdays only. This last recommendation threatened to cause further problems for the greyhound racing fraternity, since motor cycles and greyhounds frequently shared the use of the same stadium. The Cabinet, in approving the Fuel Committee's recommendations, also decided that the cricket authorities should be approached to see if the forthcoming series of Test matches against the visiting South Africans might be rescheduled 'with a view to reducing the risk of loss of industrial production'. It also considered extending the ban on mid-week matches to ice hockey and lawn tennis, though eventually deciding that they did not attract large enough attendances to pose a threat to industry.[47] Thus what were arguably the most popular spectator sports in the country, some of them particular

favourites of the mining communities, were for all practical purposes confined to Saturdays, since the government would not relax the statutory
obstacles to Sunday fixtures. Life, as a result, became just a bit grimmer,
more lacking in colour and interest, than it had been.

At the height of the fuel crisis, as that phenomenon was officially recognised, a leading article in *The Times* drew the explicit parallel between
current events and the experience of the recent past. 'The state of emergency
through which we are now passing,' it observed:[48]

> brings back memories of wartime. The darkness of the streets and roads;
> the austerity in domestic lighting ... the feeling of being cut off from our
> friends and the desire to stay safe indoors; the tendency ... towards
> avoiding unnecessary travel – all these things have a suggestion of bad
> times past.

Being the third leader, the tone of the article tended towards humour rather
than seriousness, but there was a serious point behind it nevertheless.
Indeed, not only were conditions of everyday life during the first quarter
of 1947 as difficult and unpleasant as they had been at all but the most
dangerous stages of the war, they were in various respects – thanks to
the combined effects of the weather and the fuel famine – significantly
worse. Meanwhile the spirit that had reputedly carried people through the
war, making them willing at least to put up with deprivation and discomfort
in the hope of victory and the expectation of post-war improvement, was
a rapidly wasting asset. The steady decline in co-operation with the power
restrictions indicated that public patience with controls was now easily
exhausted, when privation no longer enjoyed the justification of war. It
could almost be said that public perceptions of war itself were changing
in the light of experience in January, February and March 1947. The press
made numerous attempts, especially from mid-February, to summon up
again the wartime spirit. But in all these evocations of the war – from the
Daily Mirror to *The Times*, from *Picture Post* to *Vogue* – it is possible
to detect a rising note of fond nostalgia. By comparison with what people
now had to endure, even the war seemed to be assuming the character of
'the good old days'.

6 Come were but the spring

EMERGING FROM THE CRISIS, MARCH–APRIL 1947

Gone were but the Winter,
  Come were but the Spring,
I would go to a covert
    Where the birds sing.   Christina Rossetti, *Spring Quiet*

March proverbially comes in like a lion, and in 1947 it amply lived up to that reputation. Its early weeks witnessed what many people were to experience as the worst snowstorms of a winter that had already excelled in that kind of phenomenon. The first, spanning the 4th and 5th of the month, affected mostly the midlands and the south of England. Over most of the area the level depth of fall exceeded twelve inches, and there was drifting to a depth of up to thirty feet in places. All roads between the midlands and the south were blocked, and on the railways new epics of endurance by passengers and train staff were recorded. The most memorable, perhaps, was the twenty-six-hour odyssey of the Wednesday 1.50 p.m. from Wolverhampton to London.[1] More ominously, the Ministry of Fuel and Power reported that the storm had caused serious interference with the production and movement of coal, not much more than twenty-four hours after the restrictions on the industrial use of power had been raised. For a moment the security of the resumption of industrial activity hung in the balance, but, while coal deliveries to factories, gasworks and power stations faltered, they did not fail completely.

By 10th March the south and midlands were beginning to thaw out, but as they did so a final blizzard blotted out central and southern Scotland, Northern Ireland and the north of England on 12th and 13th March. Conditions in the areas affected were at least as bad as in any previous storm that winter, with the usual accompaniments of heavy drifting, blocked roads and railways, and so on. Once again, major coalfields – the east and west of Scotland, Northumberland and Durham – were badly affected. Yet again there was concern about maintaining fuel and power supplies, but in this case, too, the fears of further breakdown were not realised. And this blizzard, it gradually began to dawn, was the last fling of the great freeze-up. As the *Meteorological Magazine* soberly recorded, 'The end of the wintry spell over the country as a whole can be taken as March 16, 7½ weeks after its onset.'[2] But, as if to demonstrate that he had other weapons at his disposal than snow, frost, fog and freezing wind, the weather god chose to mark the end of the freeze with an exceptionally severe, though temperate, gale. Winds of nearly 100 m.p.h. were recorded, and there was widespread damage to buildings, particularly in London and the west midlands. Two people were crushed to death when their house in St John's Wood was blown down as they slept. Others narrowly escaped a like fate as roofs were blown off and chimney stacks collapsed.[3]

The spread of the thaw which had begun in the south of England on the 10th was accompanied by general, and at times very heavy, rain. In fact it was the wettest March on record in England and Wales, and it was succeeded by an April that was no dryer and which brought further severe gales in its first and last weeks.[4] But at least the weather was now warmer: the ordeal by snow and cold was well and truly over. Unfortunately it rapidly became apparent to people in the midlands and the south-east that they had simply exchanged that ordeal for another, this time by water. The accumulated snow cover of January, February and early March was converted by the thaw into a colossal volume of meltwater, to which was added the volume produced by the heavy rainfall that came with the thaw. The ground – frozen to a depth of several feet by the prolonged and intense cold – took longer to thaw than the snow. As a result, the combined meltwater and rain, instead of soaking into the earth and gradually draining into the river systems, ran precipitately off the iron-hard ground into the rivers with a speed, and at a volume, with which their normal bounds could not cope. 'The effect,' as a Ministry of Agriculture press statement put it, 'was as though the greater part of England was a built-up area.'

Nor, after the ground had eventually thawed out and all the snow had melted away, did the situation immediately improve. Continued heavy rain, coupled with abnormally high spring tides, went on placing demands on England's natural and man-made drainage facilities which strained them to – and in some cases well beyond – their limits. The result, according to the Ministry of Agriculture, was the occurrence of flooding 'on such a scale in practically all the main river systems of England at the same time' as to be 'unique in modern times'.[5] Beginning on 12th March with the rivers Welland, Medway and Avon, the floods reached their peak towards the end of the third week of that month and continued to present serious problems until mid-April.

These floods came to affect no fewer than thirty-one counties, from the Yorkshire river Ouse southward through the Trent river system in Nottinghamshire and Lincolnshire, the rivers and man-made waterways of the Fenlands, to the Thames and its tributaries. To the west, the counties through which ran the rivers Severn and Wye were also seriously affected. The flow of the Thames at Teddington increased from 3,600 million gallons per day – slightly lower than normal for the time of year – on 11th March to a peak of more than 13,500 million gallons per day on the 20th. Thousands of acres of riverside land downstream from Reading were flooded as the Thames spread out from its normal course to a width of more than three miles just below Chertsey, in the worst floods the area had suffered for more than fifty years.[6] Ironically, Londoners in the capital's north-eastern boroughs experienced a water shortage as all this was happening. Water from the Thames and its tributary, the Lea, flooded the filter beds that purified the water supply of Enfield, Stepney, East and West Ham and other suburbs. Even when the supply was restored, instructions to boil all drinking water remained in force for ten days or so.[7]

Even harder hit than the Thames valley by the floods were the Cambridgeshire fenlands around Ely, where floodwater from the Great Ouse spread rapidly over the flat landscape as the river's banks were breached in five places. By 20th March over a hundred square miles of Fenland were under water, and troops with amphibious vehicles and tanks were being employed in desperate efforts to close the gaps in the river banks before the arrival of the spring tides at the beginning of April. Particular difficulty was experienced in closing the Earith Gap breach, but eventually the engineers, military and civil, were successful. On 26th March the Fenland floodwaters were reported to be receding.[8]

At least as intractable as the breaches in the banks of the Great Ouse were those near the Lincolnshire town of Gainsborough, where the river Trent burst its banks on 23rd March to cause severe flooding of the area's rich agricultural land. A week later, when the floods were thought to have been contained, some fifty thousand acres of prime farmland were submerged, with some villages flooded to a depth of six or seven feet. But any tendency on the part of those who laboured to push the floodwaters back – and at Gainsborough, as at Ely, troops were heavily employed along with civilians in trying to control the breaches – to feel that they were getting on top of the situation proved premature. The exceptionally high spring tide of 4th April again overwhelmed the flood defences around Gainsborough. This time Dutch engineers from Walcheren were brought in to supplement local expertise, with their experience of rebuilding the sea defences of the Netherlands and the special heavy equipment they had developed for the task. The Trent had to be subdued before 22nd April brought the 'eagre' – an estuarial tidal wave similar to the better-known Severn Bore, which could raise the level of the river by as much as 6 ft in a matter of minutes. Fortunately for Gainsborough and its surrounding villages, the Anglo-Dutch effort to forestall the eagre was crowned with success.[9]

The Thames, Great Ouse and Trent floods represented the most extreme manifestation of a phenomenon that made its presence felt with more or less severity throughout that area of England's heartland bounded in the south by a line drawn from Canterbury to Bristol and in the north by the York–Shrewsbury axis. In York itself 5,000 houses were flooded, and the neighbouring small town of Selby was described as 'devastated' by the waters of the Yorkshire Ouse.[10] The Severn at Worcester in mid-March was at its highest level since 1770, and floods affected land and property along forty miles of its length.[11] The Wye, the Witham, the Welland, the

Avon, the Medway and the Lea — all these and many lesser streams flowed over or through their accustomed banks, causing hardship and sometimes worse to people and livestock and damage to buildings, land and crops. It was fortunate that Britain still had large resources of mobile manpower in the armed forces, many with recent experience of civil engineering problems of a kind not too dissimilar to those posed by the floods, and with substantial reserves of appropriate equipment in the form of amphibious transport like the wartime DUKW, heavy earthmovers and small assault craft. Without the military to carry out rescue work, emergency flood-control measures and other tasks occasioned by the floods, the toll of destruction to lives and property would undoubtedly have been much greater than it actually was.

After the arrival of the thaw, the weather in March and April — though wet and at times very windy — was at least much warmer than it had been in the preceding eight weeks. April 1947, indeed, was on average rather warmer than was usual for that month, and in some parts of eastern England it was sunnier than usual, too. The more clement weather may have played an important part in reducing the pressure of demand for gas and electricity, which normally declined in March and April anyway. This reduction was reflected in the sharp falling-off in coal consumption by gasworks and power stations that became evident at the end of March. Compared with the last week of the freeze, ending on 15th March, the consumption of gas and power station coal in the last week of the month, ending on the 29th, was down by more than 10% in each case. This trend continued through April, aided perhaps by the Easter holiday at the beginning of the month and the introduction of Double Summer Time a week later. The government had decided, on the recommendation of the Lord President's Committee, to extend the period of British Summer Time as a measure that might contribute at least in a marginal way to saving coal and electricity by reducing the need for street and domestic lighting. By the third week of April, coal consumption at gasworks and power stations was nearly 20% down on the figure for the week ending 15th March.[12] These savings were achieved in spite of the growing difficulty of controlling household electricity consumption. Indeed, by late April the Minister of Fuel and Power was expressing his conviction that the current restrictions had become counter-productive.[13] The general easing of the fuel and power position that these savings typified enabled the Fuel Committee to take a more relaxed attitude to its business, and to contemplate the easing of yet more of the emergency measures imposed in February. It even felt able to agree to the export of coal, admittedly in quite minute quantities, to traditional dependants like Eire, Gibralter and Malta.[14]

But as the thaw lightened the Fuel Committee's burden it increased the pressure on government and governed in other directions. In particular, as the fuel crisis moderated, the food crisis went from bad to worse. As *Picture Post's* mythical housewife, Mrs Jones, knew only too well, food was more of a problem now than it had ever been when the war was still on. Indeed, we have already seen that in the summer of 1946 food was regarded as much the most pressing problem facing the government. From the end of the war to the beginning of 1947, during the Attlee government's tenure of office, the bacon ration had been halved, as had the ration of margarine and cooking fat; the supply of cheese had been reduced and bread rationing had been brought in. Most recently, at the beginning of March, it had been announced that the ration of sweets was to be halved, ostensibly because of the weather. The only compensation for all these deprivations had been a twopenny increase in the meat ration.[15] The calorific value of the food consumed in working-class homes had fallen, young Dr Pyke of the Ministry of Food calculated, from 102% of what was necessary to maintain physical efficiency at the beginning of 1945 to 93% by the summer of 1946. And he noted that post-war children had lower average body weights than wartime children of the same age.[16]

The food problem was largely one of foreign exchange, above all dollars, with which to finance imports. The country had made great strides during the war towards growing its own food, but it remained in 1947 still some way short of complete self-sufficiency, especially in fats, meat, grain and dairy products. The sterling area — which was to say in essence the empire — could make up some of the deficiencies without cost to Britain's slender dollar resources. But substantial residues — 40% in the case of edible fats, for instance — had to be bought in from non-sterling sources, of which the United States was by far the most important.[17] Such suppliers required payment in dollars, but as long as Britain's balance of payments remained in deficit and she had to draw on her reserves to make up the difference between what she imported and what she exported, her dollar resources had to be husbanded with the utmost care. The American loan, which was Britain's main source of dollars, had to be stretched as far as it would go. With this in view, dollar-financed food imports of meat, butter, bacon, eggs and cheese had been cut back in 1946 to very low levels. Meanwhile the government exhorted farmers to expand their production still further. Typical of these exhortations was a speech by Lord Huntingdon, joint Parliamentary Secretary to the Ministry of Agriculture, to a farming audience in Cambridge on 1st March.[18] Food, he was reported as saying:

> was the first of our needs. We could not produce all the food we wanted, but the more we produced, the more foreign exchange we saved, either to provide the food we did not produce or equally necessary things. It was every bit as important to achieve high production now as it was during the war.

Unfortunately the forces of nature seemed to be conspiring to prevent the achievement of these aims.

The 1946 harvest had been delayed by bad weather. As a result, although the autumn weather was quite good, preparations for the coming year in agriculture had been set back. The heavy, continuous rain of late November had imposed further delays in cultivation and in the sowing of crops like winter grains and pulses. Continued wet weather in December and early January gave rise to concern about the availability of winter feed for livestock and about damage by water to emergent winter wheat and oats, as well as to potatoes stored in clamps in the open field. Then came the blizzards of January, February and early March, and their effect was catastrophic. Fieldwork in preparation for the spring sowing had to be abandoned for weeks. Winter-sown crops, at an early and vulnerable stage in their growth, were damaged by frost, as were potatoes and root vegetables in store. Fodder was running short, and what there was often could not be taken to the animals because of drifted snow. Mortality among livestock was tremendous, particularly among hill sheep and upland cattle, which traditionally wintered in the open on exposed hills and moorland.[19] The Ministry of Agriculture's monthly report on farm conditions in England and Wales at the beginning of March[20] recorded bleakly that:

> *Hill sheep* have suffered severely from the exceptional wintry conditions and blizzards, and many have been buried in deep drifts. Losses are already known to be heavy, and in many areas ... it is feared that before the thaw takes effect the death rate may well be even more serious ... On exposed and snowbound upland farms winter keep is rapidly becoming exhausted and cattle are already on a bare maintenance ration.

It was only when the thaw came, however, that the full extent of the holocaust was exposed.

The thaw did not bring an end to the problems of the food producers. Instead, it created new ones as the floodwaters swept across the farmlands of Lincolnshire, East Anglia, East Yorkshire and the Severn and Wye valleys. Crops which had survived the snow and frost were destroyed by this new menace. Much livestock was drowned and more was left starving, some so far gone that it had to be shot.[21] Root vegetables and potatoes in store were either swept away or rotted by immersion. Gradually, as information filtered back from the Ministry of Agriculture's regional officers and the County Agricultural Committees, it became possible to build up a picture of what had happened. The Minister of Agriculture, Tom Williams, in a phrase which for once represented the sober truth rather than political hyperbole, described it in the Commons on 24th March as 'a disaster of the first magnitude'.[22]

By mid-April Williams was in a position to define the disaster in detail. In all, he estimated that nearly 1·5 million hill and lowland sheep had been lost, mostly as a result of the snow, together with more than 2·5 million lambs. In total this amounted to more than 20% of the entire national flock. Cattle losses were on a lesser scale, at 50,000 head. Crop losses had been extremely serious. 116,000 acres of winter grain had been destroyed by frost or flood, and the disruption of preparations for the spring sowing meant substantial reductions in the acreage sown with spring grain – a fifth of the planned wheat acreage for 1947, for instance, half a million acres in all, remained unsown. Of the 1946 potato crop, 75,000 tons had been ruined in store, and the 1947 crop was also 'likely to be reduced, though by an unknown amount'. The acreage under sugar beet would also be reduced, if only marginally, and there had also been 'a substantial loss of vegetables'. The total value of the losses Williams put at a minimum of £16·5 million, and they could – if 1947 crop yields were adversely affected – go as high as £36·5 million. 'These losses,' he concluded, 'represent a serious disaster, both from the standpoint of our national economy, but particularly to large numbers of the smaller farmers ...'[23] They also, of course, amounted to a severe reduction in the supply of foodstuffs available to the public. The half-million acres of unplanted wheat, for example, represented the loss of a month's bread ration.[24]

Such news could hardly have come at a less opportune time. The government had recently become aware that stocks of food and animal feeding-stuff had been run down during the past year, in some cases to a considerable extent. In the case of wheat and flour, for instance, the stock at the end of January 1947 was only a little more than half what it had been a year earlier. Stocks of imported meat, of bacon, butter and high-protein oilcake had fallen to a comparable extent, and there had been a serious decline in stocks of potatoes, vegetable oils and pulses as well. When Attlee learned of these heavy stock reductions on 7th March he was extremely perturbed and demanded that the Lord President's Committee investigate the state of affairs as a matter of urgency. Dalton, temporarily in charge of the committee, reassured the Premier: although 'stocks would undoubtedly reach very low levels this year, there was no serious risk of a breakdown in supplies, or of our having to make further cuts in rations, except, probably in tea'.[25] But that had been before the extent of the agricultural disaster had been properly appreciated.

Ordinarily it might have been possible to rebuild food stocks by importing. But Attlee and his Chancellor were both painfully aware that, as far as the balance of payments was concerned, these were not ordinary times, and that Britain's capacity to import food or anything else was becoming increasingly insecure. In November 1946, less than a year after the ratification of the American loan agreement, Dalton had felt it necessary to warn the Cabinet that the loans from the United States and Canada, together with other prospective sources of external finance for 1947 and 1948, were being used up far too rapidly. If the dissipation of these resources was not slowed down, Britain would be unable to pay her way in the world by 1949, and Dalton outlined the measures that he thought necessary to accomplish such a check to the process. But the position did not improve. Instead, in March 1947, with the floods at their height and awareness growing of the scale of damage to home food production, the Chancellor was apprising his colleagues of 'a looming shadow of catastrophe' hanging over the balance of payments. If Britain went on drawing on her dollar credits the way she was now doing, they would be exhausted, he predicted, by the beginning of 1948.[26] In these circumstances there could be no question of compensating for any shortfall in home food production in 1947 by importing more. The country would once more just have to tighten its belt, even if the occasion for doing so could be delayed a few months yet.

Meanwhile, measures were being taken to make good the damage and alleviate the hardship caused by the blizzards and the floods. In practice a distinction was drawn between the losses sustained by farmers and those experienced by other people. In the latter category the main concern was with householders and their families whose dwellings had been damaged by the floods and whose furniture, clothes and personal effects might have been destroyed or spoiled by water. At a time when the supply of clothing and household goods was still to a large extent under government control, such losses could not be made good without making exceptions for distressed families or individuals under the appropriate rationing schemes and so on. In fact the government found itself involved in substantial ways in the compensation of both classes of victim, but left the actual administration of compensation largely in the hands of private, or at least non-government, bodies. Farmers were to be compensated for their actual losses of crops and livestock, as well as for any consequential decline in their future earnings, by a fund administered by the National Farmers' Union.

Its main source of revenue was to be a series of voluntary levies on sales of farm produce, with the government promising to match, pound for pound, the amount collected by the farmers themselves. Much of the work of providing relief for householders was undertaken by local authorities, with the central government undertaking to reimburse them at least in part for any such expenditure. In addition, the Lord Mayor of London opened a national flood-relief fund on 24th March, with the news of a central government contribution of a million pounds.[27]

The Lord Mayor's Fund swelled rapidly with contributions from people in all walks of life both at home and abroad. The Kind and Queen − in South Africa on a state visit throughout the period of both freeze and flood, a fact that drew some adverse comment from their subjects − gave £1,500, and further donations followed from other members of the royal family. £10,000 was donated by the Gold Coast Legislative Assembly. Help in kind also flowed in from abroad, in the form, for example, of the A£300,000, allocated by the Australian Red Cross to provide relief aid, mostly in the form of food. By the end of April the fund's value in terms of cash contributions alone, and excluding the government's million pounds, stood at £1,266,566.[28] The National Farmers' Union Agricultural Distress Fund, inaugurated on 30th March, grew less rapidly. By mid-April it stood at £135,000, to which must be added the proceeds of the government's undertaking to match private donations. Compared with the Lord Mayor's Fund and the scale of farm losses, the amount was not particularly impressive; but the Minister of Agriculture pronounced it at least 'a promising start'.[29]

The pace of activity in the Cabinet Fuel Committee in February had been quite frenetic. Members received daily reports on the fuel and power situation in all its essentials, together with a regular stream of other papers from individual Ministers and civil servants, and from the committee's subordinate institutions. In the seventeen days of February following its creation the committee itself met eight times, with a further four meetings in the first week of March − including a double session on 7th March that took up most of the day.[30] Thereafter, however, as the production and distribution of coal and the supply of gas and electricity reverted to a sounder footing, there was a rapid winding down in the sense of urgency that governed the committee's deliberations. It met only twice more in March, after the first week, and only three times altogether in April. In May the committee was not convened at all. Similarly, the medium through which the committee discharged its key function of monitoring the state of fuel and power supplies appeared less often. The daily fuel situation reports became twice-weekly at the beginning of March, and from 1st April they were compiled only fortnightly, on which basis they continued right through the 'coal summer' until the end of October.

Although the February restrictions on the household use of fuel and power stayed in force for the remainder of the 1946–47 'coal year', there was, as has been indicated, a steady easing of restrictions on other types of consumption after the removal of the ban on industrial use of electricity in the Black Areas on 3rd March. The weeklies came back on the newsstands, office and shop lighting made a reappearance, the full range of BBC radio programmes and even the television service returned to the air waves, and so on. All these things, of course, signified the improvement of fuel and power supplies, but the position remained fundamentally insecure and, for the health of the economy and the progress of the reconstruction programme, dangerous. Above all, manufacturing industry remained perilously under-supplied with coal, threatening the whole basis of recovery in production, exports and living standards. During the period of acute emergency, when gasworks and power stations enjoyed an absolute priority in the allocation of available supplies of coal, industrial coal stocks – as we have seen – had continued to decline from even the dangerously low levels which they had reached by early February. When the resumption of industrial activity in the Black Areas was permitted to take place, arrangements for supplying coal to industry were in complete disarray. The 'Cripps plan' which had come into effect on 20th January had collapsed almost as soon as it had been introduced. Individual regions, through their Boards for Industry and their Coal Allocation Committees made whatever arrangements for supplying industry, particularly 'non-essential' industry, their local resources of coal from day to day permitted. The resulting variations in supply had led, it was said, 'to anomalies and hard feelings ... little or no regard has been paid to priorities, and it has been difficult to provide indignant industrialists with acceptable explanations'.[31] So arbitrary, haphazard and unpredictable had the situation become by early March that Whitehall was being bombarded with demands from the regions for the re-establishment of a coherent national system of coal allocations and deliveries to provide a stable basis on which industry might manage its activities. Almost *any* arrangement would do, at however low a percentage of actual requirements, provided it was orderly and settled.

The response to these pleas, transmitted by teleprinter from the Board of Trade to Regional Boards for Industry on 7th March for implementation three days later, was a plan which – while it certainly offered what industrialists claimed to want by way of standardised national arrangements − did so at a level of deliveries that offered many firms little prospect of more than merely ticking over.[32] What this arrangement (described by the Board of Trade as 'interim' with perhaps more hope than faith) did was to restore in its general principles the 'Cripps plan' of January. Ominously, however, it was made clear that the restoration would be subject to 'certain modifications of the figures and of the priorities'. The most important of these was that firms to which the lowest order of priority had been assigned − those outside the 'essential' public utility, iron and steel and food-processing categories − were to be allocated coal at the rate of one third of their weekly requirements rather than half, as laid down in the original 'Cripps' formula. Any supplementary allowances assigned by the Regional Fuel Allocation Committees from their coal pools would, however, continue to be based on the full weekly requirement. To clarify by example, a firm which on 20th January had been given the basic 'Cripps' ration of 50% of its needs plus a supplement from the regional pool of 30% would, before the weather disrupted things, have been receiving 80% of the coal it needed. Under the interim arrangement of 10th March it would receive the revised basic ration of 33⅓% together with its 30% supplement, thereby getting 63⅓% of the coal it needed to maintain what was now generally understood to be the merely notional concept of normal production. The real problem, of course, lay with those firms whose activities were not deemed to be of sufficient national importance to merit a supplementary allocation from the pool. As if to reinforce the weakness of their position, a further instruction from the Board of Trade to Regional Board chairmen on 10th March made it clear that such firms could by no means rely on receiving their basic ration of one third of requirements. 'If availabilities fall below the total commitments in any region,' this new instruction read, 'the beneficiaries of the Pool will receive their supplies in full, while other firms may receive rather less than the 33⅓% basic allocation.'[33] In true biblical style, he that had not the priority status that entitled him to an allocation from the pool was to be deprived even of that which he had.

The new arrangement was intended to run at least to the end of the current 'coal year' on 30th April. The reactions of industry to this prospect were less than enthusiastic. The best that could be said for it, as the Board of Trade's summary of reports from its regional officers for the week ending 8th March put it, was that 'industrialists are beginning to realise that even this is better than nothing'.[34] Some local officers plainly did not have even so high an opinion of the scheme. From Manchester the North West Regional Controller described it as 'catastrophic to local industry', which cold not understand why − when coal production was running higher than in January — the industrial allocation should be set so much lower. From Bristol came the complaint that the South West Regional Fuel Allocation Committee could not fulfil its obligations under the new scheme with the amount of coal at present available to it, with the prediction of continued unemployment on a large scale.[35] At the end of the scheme's first week of operation, complaints flooded in. Regional pools were castigated for their inadequacy, so that even 'priority' firms were not getting their due; actual coal deliveries were not always matching up to allocations; expressions of apprehension about closures and unemployment were quite general. The textile and consumer goods industries were particularly hard hit. Yorkshire woollen and Lancashire cotton mills, key suppliers to the export drive, were each receiving little more than half the coal they needed, and protest meetings were already being reported from Manchester.[36]

The government probably did its best to respond to these problems. But it had only very limited room for manoeuvre. The management of coal supplies had become a 'zero sum' game, in which improvements granted to one category of consumer could be given substance only at the expense of some other category. Nevertheless, at the beginning of April larger tonnages of coal than hitherto were released to the regional pools, giving local fuel allocation officers a small margin at least of flexibility. Altogether the pools were expanded to the tune of 100,000 tons per week, transferred to industry from the task of building up the coal reserves of power stations, which the thaw had made a matter of rather less urgency.[37] On 10th April it was announced that this enhancement of industrial coal supplies would enable the basic allocation to be raised back to the original 'Cripps' level of 50% with effect from the 14th of the month. That was the good news. The bad news was that the 'Cripps plan' would not cease to operate at the end of April but would be extended to the end of May, by which time the government hoped that a new system of industrial coal allocations on a more generous scale might be brought into operations.[38] Until then industrialists would just have to make the best of things under the constraints of the 'Cripps plan'. They did not like it: one of their number — George Dickson, the acting chairman of the South East Regional Board for Industry — described the situation as so bad that 'full employment as an objective has been buried in the phrases of the economists' textbooks'.[39] But the Board of Trade's regional reports, collated even as Dickson spoke, suggested that from mid-April industry was no longer experiencing the acute difficulties that had been plaguing it a month earlier. That is to say, no special fuel and power problems were being encountered beyond that of coping with the dearth of an essential fuel-cum-raw material that was now merely chronic rather than extreme.[40]

As well as doing its best to overcome the short-term problem of fuel supplies for industry in the immediate aftermath of the most acute phase of the fuel crisis, the government had also to take cognisance of the longer-term problem of avoiding any repetition in future winters of the sort of disruption to industrial, commercial and domestic life from which the country was only beginning to emerge in mid-April. In fact, even as matters had been at their most serious in February, the longer-term problem had not been set aside. Attlee, for example, had defined the task of the Fuel Committee from the outset as being 'to keep the immediate fuel situation under review' and also to 'supervise the preparation of plans for avoiding a fuel crisis next winter'.[41] At its fifth meeting, on 24th February, and all subsequent meetings, the longer-term issue came to dominate the committee's proceedings. Ministerial perspectives had changed a lot since the old Ministerial Coal Committee had blithely dispersed in April 1946 in the confident expectation of not having to worry about coal again until the eve of the 'coal winter' in October. Now, in effect, Attlee was reminding his colleagues that April itself was the eve of the next 'coal winter' for all practical purposes. 'Next winter,' he pointed out to them on 17th February, 'will be upon us in little more than eight months' time, a desperately short period in which to remedy the situation into which we shall emerge from the present crisis'.[42]

Various members of the Fuel Committee − Attlee himself, Shinwell and his Permanent Secretary Fergusson, Lord Hyndley of the National Coal Board − produced their individual analyses of the long-term problem and of possible solutions to it. These differed somewhat in their details, but were united on the essential features of the problem, which remained the same as they had been in the summers of 1945 and 1946. The only differences were of degree: with each year's passing, the problem became that much more difficult to solve as the gap between foreseeable demand and predictable supply got wider and the scale of the coal-stocking requirement got larger. The precise parameters of the problem for the 'coal year' 1947−48 were set out for the Fuel Committee towards the end of February by both the Minister of Fuel and Power and the Permanent Secretary, using data compiled by their Ministry's very competent statisticians. Their prognostications did not make soothing reading for those to whom they were presented.[43]

Assuming that a coal stock of 8 million tons had to be retained at the end of the accounting period on 30th April 1948, and that a saving of

5 million tons of coal could be achieved through the coal-to-oil conversion programme in the twelve months prior to that date, the amount of deep-mined and open-cast coal required for the 1947–48 'coal year' was reckoned at 199 million tons. But, on the assumption that present trends and policies with regard to coal production continued, and allowing for the introduction as promised of the five-day week for miners in May 1947, estimated output for the period could only be put at 180 million tons. The 'gap' of 19 million tons would, it was thought, make its presence felt chiefly during the winter segment of the 'coal year'. It was a much larger shortfall than anything that had been predicted for 1946–47, and not everyone who saw the Shinwell–Fergusson calculation agreed entirely with the accuracy of its figures or the plausibility of the assumptions on which they were based.[44] But nobody could argue away the probability of a more or less substantial excess of requirements over supply.

As well as the coal problem, there were difficulties with gas and electricity, which could to some extent, indeed, be regarded as facets of the coal problem rather than distinct from it. For if more coal were available, especially for household heating, the pressure of demand for gas and electricity as substitutes might sensibly diminish. But the most important problem facing the Fuel Committee in its consideration of future gas and electricity supply lay in the large and apparently widening gap between the growth of demand for the two commodities and the plant capacity that was likely to be available to produce them. The Central Electricity Board, for example, felt that it would be able to provide during the winter of 1947–48 'a firm output' of about 9 million kW, against an anticipated peak demand for 10·5 million kW. The Board had in hand a large-scale programme of plant replacement and expansion, but it would not be until 1950–51 that capacity would be expected to match demand. The state of the gas industry's capacity to meet the demand that existed for its product could be seen in the way gas pressures had plummeted at the end of January – by as much as 80% in some districts. Once again, a considerable programme of new construction had been authorised, but at present rates of progress (as Shinwell pointed out to the Fuel Committee on 8th March) it would take two years or so to come to anything.[45]

There was nothing new, therefore, in the nature of the problems with which the Fuel Committee had to wrestle if a repetition of the fuel crisis was to be avoided in future years. But the problems were easier to state than to solve, though solved they had to be if the government was to have any hope of seeing its plans for economic and social development fully implemented and its own credibility as an administration protected. There were, obviously, two main lines of approach to the matter of bringing supply and demand for fuel and power into some kind of equilibrium. Measures could be taken to increase the supply, while attempts were made to bring demand under control. Looking no further than the immediate needs of the 'coal year' 1947–48, the latter course of regulating and restricting demand seemed to Ministers to offer the best prospects, together with the increased exploitation of oil as a substitute for coal both in manufacturing and in the production of gas and electricity. But the possibilities of increasing the supply of coal, gas and electricity even in the short term could not be neglected. It was important to secure the most rapid progress possible in the CEB's efforts to bring new generating plant on stream and to hasten the construction of new gasworks, even if it might take two years or more before such efforts paid off in the form of substantial increases in supply. Similarly, efforts to recruit more labour and to improve the efficiency of the mines had to be kept up in order to maximise the availability of coal. After their recent experiences Ministers were only too acutely aware of the need to monitor closely the patterns of activity and trends of production in all aspects of the fuel and power sector, especially through the summer of 1947. The continued flow of regular situation reports from the Fuel and Power statistical staff through the summer made this possible. There was particular concern about what might happen to coal production when the miners went over to the five-day week at the beginning of May. Much would depend on how this shortening of their working week would affect their productivity and absenteeism.

With the prospects of short-term growth on the production side of the fuel and power equation so uncertain, discussion in the Fuel Committee and the Cabinet tended to concentrate on the demand or consumption side. There was particular emphasis on the need to protect fuel and power for industry by restricting consumption on the part of households and commercial premises like shops, offices and places of entertainment.[46] Special attention was directed at controlling the domestic consumer, particularly in the light of that creature's evident unwillingness to observe for long any voluntary code of restriction. Ministerial inclinations at first tended towards the imposition of a formal scheme of domestic fuel rationing. Such a scheme was already available to the Fuel Committee at the end of February, having been drawn up by G. L. Watkinson of the Board of Trade, who had been involved in the formulation of the abortive Beveridge coal-rationing scheme of 1942.[47] Watkinson aimed at quite dramatic cuts in domestic gas and electricity consumption, to the tune of 20% and 40% respectively, in the coming 'coal year' by laying down for each household a standard allowance of gas and electricity. This, it was claimed, would be sufficient for all essential purposes, but not for such frivolities as space-heating, constant hot water or refrigerators. Failure to live within the standard allowance would be punished by deductions from the offending household's coal supply or, in the case of all-electric homes, by prosecution under the Defence Regulations. The scheme, intended for application to commercial premises as well as homes, was calculated to cut coal consumption by up to 5·5 million tons in a full year, as well as relieving to a large extent the pressure on generating and gas-making plant.

It was clear that when the Watkinson scheme was presented to the Fuel Committee on 25th February many were taken aback at its austerity and felt that it might be too severe for the public to accept. In that event, it was felt, the scheme was unlikely to effect the savings that were expected of it. But Watkinson had powerful supporters as well, not the least being Gorell Barnes, Attlee's private secretary, who pressed the Premier to push the plan through without delay. He was particularly impatient with the idea that the scheme was too drastic for the times, which to him revealed 'an extra-ordinary failure to appreciate … the extreme seriousness of the position'. If the scheme was administratively practicable it should be put into effect. Clearly, Douglas Jay's departure in June 1946 had done little to moderate attitudes in the Prime Minister's private office. But in the end the stern counsels of the advocates of, as it were, 'Watkinson now!' did not prevail. Most of the politicians, Attlee among them, were willing enough to admit that something like Watkinson's plan was necessary, but few were disposed to face the political consequences of introducing it. The issue was mulled over for six weeks or so, and finally resolved only a couple of weeks before the new 'coal year' began.[48]

What emerged bore little resemblance to Watkinson's plan. Instead of formal rationing backed up by penalties, there was another scheme for voluntary cuts in gas and electricity consumption on the part of domestic and commercial users.[49] The only element of compulsion was a ban on the use of gas and electricity for the purpose of space-heating at home and in both commercial and industrial premises, to apply to the summer months from May through September. And even then, as Sir Guy Nott-Bower of the Ministry of Fuel and Power told the press, these statutory prohibitions were essentially a sham. It was not proposed, Sir Guy announced, to use police or snooping or any method of the sort to enforce them, but to rely instead on the Englishman's natural inclination to obey the law when he thought it justifiable.[50] Apart from observing the ban on space-heating, households were being asked to cut their gas and electricity consumption from May to September to three-quarters of the levels for the same months of 1946. Similar voluntary percentage cuts, varying according to the type of undertaking and its peculiar needs, were expected of commercial concerns. The whole thing was to be backed up by an elaborate publicity campaign devised by the advertising agency Wood & Partners, with the central slogan 'That's the way to save 2,500,000 tons by winter' − not, perhaps, the most inspired example of the copywriter's art.[51] Reinforcing the message of the campaign's leaflets and press advertisements was a so-called 'Sales Force', recruited for the most part from women's organisations like the Women's Institute, the Mothers' Union, Townswomen's Guilds and Women's Voluntary Service, and headed by the energetic President of the WVS, the Dowager Marchioness of Reading. Some of these organisations had been consulted during the formulation of the policy they were now helping to implement, and had been instrumental in ensuring that the restrictions were voluntary rather than compulsory.[52] Now they would distribute leaflets and visit people in their homes to show them how to keep track of their gas and electricity consumption, and generally help to spread the gospel of fuel economy. To assist the efforts of the 'Sales Force', the Chancellor of the Exchequer in his budget of April 1947 reimposed the $66\frac{2}{3}$% purchase tax on household electric heaters which he had lifted only two years before. It was, he said, 'an unpleasant but necessary method of fuel economy'.[53]

As well as trying to persuade domestic and other non-industrial consumers to curtail their demands on the country's overstretched generating capacity, attention was given to reducing the industrial load on the system at peak periods. A ban on the use of electricity and gas for industrial space-heating was, of course, to be imposed in the summer. But greater significance was attached in the Fuel Committee to the possibilities of persuading industry to reorganise its work patterns in such a way as to shift peak industrial demand for electricity to periods of low domestic and non-industrial demand, so that the risk of 'load shedding' at such classically vulnerable points of the day as 8.00 to 9.00 a.m. and 4.00 to 6.00 p.m. might be reduced and even, with luck, eliminated. The Fuel Committee considered this matter, under the heading of 'Staggering hours of work in industry', at considerable length in March and April, but to little immediate effect. None of its proposals was received with any enthusiasm by managers or trade unions in manufacturing, nor indeed by the electricity supply undertakings, and no agreed scheme was ready for introduction at the start of the new 'coal year'.[54]

Steps were, however, taken to control the direct consumption of coal by industry through the summer of 1947 by formulating a new set of coal allocations to operate from the end of May − when the resurrected 'Cripps plan' was due to finish − until the end of October. At first, when the Coal

Budget had been presented to the Fuel Committee early in March, it had been agreed that industry should be supplied during the 'coal summer' with 17·6 million tons, against an estimated requirement of 26·2 million tons. That is, industry was to be given two-thirds of what it required to maintain full production and full employment. After these figures had actually been announced, the members of the Fuel Committee had their implications drawn forcefully to their attention by the man who carried most of the political responsibility for maintaining most of the country's industrial effort, the President of the Board of Trade. And the implications, as spelled out by Cripps in a long and detailed memorandum, were horrendous.[55] For a start, he pointed out, the loss of one third of its coal requirements over the summer months would actually render the position of industry in general worse than it had been over the past few months. Coming on top of 'the present disruption and shortages', the effects of the proposed cut would be catastrophic:

> ... we should be starving industry of raw materials and ensuring that not only the basic industries but also all subsequent stages of manufacture will suffer ... It would probably imply a slump in the output of steel to an annual rate of about 9 million ingot tons as compared with 12·7 million ingot tons achieved in 1946 when there was an acute overall shortage of steel. It would involve a reduction of one third or more in the output of basic chemicals ... In the textile industries we should be faced with the complete abandonment of our export trade and all hope of maintaining the clothing ration ... There would be a grave shortage of all kinds of paper and packing materials, a drastic curtailment in the production of building materials, a famine in pottery and many other household goods, and a complete disorganisation of the engineering industry ... Even the food processing industries could not wholly escape.

Presented with this stark vision of industrial apocalypse, Cripps's colleagues in Fuel Committee and Cabinet were only too happy to go along with his suggestion that the summer coal allocation for industry should be raised from two-thirds of what was required to 86·8% — a figure based on maintaining deliveries at the level of the summer of 1946. Out of this, industry would be expected to operate at the best possible level of activity while building up a coal stock for the winter equal to three weeks' consumption. Aneurin Bevan was not happy about the effects of Cripps's proposal on the house-building programme, but with the minor modifications needed to accommodate him the revised allocations were accepted by the Cabinet for implementation from 1st June.[56] It would be fair to ask where Cripps thought the extra coal to support his upward revision of industrial allocations might come from. He did not, in fact, propose to shift coal to industry from other consumers, but claimed to detect developments in the coal industry — mainly with regard to recruitment and productivity — which held out the possibility at least that more coal might be available in the summer than had been anticipated in the Coal Budget. His optimism was not, as we shall see, entirely without foundation — though recent experience must have engendered some tendency to scepticism where sanguinity about the future performance of the coal industry was concerned. In fact the impending introduction of the five-day week in the mines made the summer coal production position extremely hard to foretell. Ministers perhaps had to accept Cripps's favourable prognostications: he had done an excellent job of setting before them the economic consequences of their not being realised.

It was the government's hope that the domestic and non-industrial economy campaigns together would achieve a saving of 2·5 million tons of coal during the summer of 1947, and the ban on industrial space-heating an additional million tons.[57] A further saving would, it was hoped, be achieved by postponing the introduction by the railway companies of their summer timetables for a month, and then running summer passenger train services at a level 10% lower than that of 1946. This would put passenger schedules for the summer of 1947 on a par with those of the worst period of the war, with the aim of reducing railway coal consumption by a mere quarter of a million tons in the May–September period.[58] But so desperate were Ministers to find scope for coal savings of *any* size that even this meagre amount could not be passed up.

As we have noted, an additional cut in the consumption of coal amounting to some 5 million tons in the full 'coal year' (2 million in the summer alone) was anticipated from the conversion of industrial plant from coal burning to oil firing. The coal-to-oil conversion campaign had failed, of course, to achieve the results expected of it in 1946 and was rather in the doldrums at the beginning of 1947 because of material and equipment shortages. But the events of February and early March had given the campaign a new impetus, as did the prospect of continuing coal shortages even after the acute crisis had passed. Attlee himself demanded the exploration of 'all means of accelerating and expanding this programme regardless of cost' and the overcoming by 'whatever assurances or guarantees are necessary' of the hesitancy of industrialists with regard to switching from coal to oil.[59] By early March the Ministry of Fuel and Power was attempting to give effect to the Prime Minister's wishes by trying to breathe new life and urgency into the conversions that had already been put in train before February while canvassing industry for as many new conversion projects as might be practicable. Even conversions which had previously been turned down were being resurrected. Preparation was being made by the Ministry, in short, for coal-to-oil conversion *à l'outrance*. Attlee's fears about the reluctance of industrialists to participate — because of their doubts about the duration of the coal shortage or the continuance of the subsidy of £1 per ton on fuel oil burned by converted plant that Dalton had brought in the previous August — proved groundless. Applications for authorisation to convert plant flowed in. By the beginning of March approved schemes in the pipeline were running at the level necessary to secure a 5 million ton coal saving once they were all operational. The long-term prospects of conversion as a means of solving the coal problem looked immensely attractive, and officials looked forward to coal savings of up to 17 million tons by 1950–51.[60] Indeed, as one official enthused,[61] the programme of coal-to-oil conversion:

> could go on indefinitely until it eventually began to cause unemployment and the closing down of pits in the coal industry. This state would probably be reached before technical problems and oil supply limitations stepped in to close the campaign. It is essential, therefore, that a limit should be set solely from the *coal* point of view.

He might have been wise to temper his excitement at the potential of the conversion programme with the remembrance of the high hopes that had been reposed in it in 1946, and their subsequent non-fulfilment.

By late March it was beginning to look as if recent history might be in danger of repeating itself. Once again, shortages of the technical equipment and materials necessary for the completion of conversion projects were beginning to make themselves felt. There was a particular shortage of steel. Applications from industry for authorisation to go over to oil were running dangerously ahead of the resources available, and on 20th March it was thought necessary to grant no further authorisations. But applications continued to pour in, and industrialists became increasingly impatient with what they saw as bureaucratic obstruction of a sure way to by-pass the coal bottleneck.[62] By mid-April, as a result of this pent-up pressure of demand, serious concern was being expressed by Shinwell's officials about the future of the whole conversion programme. There was, accordingly, a distinct note of caution about Shinwell's own progress report on coal-to-oil conversion, delivered to the Fuel Committee on 14th April. Noting that 750 projects had been carried through by 20th March, offering an annual coal saving of 1·5 million tons, and that a further 1,170 projects were being implemented at a potential annual coal saving of 5·3 million tons, he observed that the ceiling of the existing programme had been reached. In fixing a ceiling for future projects, the government, Shinwell said, would have to consider not only 'the practicability of

increasing the target' but also 'the desirability of doing so'.[63] The government was, in fact, concerned about increasing the country's dependence
on oil from several points of view: the security problem posed by relying
on an external source of basic fuel, the foreign exchange cost of uncontrolled oil imports, the shortage of tankers (especially sailing under the
British flag) to maintain oil supplies, and so on. Some Ministers may have
found their early zeal for conversion modified by recognition of the long-
term possibility of oil-induced pit closures. At any rate, Shinwell at least,
by late April, was openly voicing to the Fuel Committee his conviction
that things had gone just about far enough in the field of coal-to-oil conversion. 'He did not believe,' the committee's minutes of 21st April
recorded, 'that as a matter of long-term policy the programme should be
greatly expanded ...'. But at least there seemed every prospect of the
programme effecting substantial reductions in the short term in coal
consumption: projects already in hand, Shinwell informed the same
meeting, should save 8 million tons of coal in a full year.[64]

Although in the short term the prospects of increasing the supply of
coal seemed to offer fewer returns than the control and reduction of
demand, if only because coal production was a labour-intensive business
and newly recruited miners took time to become effective, the government
did not entirely neglect that side of the equation in March and April. Even
the possibility of importing coal, which had only recently been rejected
when the crisis was at its height, was revived in March, primarily as a way
of building up stocks for the winter. The amounts that might be available
− a quarter of a million tons per month from the United States plus in-
determinate though substantial amounts from South Africa and Poland −
were not inconsiderable, and the Fuel Committee considered the matter
at some length through March and April.[65] But the problem remained
that, as in February, Britain could be supplied only at the expense of
countries whose need for American coal was even greater than her own.
In any case, shipping space to handle bulk coal cargoes was in short supply.
Furthermore, the terms on which the Poles were offering their coal were
regarded as too high. As awareness of these difficulties grew in the committee, interest in importing coal in large amounts declined, and members
devoted their efforts instead to securing the expansion of home production
by increasing the size and improving the efficiency of the mining labour
force.

In the *Economic Survey* for 1947 the government had set itself the target
of increasing the number of workers on colliery books from the level of
just over 690,000 to which it had sunk at the end of 1946 to 730,000.
The sort of intake into the industry that might enable that target to be

met constituted, as Attlee put it, 'a severe recruiting problem'. It meant that the net outflow of workers to the tune of some 1,500 per month that had characterised the second half of 1946 would have to be reversed and turned into a net *intake* of 3,000 per month.[66] How was this turn-round to be achieved? Greater efforts must be made, Attlee suggested, to make mining an attractive option for British workers. Existing programmes for the recruitment of Polish and Irish workers should be intensified. And further possibilities of recruiting foreign labour should be explored. Attlee suggested bringing in Italians and European war refugees ('displaced persons'). His secretary, Gorell Barnes, talked of German prisoners of war and refugee Spanish Republicans from the Asturias.[67] As far as would-be British recruits were concerned, Attlee shrewdly pointed out that recent events had highlighted the relative security of coal-mining employment. That attraction might be augmented by the fact that the government was proposing further additions to miners' food rations, to which extra meat had already been added in October 1946. Extra fat, sugar and 'points' — the device by which scarce foods that were not formally rationed were controlled — were now on offer exclusively to miners as an inducement to new recruits and an incentive to those already in the industry.[68] A publicity campaign organised by the Central Office of Information, which began to roll just as the fuel problem became manifestly critical in February, extolled the advantages of following a career in mining.[69] In newspaper advertisements, posters, leaflets distributed by the labour exchanges, public exhibits and even films, the message was proclaimed that coal mining was now 'The most important job in the country'. The campaign aimed partly at increasing public awareness generally of the crucial part coal played in the country's prospects for economic and social progress. But its primary intention was to provide coal mining with a more positive image, with a view to overcoming the known resistance to colliery work among non-miners and to increasing the morale and hence the commitment of the existing labour force.

At the end of April 1947 the success or failure of the government's efforts to control the consumption of fuel and power and to improve the supply remained to be seen. The objective was the long-term one of securing the fuel position in the winter of 1947–48 and beyond. All that could be said, as the 1946–47 'coal year' drew to its close, was that there were some encouraging signs to be seen. The coal-to-oil conversion programme, for example — with all its problems in regard to materials and equipment — looked as if it could well achieve the coal savings expected from it in the Coal Budget. In coal production itself, there appeared to be grounds for at least cautious optimism. The hoped-for upswing in recruitment to mining seemed to be under way: in the first quarter of 1947, although more than 12,000 men had left the mines, nearly 27,000 had come in, and the number of wage-earners on colliery books had risen from 692,000 in December 1946 to 710,000 in April.[70] There was hope that this trend might continue and that the statistics of absenteeism and productivity – already looking better than they had done for a year or more[71] – might also go on improving. There were still, of course, serious problems to be faced, like the delays experienced in the construction of new power stations and gasworks. And above all, perhaps, there was uneasiness about the effect on coal supplies of the introduction of the five-day week for miners at the start of the new 'coal year' in May. The government had considered postponing the event, but Attlee reported after meeting the executive of the National Union of Mineworkers in March that the union was unlikely to accept any postponement voluntarily. The government could not bring itself to exercise compulsion, at least until there was clear evidence that the operation of the five-day week was seriously undermining the security of fuel and power supplies for the winter. In the meantime Attlee felt that he had no option but to authorise the introduction of the new working arrangements as scheduled on 5th May, on the terms agreed between the NUM and the Coal Board. These, to be sure, seemed to offer compensation for the reduction in hours of work in the form of increased productivity. The miners' leaders had assured the Prime Minister that 'a much better spirit' now existed in the mines and that accordingly the five-day week *need* not involve any loss of output. They even promised to consider the Premier's request for efforts to secure an increase in output. And with that the government had to be satisfied and let the five-day week go ahead, though fears remained among members of the Cabinet about how it might all turn out.[72] Thanks to the continued compilation of regular, detailed reports on the state of fuel and power supplies for the Fuel Committee, it would at least be possible to recognise any threat, whether from the five-day week or from any other quarter, on the approach to the day of reckoning at the end of October, when the prospects for the winter would stand revealed. Meanwhile Ministers and officials could turn to the task of calculating the damage that the fuel crisis in its most virulent form had done since January to their hopes and plans for economic recovery and progress.

7
The end of it all
COUNTING THE COST

... and the end of it all will be that the country will be called upon to pay the bill.

J. Keir Hardie, House of Commons, 28th June 1894

The Attlee government was committed by its 1945 general election manifesto to the creation of an economy 'planned from the ground up'. To carry out such a pledge, the government had to equip itself with the best service it could muster for the collection and analysis of information about the workings of the economy, and this it had arguably done. Attlee had the advantage, of course, that technical experts recruited to manage the wartime mobilisation of economic resources were still, by and large, in the government's service when Labour took office. A considerable body of expertise, as well as an administrative framework capable of being adapted to the new government's purposes, was already in place. The names that terminated the memoranda circulating in Whitehall in the spring and summer of 1947 on the subject of the fuel crisis and its impact remain in many cases familiar and respected to this day among social scientists. No previous peacetime government had been better equipped to monitor and assess the effects, both immediate and longer-term, that the crisis might have had on the country's economic life and prospects.

But even the galaxy of talent available to the government faced certain difficulties in making a precise assessment of the specific impact of the fuel crisis *per se* on industrial output, exports and the balance of payments. For one thing, the fuel crisis could not in practice readily be separated out from the other problems that were operating in and upon the economy at the time − problems like the labour shortage, or the dollar shortage, or indeed the appalling weather of January, February and early March. They were all simultaneous in their impact and so closely intertwined that their individual effects simply could not be distinguished from each other with any certainty. Thus it was not possible for contemporaries − nor is it any easier now − to say exactly how far any drop in the level of exports in, say, February and March 1947 might be the result of a decline in production for export due to fuel and power shortages, and how far it might be the fault of the weather in disrupting the transport of goods from the factory to the port of shipment. As a result, in government circles, the phrase 'the fuel crisis' came to be employed as a kind of shorthand term to describe the whole gamut of problems that came together in the early weeks of 1947. To the extent that the phrase had any precise definition in official terminology, it was a chronological one. 'The fuel crisis' in Whitehall's book was the term employed specifically to describe what happened from the beginning of the second week of February − when the statutory fuel and power restrictions were put into effect − until the beginning of March, when power was fully restored to industry.

Clearly, such a definition leaves much to be desired. There were other problems than those of fuel and power to contend with during that period.

And in any case, the crisis in fuel supplies had actually declared itself in its acute form at the turn of the year, if not earlier, when the highly restricted set of industrial coal allocations proposed by Cripps on 6th January had had to be adopted. As to the termination of this acute phase of the fuel crisis, it seems absurd to argue that it could have come about before the 'Cripps plan' gave way to something more like the levels of fuel allocation prevailing in the latter months of 1946. That did not occur until the end of May. A further problem of chronology is that of knowing when the effects of the fuel crisis — even by its dubious and narrow official definition — actually worked themselves through the economic system. As late as 31st July 1947 an official report[1] could explain the depressed state of exports at that time as being:

> ... mainly due to an unexpected fall in engineering products owing to the difficulties and shortages experienced in the early part of this year, *the impact of which has not yet made itself fully felt on long cycle production* [the emphasis is mine].

Efforts to gauge the impact of the fuel crisis must also have been hindered by the lack of a stable *status quo ante* to provide a base for calculating losses to production or trade. British economic life in 1946—47, and indeed that of the world at large, was still in a state of flux and instability caused by the transition from war to peace. Wartime structures, relationships and patterns of activity were dissolving or being modified. Economic activity was at the mercy of sudden changes in the flow of trade or finance, of hastily contrived changes in commercial policy, of abrupt swings in currency exchange rates, and even of the vagaries of the weather, to a greater extent than would have been the case in more settled times. The trouble was that in late 1946 and early 1947 there could be no firm conception of what might constitute 'normality' in economic terms. There was therefore no stable basis for defining, for example, what the level of industrial output or of exports in February or March 1947 might have been without the intervention of acute fuel and power shortages and the consequent large-scale closures of industrial plant.

The difficulties in the way of assessing accurately the impact of the fuel crisis did not, of course, stop the government and other agencies from making the attempt. Even before some of the major restrictions on industrial and domestic fuel and power consumption had been lifted, the effort was being made to measure the extent of the setbacks they had caused to the country's development and the government's plans. On 17th April Cripps was able to lay before the Cabinet some preliminary estimates of the harm to industrial production since the beginning of February. As well as suffering the compulsory loss of electric power over a wide range of industrial activity in England's three principal manufacturing regions for two or three weeks, industry – by Cripps's reckoning – had been deprived of about two million tons of coal over the period he had under review. This amounted to about four weeks' coal supplies at the rates of allocation laid down by the government at the beginning of January. The effect of all this, Cripps announced, had been to reduce steel production 'to the lowest level since the depression of the early thirties'. In addition, the output of nearly every important raw material had suffered severely; he singled out chemicals, paper, textile yarns and building materials as having been particularly hard hit. The cost to the economy in lost exports alone amounted, 'at a moderate estimate', to £100 million.[2]

As time passed, and the flow of information about what had happened to individual industries improved, it became possible to build up a more detailed and circumstantial picture than Cripps had been able to present. It showed that, if anything, the industrial situation in February and March had been even more daunting than he had suggested. Early in May *The Economist* tabulated the information then available from both government and industrial sources under the headline 'Fuel crisis post-mortem'.[3] The paper quoted an official estimate made early in March that, during the crisis period as officially defined, total industrial output had fallen by some 25%. In *The Economist's* view, this figure seemed to err on the side of optimism. But the full seriousness of the position was more graphically portrayed in the statistics of the individual basic industries, presented by the paper in a simple table which measured their output in February and March as percentages of their January production. Let the figures speak for themselves:

Volume of production (January 1947 = 100)

	February	March
Electricity	79	85
Steel ingots and castings	86	82
Bricks	65	73
Cement	44	83
Cars (private)	40	88
Cotton yarn	50	101

In fact, as *The Economist* implied, the use of the January level of production as a baseline put, if anything, an unduly favourable gloss on what had happened. January, it was pointed out, 'was only a "good" month when compared with the two which followed'. And indeed the official statistics presented in the *Monthly Digest of Statistics* indicate that industrial output in January 1947 was lower by a margin of about 5% than it had been in October or November 1946, before the fuel crisis clearly entered into its acute phase. This highlights the problem that no recognised 'normality' in the pattern of post-war economic activity had yet been established, against which the severity or otherwise of short-term fluctuations could be judged. It is impossible to say with certainty whether January's reduced rate of industrial output represented a 'normal' pattern of seasonal fluctuation, or whether it reflected only the disruption of activity in industries like cotton textiles, cement and car manufacturing that was already occurring as a result of fuel and power cuts from Christmas 1946 onwards.

When *The Economist* published its post-mortem in May there was still a highly provisional look to its calculations. The full effects of the fuel crisis in its acute form were still very far from having worked themselves out of the system. Indeed, it might plausibly be argued that, with industry still operating on the 'Cripps plan' coal allocations, the crisis remained acute even then. Fuller information and more mature calculation, however, served more or less to confirm the state of industrial affairs that *The Economist* had postulated. This may be seen, for example, in the index of industrial production compiled by the Central Statistical Office, and published in the *Monthly Digest* from June 1948 onwards.[4] The index showed that in February total industrial output was more than 20% lower, and manufacturing output nearly 25% lower, than in January. The corresponding March figures still remained some 6% lower than January's. Only in April were January's output levels in manufacturing and in aggregate industrial terms regained, and then only just. This meant, of course, that April's levels remained significantly below those of October or November 1946, before the fuel and power problem began to exercise an obvious effect on industry. Even in April basic industries such as textiles, building materials, ironfounding and paper-making continued to be bedevilled by unemployment and short-time working as a result of fuel shortages.[5]

In fact, taking the first three months of 1947 together, production levels in British industry were barely above those attained in the corresponding period of 1946. This must have represented a severe setback to the government's hopes and expectations of industrial growth. It was clear in ministerial pronouncements and other official statements that rapid industrial growth was a central assumption in government plans for 1947, even though care had been taken (for instance in the *Economic Survey for 1947* which set out those plans) to avoid an overt commitment to any specified rate of growth. Yet here they were, at the end of the year's first quarter, in effect no further forward than they had been a year before. Looking at the index of industrial production's calculations for individual industries, it is apparent that some key sectors which had been among those hardest hit in February were still operating in April at levels of activity lower than January's. Particularly worrying for a government with an acute housing shortage to deal with, and with an already disappointing construction record, was the inclusion in the list of the brick, cement, glass and non-ferrous metal industries.

Any concern that the government may have felt about the implications of the fuel crisis for its house-building programme paled into insignificance beside its worries about the effects of the crisis on the export trade. The rapid recovery of exports from their extremely low wartime levels was a matter of transcendental importance to all hopes and plans for social and economic progress. As the *Economic Survey for 1947* put it;[6] 'Without exports, we cannot get food and we cannot get raw materials, and without these we cannot hope to increase our standard of living – or even maintain it.' Cripps's initial 'moderate estimate' of 17th April, that the fuel crisis had cost £100 million in lost exports since the beginning of February, was rapidly superseded by a figure twice that size, formulated by the Treasury's Balance of Payments Working Party. In a report dated 18th April the working party noted that 'We now face a crisis in our external financial position', with nearly half the credits available under the American loan having been used up. One of the principal causes of this state of affairs lay in the fact that 'the fuel crisis has cost us two months' exports and has set back the export drive by nine months; this is equivalent to a loss of export income of £200 millions'.[7]

This is not the place for a detailed account of the melancholy history of the balance of payments in the spring and summer of 1947, as the 'looming shadow of catastrophe' that Dalton had seen hanging over it in March darkened and deepened into the reality of the convertibility crisis of July and August.[8] Suffice it to say that the introduction of free convertibility for sterling on 15th July, as required under the terms of the American loan agreement, stripped the country of almost its last dollar resources. The government was forced to renege on convertibility on 20th August, with dire results for national pride and international financial standing. It was also obliged to bring in a package of emergency measures designed to cut overseas expenditure, which deprived the public of some of their remaining imported pleasures. The chief restrictions were on imports of American foodstuffs, tobacco and Hollywood films.

Nor is it the place to consider in detail the competence of the government's handling of the balance-of-payments problem in the lead-up to convertibility, though we may note certain apparent similarities with the handling of the fuel and power problem during 1946. There seemed to be the same fatal inability to translate awareness of the problem and its political consequences into any kind of effective remedial action before a thoroughgoing crisis broke. In both cases Ministers were open to accusations of undue complacency in their public statements. Shinwell's remark that everyone knew there was going to be a coal crisis except him was matched by Dalton's reassurance a week before the introduction of convertibility that:

> in large measure 15 July has already been discounted and the additional burden of assuming these new obligations under the Anglo-American Loan Agreement will be noticeably less than many people suppose.[9]

Dalton was arguably drawing as heavily as the colleague of whom he had been so critical on the example of Mr Micawber.

What is germane to this account is the matter of the extent to which the impact of the fuel crisis on the export trade contributed to the weakening of the balance of payments which laid Britain open to disaster and humiliation on the advent of convertibility in July. Informed opinion was in no doubt that the connection between the two crises was direct and powerful. For example, Treasury assessments of the deteriorating foreign exchange position during May and June, on the approaches to convertibility, uniformly assigned to the fuel crisis and its £200 million of lost exports a leading role in the country's growing financial debility. Typical of the *genre* was a paper presented to the Cabinet by the Chancellor of the Exchequer on 5th June.[10] It listed, presumably in order of importance, seven distinct factors in the deterioration in the balance of payments. First was an increase of 10% to 15% in world prices, which threatened to add £200 million to the import bill. In second place, but quantitatively equal in its impact on the position, was the fuel crisis, which 'has cost us two months' exports and has set back the export drive by nine months; this is equivalent to a loss of export income of £200 millions in 1947'. When the convertibility crisis was in full swing in early August, and precious dollar resources were melting away faster than ice cream in the heat wave that marked the high summer of 1947, Attlee ascribed to the fuel crisis the principal role in the failure of export earnings to reach the levels required to prevent unexpectedly heavy drawings on Britain's dollar credits to pay for her imports. And even when sufficient time had passed for a more considered judgement to be made, this view remained the Treasury orthodoxy. An appreciation prepared in 1962 by the man who had been in 1947 the Assistant Secretary in the Treasury's overseas finance division placed the fuel crisis and its lost £200 million of export earnings high among the causes of the collapse in the balance of payments that precipitated the convertibility crisis.[11]

There may be reason to doubt the precise accuracy of these contemporary perceptions. Reading the numerous papers on the balance of payments that circulated in Whitehall and Westminster between April and August, one is immediately struck by the way in which the phraseology of the Balance of Payments Working Party paper of 18th April is employed almost verbatim in one document after another. It looks very much as if the original formulation by the working party became the conventional, stereotyped 'Treasury view', the accuracy and authority of which were simply never questioned. But what was the provenance of this calculation that the fuel crisis cost the country £200 million in lost exports? Is it actually as reliable and authoritative as was assumed at the time, and has generally continued to be assumed ever since?

Sir Alec Cairncross claims that the figure originated with him when, as a Board of Trade official, he was asked to supply Cripps, as President of the Board, with an estimate of the cost of the fuel crisis. He admits, however, to having no recollection of how he arrived at the figure.[12] Lest it be thought that Sir Alec may have plucked the figure from the air to keep his Minister happy, the papers of the Central Economic Planning Staff (of which he was a member) give some clues as to the probable basis of his calculation.[13] It appears that during the compilation of the *Economic Survey* for 1947, just before the full force of the fuel crisis broke over the country, the planning staff had set a target for total exports (i.e. exports of goods produced in Britain plus re-exports) for 1947 of 150% of the volume of exports achieved in 1938. This target was expressed in monetary terms as £1,300 million. Just before the *Survey* was due to go into print, however, this target was revised downwards because of the effects of the fuel shortages that had already been experienced before the beginning of February. The new target was to be 140% of the 1938 volume of exports, or £1,200 million at 1947 money values, and this was duly published in the *Survey* in mid-February. But when the full effects of the fuel shortages and power restrictions of February and March began to be recognised, the Board of Trade — as the body chiefly responsible for looking after overseas trade — made a further downward revision in the target, to £1,100 million. It seems likely that Sir Alec may have informed Cripps of this second revision just before the latter presented to the Cabinet his 'moderate estimate' of 17th April that the fuel crisis has resulted in the loss of £100 million in exports *since the beginning of February*. The next day, adding the two downward revisions of the export target together, the Balance of Payments Working Party came up with its definitive figure for the *overall* loss of exports due to the fuel crisis of £200 million.

What we have, then, in this figure of £200 million is emphatically not a careful calculation of known loss to real export transactions. It is instead no more than an estimate, made quite early in the year, of the extent to which exports *might* undershoot a hypothetical target for the level of exports to be achieved in the full year. It was, in other words, a tentative, provisional estimate of possible loss, based on certain assumptions about the future flow of goods for export which might or might not be fulfilled in practice. As things turned out, it was already becoming apparent by the beginning of June that April's worst fears were not necessarily going to be realised. Exports in May were significantly higher than expected, and it seemed possible to think in terms of revising the year's export target yet again − this time upwards, to £1,150 million.[14] Such a revision would immediately reduce the loss to exports attributable to the fuel crisis from £200 million to £150 million. But the calculation was qualified by the thought that

> The effects of the fuel crisis are bound to be felt for many months to come and the current rate of exports is sustained by work done ... before the electricity crisis in February.

This consideration raised doubts about the economy's ability to maintain the unexpectedly favourable trend in exports currently being achieved, as the reduced levels of export production attained in February and March fed through to the trade statistics of July and August. In the event, however, total exports for 1947 came close to reaching the *Economic Survey's* target of £1,200 million. They fell short by less than £2 million, a margin so small as to be insignificant.[15] This does not, of course, mean that the loss of exports due to the fuel crisis was equally insignificant, but it reinforces the suspicion that the conventional assumption that the fuel crisis cost the country £200 million in lost exports probably errs on the side of excess. The true figure, on the other hand, does not seem readily susceptible to precise measurement. The view recently expressed by Sir Alec Cairncross, that 'it would be reasonble ... to take £100 million as a minimum estimate of the loss',[16] may indeed be none too wide of the mark. If less than contemporaries believed, it remains a substantial figure, and one which − in the circumstances − the economy could ill afford to forgo.

Whatever the exact figures that might be attached to the economic losses sustained as a result of the fuel crisis in terms of reduced exports or cuts in industrial output, there is no doubt they were severe. The setback to the country's post-war revival was a heavy one. It has been suggested that it was also unnecessary . Specifically, the charge has been made that 'For a minute economy in fuel — the coal equivalent of the electric power of which the factories were deprived in February — something like a quarter of February's manufacturing output was thrown away', and that this loss need not have taken place.[17] That the saving in fuel achieved by depriving the so-called 'non-essential' industries of their electricity supplies was very small seems unarguable. The total saving in power-station coal consumption between 10th and 28th February — virtually the entire effective period of industrial restriction — was 513,850 tons.[18] By comparing the scale of power-station coal savings before and after the resumption of industrial electricity supplies, together with the difference between the saving in those areas where industrial restrictions applied and those where they did not, it seems likely that about half this total saving can be attributed to the industrial restrictions. That is to say that in February 1947 something like a full week's industrial output was sacrificed for the sake of saving some 260,000 tons of coal, or less than half a day's coal production. Put in those terms, the achievement seems wildly out of proportion to the cost.

The question is whether the government had any alternative to the imposition of the industrial power restrictions of 10th February. The object of the exercise was to enable power-station coal stocks to be built up so that a complete collapse of electricity supplies might be avoided, with all that such a thing entailed by way of the disintegration of the apparatus of civilised existence. Ministers had had the meaning of such a breakdown put to them by Shinwell at the beginning of January: households deprived of the means of heating, lighting and cooking; mass unemployment; the collapse of essential services like transport, sewage and water supply.[19] It was a prospect to be avoided at all costs, to be sure. But was it really the prospect the country faced at the end of the first week in February? Was the situation then truly so grave as to render essential the acceptance of a considerable decline in industrial output, near-record unemployment (albeit only for a short time, as it turned out) and the large-scale loss of sorely needed exports so that an even worse fate could be avoided? A review in detail of the power-station fuel supply position makes it hard to accept that this was the case.

On 7th February, when the decision to impose the cuts was taken, power-station coal stocks in the 'Black Areas' remained — on average at least — above one week's consumption. London and the South East had 254,000 tons, or 9·2 days' supply. The North West and Midland regions carried stocks equal to seven and a half days' consumption.[20] Admittedly, stocks at individual power stations were sometimes rather lower than the regional averages; but the overall situation even in these, the worst-hit parts of the country, hardly amounted to the last extremities of fuel supplies in the electricity generating industry. It is interesting to note that the power-station coal position early in February was not much different from that of the gas industry. But there was no suggestion of shutting down *gas* supplies, even in London, where gas-coal stocks were at their lowest. Compared with the coal stocks remaining to the railway companies in mid-February, power stations actually looked positively well supplied. By 26th February the railways had only four days' supply in hand. In fact, following the imposition of the electricity consumption cuts on 10th February, power-station coal stocks in the areas most at risk increased quite rapidly. By 12th February, when the Fuel Committee met for the first time, there had already been a significant improvement. And in the two weeks following 7th February power-station stocks in all the 'Black Areas' taken together increased from 529,497 tons to 834,588. The increase, 305,091 tons, would have been more than enough to keep industrial electricity supplies going thoughout the three-week emergency period.

There is an obvious contrast between the amount and the quality of information about coal supplies and stocks available to the government before and after the establishment of the Fuel Committee on 12th February. The committee, through its detailed daily situation reports, operated at a great advantage over its predecessor, the Ministerial Coal Committee, or even over the Cabinet itself as it operated before the emergency was declared. It enjoyed a far superior basis for decision-making and for the 'fine tuning' of supplies. The considerable improvement in the government's ability to control the fuel and power situation conferred by this superior intelligence (using the word in the military sense) could surely have been used, not to build *up* coal stocks at power stations at the expense of industrial activity, but to keep them steady while maintaining it. There may have been a case, before the sort of data contained in the daily reports was available, for declaring a short industrial holiday while the true coal supply position was ascertained. But once the details of the position had been established, and control over it imposed − and it is worth recalling in this connection how quickly the Fuel Committee passed from concern about the immediate crisis to consideration of the longer term − it is hard to see any justification for keeping the stoppage going for another two weeks. At the centre of the decision to do so was the desire to build up power-station coal stocks in the 'Black Areas' to a minimum of two weeks' consumption. This, however, seems to have been a wholly arbitrary figure, not based on any explicitly stated operational considerations: 'The Central Electricity Board *felt* that it would be necessary ...'.[21] The Ministry of Fuel and Power took the view that a stock equal to one and a half weeks' consumption would be enough 'to take the risk of relaxing the restrictions'.[22] But the CEB view was allowed to prevail, perhaps because by then Shinwell's Ministry was seen to have taken too many risks that had not come off. The result was, however, that the industrial stoppage was prolonged by some days in the midlands and by over a week in the other 'Black Areas', over and above what would have been the case had the Ministry's more sanguine view prevailed. With hindsight, the risk entailed by accepting the suggestion of Shinwell and his associates hardly seems to have been a very serious one.

It is perhaps worth noting that the cuts in domestic and non-industrial electricity supply during February and March resulted in a reduction in power-station coal consumption of the order of 15% to 18%.[23] Had similar restrictions been put into operation, and enforced in such a way as to achieve similar savings, from the start of the 1946−47 'coal year' on 1st May 1946, something like half a million to a million tons more coal might have been available by the end of January 1947. If this extra supply had been on hand, the breakdown of industrial electricity supply in February could with ease have been avoided altogether.

It can also be argued that if such domestic and non-industrial restrictions had been brought in during the 1946 'coal summer' the disruption experienced in homes and commercial premises at the peak of the crisis might have been much reduced. Public awareness of the dangers of the fuel situation would have been heightened, and people might have been better prepared for difficulties in the winter. There would have been time to think, to conserve and stockpile domestic coal and alternative fuels. No doubt there would still have been inconveniences had the sort of measures introduced in February been brought in ten months or so earlier. But the more favourable circumstances of the summer might have made them easier to cope with and perhaps have saved people from the serious hardships created by lengthy cuts in heat, light and power during the hardest winter in living memory. Who knows, had such steps been taken from May 1946, it might actually have been possible to increase domestic fuel and power supplies when the going got really hard in the first quarter of 1947.

Any discomfort or inconvenience that the public might have been obliged to undergo had domestic fuel and power cuts on the lines of those imposed in February 1947 been applied instead from May 1946 would certainly have been slight by comparison with the experience of most of their European neighbours. Léon Blum may have been striving for effect when he wrote to Attlee in January 1947 that the fate of democracy, socialism and economic growth in France, and Europe generally, hung in the balance for want of one or two million tons of coal per month. But a more sober assessment of the European coal situation by one of Attlee's staff economists did not conflict fundamentally with the picture Blum had painted.[24] In December 1946, it pointed out, Britain was unique in Western Europe in consuming more coal than she had done before the war. Western European coal consumption in general was down to about two-thirds of the pre-war level, and in some countries down to between one third and one half of that. It was also noted, however, that Britain was additionally unique in allowing her fuel and power problems to manifest themselves in the form of industrial shut-downs and unemployment. Elsewhere it had been the *domestic* consumer who had borne the brunt of the fuel famine, while the work of industrial reconstruction was safeguarded. By the standards obtaining among domestic consumers of electricity on the Continent, the British had hardly been required to make any serious sacrifices or to accept any significant inconvenience in terms of domestic comfort since the end of the war.[25]

It may be, of course, that they would not have been willing to do so. The government certainly seems to have been reluctant to put the matter to the test, even when − at the start of the 'coal winter' in November 1946 − it was admitted by the Minister of Fuel and Power himself that substantial economies would have to be made to avoid a crisis before the end of the 'coal year'. But the evidence, for instance, of the Mass Observation surveys of February 1947 suggests that there remained a reservoir of willingness to support economies if the gravity of the position were made sufficiently obvious. It should have been tapped much sooner, so that, instead of having to be overcome, the acute problems of the period between late January and mid-March might have been averted or their severity at least reduced.

Those who in the spring and early summer of 1946 foresaw a fuel crisis in the coming winter were often as alive to the dangers such an event would create for the Attlee government in political terms as to the economic problems it would cause. Douglas Jay, for example, repeatedly pointed out to Attlee that a fuel crisis bringing industrial disruption in its wake would seriously undermine the government's standing with the electorate and might − coming hard on the heels of the coal industry's passing from private to public ownership − discredit not only the newly formed National Coal Board but even the very concept of nationalisation itself.[26]

There is, indeed, evidence that the government's credibility suffered quite a severe jolt, but also that the setback had little lasting effect. The most striking evidence of the government's reduced standing with the British public is perhaps to be found in the results of public opinion surveys conducted by the Gallup organisation's British subsidiary, covering the period from August 1946 to May 1947.[27] A poll conducted in March 1947 showed a sharp drop, compared with a similar survey of the previous August, among those expressing approval or satisfaction with the government's record, from 46% of those interviewed to 39%. Those expressing disapproval or dissatisfaction increased more than proportionately, from 41% to 54% of the respective samples, as a result of a steep decline in the number of respondents offering no opinion either way. As with the standing of the government as a whole, so with the reputation of its leader. Those who approved of Attlee as Prime Minister had numbered 52% of Gallup's sample in December 1946, while 30% had disapproved and 18% offered no opinion. The next time the question was put, also in March 1947, Attlee's support had diminished by six percentage points, while those who were dissatisfied with him had grown by no less than fifteen points, again partly as a result of a sharp reduction in the proportion of 'Don't knows'.

Remarkably, however − especially in view of the fact that restrictions on the use of electricity in homes, shops, offices and places of entertainment remained in force − both Attlee and his government had, by May, regained much of the esteem in the eyes of the public that they had earlier lost. Since March those expressing satisfaction with the government's record had risen from 39% to 42% of the Gallup sample. They were still outnumbered by the dissatisfied, but the proportion in this category had shrunk from 54% to 48%, while those who were content to suspend judgement (or who simply had no opinion on the matter) grew in number. Attlee's personal resurgence in public esteem over the same period was even more marked − a gain of five percentage points in those who expressed satisfaction with his performance as Prime Minister, and a nine-point drop in those who did not. This put Attlee's standing back almost to the level he had enjoyed in October 1946, before the fuel problem had materialised in a form obvious to the public.

Even though people may, in the short term, have been less satisfied by the performance of the government in relation to the fuel crisis, their increased dissatisfaction seems to have done little to alter their political sympathies and allegiances. A Mass Observation survey conducted during the first week of restrictions in February recorded that, among people who had voted Labour in the 1945 general election, only a sixth put the blame for the fuel crisis on the government or any of its members. And few even of those felt so strongly about the matter as to consider switching their loyalties away from Labour. A further survey carried out by the same organisation towards the end of February, when the restrictions had begun to ease, found attitudes more or less unchanged. In fact, Mass Observation concluded, even those who had voted Conservative in 1945 were not very strongly inclined to regard the fuel crisis as the government's doing. About half the Conservative voters whose views were canvassed saw the causes of the affair in the weather, or in past mismanagement of the coal industry, or had no firm opinion at all about its origins. Of those who for one reason or another had not voted in 1945, quite a high proportion — between a third and a half by Mass Observation's reckoning — blamed either the government as a whole for the fuel crisis or the Minister of Fuel and Power specifically. But even their feelings about the matter were apparently not sufficiently strong to undermine their broadly sympathetic attitude to Attlee and his colleagues.[28]

All in all, the evidence provided by contemporary opinion sampling (which, to be sure, was less precise and sophisticated in its techniques than its modern equivalent) gives little support to the idea that the fuel crisis posed any serious threat to the government's political standing. There certainly seems little reason to believe that the fuel and power situation represented a political as well as an economic crisis for Labour. Other conventional political indicators appear to confirm that interpretation. There was, for instance, little obvious shift in the political feeling of the country against the government to be discerned in those by-elections on which the fuel crisis might have been expected to exercise some effect. There were, as it happened, only two parliamentary by-elections held in the first six months of 1947, at Normanton in Yorkshire on 11th February and at Jarrow in County Durham on 7th May — both rock-solid Labour seats. The essential loyalties of the electors of this very narrow sample of constituencies did not change. Both remained in the Labour fold, even though swings of 3·3% and 5·1% respectively (compared with 1945) towards the Conservatives were recorded. Psephologically, however, it is hard to read any significance into these results. The tide in by-elections had already, it seems, turned against the government from the summer of 1946. In the first half of that year the Labour Party was still increasing its share of by-election votes over the Tories in those contests which involved both parties. During the next six months, however, the swing was clearly towards the Conservatives, to the tune of 3·9% on average. The swings recorded at Normanton and Jarrow (which averaged 4·2%) were not in any way, it appears, out of line with the trends established in the six by-elections between July and December 1946 in which Labour and Conservative candidates were matched.[29]

One man whose reputation and standing might have been expected to suffer was the Minister of Fuel and Power, Emanuel Shinwell. Even before the turn of the year he was the subject of a growing volume of critical comment in the press, from those who, like the editor of *The Economist*, saw a fuel crisis looming while the man politically responsible appeared to do little or nothing about it. By February the frequency of press criticism of Shinwell had greatly increased and its tone had sharpened considerably, and even after the worst of the crisis was over the sniping continued. For *Picture Post's* supposedly typical working-class housewife, for example, he was 'The only member of the Government she has her knife into ... and that is because he did the unforgivable thing. He led her up the garden path ...'.[30] Feeling against Shinwell, as we have seen, ran almost as high among some of his immediate colleagues in government as it did in Fleet Street, but his stock does not seem to have fallen so low with the general public. A Gallup poll taken early in January 1947 indicated that those who thought Shinwell was doing a satisfactory job as Minister of Fuel and Power outnumbered those who did not in the proportion of five to four. Unfortunately, Gallup did not see fit to put the question again in, say, early March. However, Mass Observation's two exercises in sampling opinion about the fuel crisis in February seemed to reveal no great disposition to place the blame on his shoulders or to demand his removal. Only one in fourteen of those questioned by Mass Observation wanted to see either the government or Shinwell replaced.[31] His own constituents in County Durham evidently retained their faith in him in full measure: his share of the vote in both the 1950 and the 1951 general elections was higher than it had been in 1945, on substantially increased turn-outs in both cases.[32]

Perhaps aware that Shinwell's standing remained high with the party faithful, who did not see his shortcomings as an administrator at close range, Attlee seems to have felt unable to dispense with his service altogether, however much in private he might have liked to do so. Thus he kept Shinwell on at Fuel and Power until October, and thereafter retained him in the government, if not in a Cabinet post.[33] Any dent in his reputation Shinwell was able to overcome simply by outliving his contemporaries in the first Attlee administration. By the time of his death in 1986 he had long since ceased to be known as one of Attlee's less successful Ministers and had become a national institution – good old Manny, peer of the realm, Grand Old Man of the Labour Party and honoured centenarian, a regular guest on television 'chat shows' with his reminiscences of the great post-war days of hope and reconstruction laced with just enough acid to lift them above the general run of televised banality. Even Douglas Jay, having found common cause with Shinwell during the late 1960s and early '70s in their hostility to Britain's entry into the European Economic Community, had come to take a more mellow view of the man of whom, as Attlee's private secretary, he had been so critical.

As far as nationalisation as a policy was concerned, it did come in for some hostile comment even among Labour voters in Mass Observation's second survey of February 1947. A further survey undertaken in May indicated that by then a large number of people saw nationalisation as a major factor in bringing about the crisis. If this indeed represented the early manifestations of disenchantment with the principle of nationalisation, such as Jay had earlier feared, it hardly amounted to a rational reaction to the situation. The fuel crisis had clearly not been something that had arisen only since the formal inauguration of the nationalised coal industry on 1st January, and on no reasonable interpretation of the facts could nationalisation by itself, or any supposed mismanagemenet of coal production by the National Coal Board, be blamed for what had happened. But, as the compilers of the Mass Observation survey report rather tartly observed, people's reactions to the fuel crisis were more inclined to be emotional than rational, and were likely to be based on little real knowledge of the facts.[34]

It is perhaps fair to say that the government in general and Shinwell in particular came through the crisis with their standing in the eyes of the public less severely impaired than they had expected, or than they had any right to expect. On the whole, the evidence relating to the opinions and political reactions of the public seems to support the general conclusions voiced by Mass Observation in May 1947.[35] Most people, the organisation reported, had found the experience of the fuel crisis inconvenient and depressing:

> but *not sufficiently so* to shake more than a minority from their generally prevailing attitudes of tolerance and disinterest. Perhaps the situation was too clearly *precipitated*, at least, by forces and factors which were so obviously a matter of bad luck that some sort of sympathetically defensive feeling towards the government was inevitable.

But the report went on to present a warning that in the longer term, as people themselves became more detached from the events they had just come through — and so perhaps more susceptible to 'the propaganda of the newspapers' — their sympathy with the government might not last. 'Consciously, at least, people are not blaming the government for the situation,' the report concluded:

> but it is still possible that this criticism, which everyone must have come across at some time or another, may serve as a background support for later more violent reactions.

Having got off fairly lightly from this, its first major crisis, the government would have to beware in case any dissatisfaction with its future conduct was reinforced by delayed resentment against its past failings in the matter of fuel and power.

From a political point of view, perhaps the most significant cost to the government was in terms of its confidence in itself. There had, of course, been problems for it to deal with before January 1947 — with the Russians, with the 'dollar gaps', with food, with housing, and so on. But none of them had so obviously developed to crisis proportions. None had got so completely beyond control as to threaten so obviously to make nonsense of ministerial plans for economic and social reconstruction. Two elements of the situation in particular may have had especially harmful effects on the morale of Attlee and his Ministers. One was the fact that, of all industries, it should have been coal that had let it down. The special position occupied by the miners in the labour movement, the steps that had been taken by the government to meet their aspirations and foster the 'new spirit' in the mines, had been set at naught. Secondly, the spectre of unemployment — to the abolition of which above all other social evils the government had pledged itself — had been allowed spectacularly if briefly to raise its head again. And Ministers, reviewing the fuel and power prospects from the vantage point of February or March, must have feared a further resurgence. These things having once happened, there could be, as Hugh Dalton put it, 'Never glad, confident morning again!'[36]

8 The more distant prospects

FUEL AND POWER, 1947–51

... there was likely to be a severe fuel crisis in the next three
months, and the more distant prospects were far from
encouraging. Cabinet Minutes, 1st February 1951

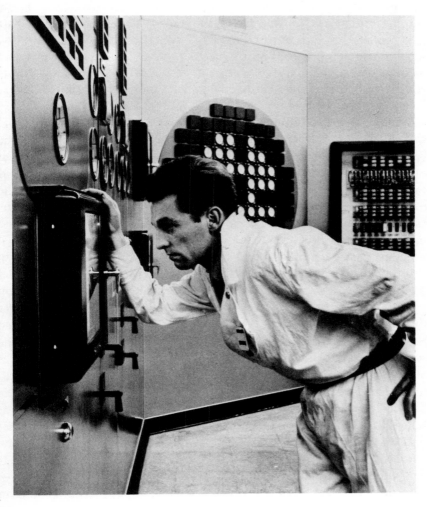

Even as the fuel crisis was at its most acute, in mid-February, we have seen how the Cabinet Fuel Committee rapidly raised its sights from the immediate shortages to look towards the fuel and power position during the new 'coal year' that was due to start on 1st May 1947. Viewed from the chill vantage point of February, the prospects could hardly have looked more bleak. According to the Minister of Fuel and Power, the aggregate requirement for coal in the new budget period would be 199 million tons. But, 'on the basis of present trends and policies', a total output of no more than 180 million tons of deep-mined and open-cast coal was likely to be available to meet that requirement. The prospective deficit on the Coal Budget, therefore, would be about twice as large as the one with which the government had been contending, none too successfully, during the current 'coal year'. Nor was that all the bad news Shinwell had to impart to his colleagues. For, as he pointed out, even if enough coal to meet the requirement in full were to be produced, there would remain the problem of inadequate electricity generating capacity, which would be serious enough to interrupt industrial activity again on a substantial scale next winter.[1]

As things were to turn out, coal production during the new 'coal year' was significantly greater than had been anticipated in February. By the beginning of May even Attlee's private secretary — perennially sceptical of any optimistic projections emanating from the Ministry of Fuel and Power — was willing to express a certain qualified contentment with the trends that seemed to be emerging in the Fuel Committee's situation reports as the old 'coal year' came to a close.[2] If maintained, they seemed to hold out the prospect of a level of output during the six months of the 'coal summer' nearly ten million tons higher than had been thought likely in February. And in spite of the introduction of the five-day week in the mines on 5th May — which Ministers had feared might result in a contraction of output — and despite a worrying rise in absenteeism among miners over the summer holiday period,[3] the trends were maintained. At the end of September, Shinwell was able to assure the Fuel Committee that the summer's output was indeed running well ahead of February's estimates and would finish up about ten million tons (roughly 11%) higher than had then been forecast.[4] During the latter weeks of the 'coal summer' and the early part of the winter there was concern that the level of output might fall, owing to a loss of labour from the industry. There had been a net outflow of over 4,000 men in the August–October quarter. But the numbers picked up again in the last two months of 1947, and output itself did not seriously falter.[5] Indeed, for two consecutive months — November and December average weekly coal output exceeded 4 million tons, a figure that had hitherto only been achieved in one or two isolated weeks since the end of the war.[6] The 4 million ton weekly average was exceeded again in February and April 1948, and in the full 'coal year' ending on 30th April production totalled over 209 million tons instead of the 180 million that had been predicted in February 1947, an improvement of no less than 16%.

This fairly remarkable excess of actual over expected production seems to have stemmed from two principal developments in the coal industry. The first was a significant growth in the size of the labour force. The number of wage-earners on colliery books – a measure essentially of the industry's maximum potential labour force – having risen from 692,000 to 710,000 during the 'coal winter' of 1946–47, then grew to a peak of 719,000 in July and August. It fell back somewhat during the next three months, to 714,000 in November 1947, but during the last five months of the 'coal year' recruitment picked up again, and the number of men on colliery books rose to 724,000 in April 1948.[7] Here was the pay-off for the recruitment and training of the men of the Polish Resettlement Corps, nearly 6,000 of whom had been taken on by December 1947, and of the policy of directing immigrants from the Irish Free State into the pits. Neither group, it has to be said, seemed very enthusiastic about its new occupation. There were complaints from the Poles that they were being discriminated against in the allocation of better-paid forms of pit work. And, to the annoyance of the Ministry of Fuel and Power, the Irish – having accepted employment in the mines as a condition of entry – showed a marked tendency to decamp to the midland car factories at the earliest opportunity.[8] Recruitment of indigenous British labour also increased, motivated perhaps by the government's campaign to make coal mining a more attractive occupation by publicising the vital role of the miner in the work of economic reconstruction, together with the advance miners had recently made in terms of wages and working conditions.

There was evidence, however, that the campaign was being less successful than the government and its publicity agencies might have hoped. An inquiry conducted by the government's own Social Survey in February 1948 – ten months after the campaign had been launched – pointed to rather disappointing results.[9] Out of a sample of 1,870 men, none of them connected with coal mining, only 5% favoured mining as a job, and only 8% of those with sons aged between fourteen and eighteen saw it as a suitable occupation for their offspring. Negative attitudes towards mining villages persisted strongly: they were perceived as isolated and lacking in amenities. And although the overwhelming majority of the sample claimed to have seen the government's publicity material, few had evidently paid it much attention: only 3% for example, could give a recognisable description of the newspaper advertisements about mining. A Mass Observation survey conducted at about the same time came to much the same conclusions.[10] It found that the standing of the miners in public esteem was high, but that few wished to join this esteemed group because the image of mining as a job remained bad. The report concluded that the people who had been interviewed:

> however much they believe that miners are 'grand fellows' who 'have a hell of a job', do not think that people who have any choice in the matter would undertake such work ... they have a long way to go before they accept mining as a possible and interesting career for someone *not* 'born to it'.

This may help to explain why the labour force did not rise to the extent envisaged by the government in, for example, the *Economic Survey* for 1947, which had set a target of 730,000, to be achieved by the end of 1947. Ministers, however, seem to have preferred to blame the raising of the statutory school-leaving age from fourteen to fifteen at the start of the 1947—48 school session. This, the Minister of Labour told the Fuel Committee, had deprived the coal industry of a whole year's intake of juveniles: and the numbers of such recruits did indeed slump after July 1947.[11]

The second development contributing to the unexpected growth of coal output was an increase in the efficiency of the industry's labour force. Overall output per man shift rose by more than 5%, from an average of 1·04 tons in the 1946—47 'coal year' to 1·09 in that of 1947—48, though it still lagged some way behind the productivity levels of the 1930s.[12] The government, while no doubt gratified by this encouraging improvement, was again rather less than entirely satisfied with it. In the summer of 1947, for reasons connected with the balance-of-payments problems then coming to a head with the introduction of sterling convertibility, it sought ways of obtaining further advances. Recognising that the scarcity of coal was a serious handicap to the production of goods for export, and indeed that in conditions of world shortage coal itself was an eminently exportable commodity, the Cabinet at the beginning of August determined to set a coal production target for the rest of the 'coal year' of 4·25 million tons per week. This when, in practice during the past three months, average weekly output had been running at about half a million tons below that figure. With the attainment of its aim in mind, the government entered into discussions with the National Coal Board and the National Union of Mineworkers to secure the implementation of undertakings given by the NUM, as a *quid pro quo* for the granting of the five-day week, to accept increased 'stints' — the agreed amounts of work that individual miners were expected to complete in a single shift.[13] It was perhaps unwise for the government to link its desire to see better productivity with a suggestion that the length of the standard shift in the mines should be increased by half an hour. Coming only a couple of months after the introduction of new hours of work under the five-day week agreement, this was not the way to induce a spirit of co-operation from a union whose members in the past had rallied to the war-cry 'Not a penny off the pay, not a minute on the day'. There were already signs that the NUM was becoming disenchanted with nationalisation — not the principle, to be sure, but the way that principle was being put into effect. A survey of miners in June had revealed among them a rising tendency to view the NCB, 'visible sign and symbol of authority', as not much different in practice from the old regime in the mines. The investigators speculated about the extent to which miners' growing hostility to the Board reflected present grievances, and how far it represented ingrained attitudes to 'the bosses' rooted in the past.[14] In any event, the NUM was in no mood to give anything away, either to the government or to the Coal Board.

The union *was* willing to consider the matter of extended stints, together with a resumption of Saturday working twice a month, but only on terms which were not acceptable to the government. For instance, the union wanted all miners who worked a Saturday shift to be paid at overtime rates: the government refused to sanction overtime rates for men who had not worked the full five shifts in the preceding week. The government huffed and puffed: disappointment and dissatisfaction were expressed in Cabinet at the unwillingness of the miners 'to make a further contribution to assist the country in the present economic crisis'.[15] When the NCB and the NUM sorted out the matter between themselves along lines that reflected the union's ideas rather than the Cabinet's, Attlee and his colleagues refused to ratify the arrangement. The two parties to it were told that 'the final decision must rest with them and that they must take full responsibility for it'.[16] The government, in effect, washed its hands of the whole affair. Once again, the miners and their representatives had demonstrated that their broad ideological sympathy with the government need not be expected to interfere with their tradition of hard bargaining in matters of wages and working conditions. But even if Attlee and his Ministers had not managed to get their way with the NUM, the arrangements agreed between the union and the Board for the more efficient use of manpower nevertheless seem to have had the desired effect, to some degree at least. At any rate, output per man shift in the seven months of the 'coal year' following the NCB–NUM agreement, at over 1·10 tons, was significantly

167

higher than the 1·07 tons of the' five months before that.[17] Better organisation of the labour force was certainly a more plausible explanation of improved productivity than mechanisation, which appeared to be hopelessly bogged down in administrative problems as well as beset by shortages of essential materials (notably steel) and an acute scarcity of suitable manufacturing capacity in the engineering industry. No significant gains in output or productivity were to be expected from that quarter in this 'coal year' at any event.[18]

Some credit for the increased production of coal was assigned to reduced absenteeism − or, to put it more positively, to increased attendance at work − on the part of miners.[19] The official figures do, indeed, show a striking change in the trend after April 1947. The proportion of possible shifts for which men did not turn up stood at 14·5%·overall and nearly 18% among face workers in that month. The comparable figures for May were, respectively, less than 10% and less than 12%. This dramatic improvement, however, may be regarded as more apparent than real, in the sense that it represented a paper gain stemming from the introduction of the five-day week. In practice the average colliery wage-earner worked *fewer* shifts in 1947−48 than he had in 1946−47 − 4·66 per week instead of 4·87. But he worked to greater effect during them, and produced enough extra coal per shift to more than offset the decline in the amount of time he spent at work.[20]

On the demand or consumption side of the fuel and power equation, matters had no more gone the government's way than they had on the supply side. Its campaigns to reduce coal consumption through the substitution of oil in industry and through rigorous domestic economy in the use of gas and electricity were both much less successful than had been hoped.

By the end of 1947 the coal-to-oil conversion programme for industry, which had been revived amid such high expectations in March, had more or less run into the sand. Conversion schemes which had not by then been substantially completed were suspended, and industrialists who had obtained official authorisation to convert their plant to oil burning began to be pressed to abandon their plans and, even where conversion had been completed, to revert to coal.[21] Throughout the summer the programme had been plagued by difficulties. There were particular problems with the provision of materials − above all, of steel − and of equipment for handling and transporting heavy fuel oil in bulk. For example, to cope with the increase in heavy oil traffic on the railways that would be occasioned by the conversion programme authorised by the government in April 1947, 1,250 new tank wagons were needed by the end of Feburary 1948. When the conversion programme was expanded in June 1947 a further 1,500 such wagons needed to be manufactured. But owing to the steel shortage, aggravated by the lack of suitable plant capacity among the railway wagon builders (who were working flat out on the production and repair of coal wagons), the production of these tankers was not even programmed to begin until September 1947. And deliveries by the end of that year would total, not the 1,000 anticipated by the Ministry of Fuel and Power and the Petroleum Board (the statutory body within which the oil companies operated under the wartime oil-control arrangements that remained in force until June 1948), but a mere 200.[22] Then came problems with the supply of oil from overseas. At the beginning of October 1947 there was a substantial increase in the world price of oil — largely as a result of the rapid growth of American demand. Oil remained quite freely available, but it was sufficiently more expensive to make industry worry about the wisdom of turning to it as a substitute for the cheap coal that was Britain's traditional fuel. What was not freely available, however, was a fleet of ocean-going tankers of sufficient size to handle the rapidly growing international trade in oil as every industrial country affected by the world coal shortage increased its oil consumption to compensate. In December the government admitted defeat and announced the curtailment of the conversion pro-gramme a long way short of the intended coal saving of 5 million tons in the 1947—48 'coal year'.[23]

At the start of that coal year the Dowager Marchioness of Reading and her 'Sales Force' drawn from the volunteer regiments of women — the Townswomen's Guilds, the Mothers' Union, the Women's Institute and so on — were let loose upon the country under the banner devised by F.C. Pritchard of Wood & Partners, practitioners in advertising: 'Fuel crisis: towards the way out — that's the way to save 2,500,000 tons by winter'. The Sales Force delivered to every household in the land a copy of the Ministry of Fuel and Power's leaflet combining the exhor-tation to domestic fuel economy with practical advice as to how it might be given effect, and then stood by to dispense further advice to house-holders thus motivated to cut their gas and electricity consumption. After a couple of months, however, there were noticeable changes in the conduct of the campaign. The nomination of a specific target — to cut household gas and electricity usage by 25% to secure a saving of 2·5 million tons of coal by winter — was dropped, to be replaced by a series of general exhortations aimed specifically at housewives under such slogans as 'Saving fuel brings you the things you want' and 'Saving fuel saves breadwinners' jobs'. Then the Sales Force was supplanted by a network of local Fuel Saving Committees, usually headed by His Worship the Mayor, in most major towns.

These measures were probably intended to remedy the failure of the scheme in its original form, though such a thing was not explicitly admitted. This failure, like others on the public relations front, was documented by the government's own public opinion samplers of the Social Survey, in a national survey of housewives' reactions some six weeks after the supposedly comprehensive distribution of the Ministry of Fuel and Power household economy leaflet. Just over half the sample were aware of having received the leaflet. Of these, fewer than half had actually read it, and only 10% of *them* knew it was aimed at securing a specified level of economy. Hardly any of the women canvassed thought they would be able to reduce their gas and electricity consumption by a quarter from the previous summer's levels, and a large minority did not see how they could cut their consumption to any significant extent at all. The survey concluded, not unreasonably, that the impact of the campaign had, thus far at least, been limited. Its report drew a very hostile reaction from the Central Office of Information, the government's publicity agency with overall responsibility for the campaign, which was nevertheless unable to undermine the survey's conclusions in any way. Nor was there any reason to suppose that the campaign in its modified form was any more successful. It was wound up on 31st March 1948, having cost £73,464.[24]

Despite the very limited success of these efforts, coal consumption during the 1947–48 'coal year' actually remained within the limits postulated by Shinwell in his review for the Fuel Committee in February. The types of saving he had anticipated had not been achieved, but actual coal consumption, at 198,873,000 tons (if the Central Statistical Office is to be believed), was just inside the 199 million tons he had predicted. For the first time in years, production had succeeded in keeping ahead of consumption. As a result, the country went into the winter of 1947–48 with its distributed coal stocks in what by recent standards was a healthy state; over 16 million tons at the end of October, compared with less than 11 million at the same point in 1946. Even more remarkably, perhaps, the run-down of stocks over the winter was small: at the end of April 1948 distributed coal stocks still amounted to over 13 million tons, as against 6 million a year before.[25]

Just as the forces of nature had conspired to embarrass those responsible for coal supplies between January and March 1947 by severely aggravating an already acute problem, so they combined in the summer of 1947 to spare their former victims further tribulation. For if there was one thing more than any other that contributed to keeping the consumption of coal within bounds during that summer, it was the weather. The terms in which the summer of 1947 is described employ nearly as many superlatives as those used to depict the winter it followed, but this time of a thoroughly positive kind. Of particular significance to those concerned with fuel and power was its warmth. May was rather wet, but a good deal warmer than any other May since the beginning of the century. June repeated the pattern: dull and damp, but much warmer than usual for the time of year. July started with a cold spell, but then became hot, with some spectacular thunderstorms and extremely heavy local downpours. The inhabitants of Wisley in Surrey were on the receiving end of four inches of rain and hailstones 'about the size of grapes' (an appropriately botanical standard of measurement for the home of the Royal Horticultural Society) which fell within seventy-five minutes on 16th July.[26] So far, so good; but August was something special, as even the unemotional scientific description of the *Meteorological Magazine's* monthly record manages to convey:[27]

> In the British Isles the month was exceptionally hot and dry, with abundant sunshine; it was also unusually quiet, northerly and easterly winds predominating. It was probably the warmest August over the country as a whole since before 1881 ... At Oxford the mean temperature for the month was the highest for August since records were first taken in 1815.

The conditions which had produced this phenomenon persisted through the first half of September, and that month went on record as the warmest September since 1901. Dry, warm and sunny weather also continued to prevail through the greater part of October. It was, in short, one of those summers the memory of which sustains the inhabitants of these islands through the six or seven mid-year bouts of cold and wet that have to be borne before another one like it comes along: one of the great summers.

Fuel and power consumption was held in check not by the exhortations of Mr Pritchard or the exertions of Lady Reading's Sales Force but simply because there was virtually no need for space-heating – and probably not much even for hot food – over the period from May to October. As early as the beginning of June, the significance of its clemency was already being officially recognised, as when Shinwell delivered a progress report to the Fuel Committee on the domestic economy campaign.[28] The actual savings that had so far been acheived, he informed the committee, seemed to represent a good response to the official economy campaign, but in fact 'were clearly very largely due to the good weather'. Coal savings of the order of those achieved in May, he went on, would – if continued through the summer – produce an overall saving of 2 million tons. But in fact, as the weather got better and warmer, the cuts in coal consumption grew as well. The result was that the Ministry of Fuel and Power's regional coal supply officers were able during the summer months to get away with providing consumers with deliveries that fell consistently well short of their official allocations. This applied across the board throughout the entire summer, to industrial and household consumers alike. House coal was once again 'very heavily underdelivered', to use a phrase employed in an earlier consideration of the subject by Shinwell's officials, to the extent of about 15% of the July allocation, 25% of August's, and nearly 17% of September's. And because of the substantial drop in household demand for gas and electricity those sectors could be cut back too. Electricity generating did not receive its full allocation of coal in any week from the beginning of June to the end of September, the shortfall in August amounting to 20%. Only in the last week of June did the iron and steel industry, for all its importance to the expansion of exports and to the refurbishment of industrial capital equipment, receive deliveries that matched or exceeded its allocation. The August shortfall was more tahn 25%, and even in September only about 90% of the industry's allocation was filled.[29] In the case of iron and steel, and indeed the manufacturing sector generally, summer holiday closures cut down the need for fuel and power. Yet in spite of the general cut-back in coal deliveries relative to allocations, the stocks held by consumers or (in the case of house coal) by retailers grew rapidly in the course of the summer. Coal merchants' stockpiles of house coal at the end of October, on the eve of the 'coal winter', exceeded those of May nearly sixfold. Even the railways, which normally made heavy inroads into their coal supplies in the summer months on account of the growth of passenger traffic to the holiday resorts, emerged from the summer with their stocks much improved. Power-station and gasworks stocks also increased substantially between May and October, by roughly 75% in each case, so that they too entered the winter period in approximately twice as healthy a position − in terms of the number of weeks' supplies they had on hand − as they had enjoyed at the same time the previous year.[30]

Nor did the advent of winter make much of a change in the situation. There were spells of cold weather, to be sure, sometimes accompanied by severe frosts and occasionally by heavy snowfalls. But they were few in number and of short duration. In general, the winter of 1947−48 was remarkable for its mildness, even warmth. Temperatures up to 64°F (18°C) were recorded in February, and up to 75°F (24°C) in March. As a matter of fact, in every month of that 'coal winter' the mean temperature was well above the established average, as part of a remarkable sequence which — as the *Meteorological Magazine* faithfully recorded — extended unbroken over a period of thirteen months to April 1948, the longest on record.[31]

As a consequence of the unexpectedly high level of coal output achieved through the expansion of the mining labour-force and improvements in its productivity, and of the effect of the unusually mild weather on the demand for coal, there were no serious problems arising directly out of coal shortages during the winter of 1947–48. The government had made contingency plans for a much harder winter than was actually experienced, and this time it was determined that any restrictions on coal consumption that might be necessary should fall on domestic rather than industrial consumers.[32] But, thanks to the mildness of the weather and the summer's successful stock-building, things never came to such a pass. This was not, however, to say that there were no problems at all on account of the inadequacies of fuel and power resources. For, as Shinwell had warned in February, even though the country might have managed to produce all the coal it required, it still had to contend with an electricity generating capacity insufficient to cater for the foreseeable peak winter demand for power. Back in February the Central Electricity Board had estimated that peak demand during the 1947–48 winter could exceed available generating capacity by a margin of about 13%.[33] In the event, when the peak of demand occurred in early December 1947, only 9% of the load had to be shed by means of power cuts and voltage reductions. But right through January the balance of demand and capacity was on a knife edge, with occasional local power cuts and more frequent national voltage reductions of 5%.[34] The problem was that, although even before the disasters of 1946–47 the CEB had instituted a large-scale programme of capital spending on new generating plant, long delays were being experienced in the construction of new power stations and the delivery of new equipment. And here there was certainly an effect of the coal shortage to be discerned, because one of the chief difficulties — as with coal-to-oil conversion and the technological modernisation of the coal mines themselves — was the shortage of steel. Only about half the amount of new generating capacity planned for 1947 was actually in service at the end of the year, and the record of the following year was to be even worse.[35] Indeed, demand for electricity was coming so far to outstrip the growth of generating capacity that — whereas the CEB had reckoned in February 1947 that capacity would catch up with demand in 1950–51 — eighteen months later the new Minister for Fuel and Power, Hugh Gaitskell, was to inform the Cabinet that capacity was likely to fall short of peak demand until 1954, and that the shortfall would be especially large during the next three winters.[36]

By the time Gaitskell addressed the Cabinet on that matter the electricity supply industry, like the coal industry in January 1947, had passed from private or municipal hands into the ownership of the State, with a single statutory body — the British Electricity Authority — in overall control. This exercise in nationalisation, accomplished on 1st April 1948, was followed after thirteen months by the nationalisation of the gas industry, this time without any central authority equivalent to the National Coal Board or the Electricity Authority. As far as the supply of gas and electricity was concerned, the effects of nationalisation were, on the whole, beneficial, if only because administration was made simpler and more efficient through the replacement of the myriad of local supply undertakings by the area gas and electricity boards, operating on a much larger scale. There were technical benefits too. As a recent study of electricity supply describes the situation with regard to generating plant before nationalisation:[37]

> The placing of orders was under the control of the undertakings rather than the CEB, and this resulted in some manufacturers having idle production facilities while others had lengthening order books and were failing to meet delivery dates. The engineers employed by each municipality and company also had their own idiosyncratic views of how each piece of machinery should be designed, and the CEB were unable to impose greater standardisation in order to speed up manufacture.

Nationalisation created a framework within which technical standardisation and the co-ordination of equipment orders was at least possible. Much the same could be said of the gas industry under the new regime. Nationalisation made possible a more sensibly planned pattern of capital investment in a new gas production plant, the creation of what amounted to a 'national grid' of gas mains, the concentration of production at the most economic sites, and so on. What it could *not* do for gas, any more than it could for coal or electricity, was to ensure that production capacity kept pace with the growth of demand. Yet again, steel shortages inhibited the growth of gas production and made it necessary for some of the new area boards to turn away business from large-scale industrial consumers.[38] It would be a long time before gas and electricity supplies could be relied upon not to falter every time the temperature dropped below freezing for a few days.

The Attlee government that came to office with such a large majority and such high hopes in 1945 had to face the electorate again in 1950. The result of the general election held in February was much less conclusive than that of 1945. The Labour Party resumed office under Attlee with an overall majority of only three seats in the Commons, compared with 146 in 1945.

Governing with such a slim margin was extremely difficult, and Attlee determined — apparently quite on his own initiative[39] — to call another general election in October 1951. It was a gamble he was to lose. The resurgent Conservatives, though polling a slightly smaller number of votes than Labour (which actually took a higher percentage of the total vote than in 1945) emerged with a clear majority of seats. Churchill came back to office as Prime Minister, and the Attlee years were over.

After the summer and early autumn of 1947, when the government still thought it necessary to prepare for the possibility of winter energy problems, fuel and power rather tended to fade from the agenda. There were, as we have seen, some problems of electricity supply at the beginning of the 1947–48 winter, but nothing quite so serious as had once seemed probable. After that, during the rest of the Attlee government's first term, other problems than fuel and power came to absorb the attention of Ministers and civil servants. It was not that the supply of coal or gas or electricity was thereafter quite secure and no longer a matter of concern. Every so often there are to be found indications in, for instance, the deliberations of the Cabinet that the fuel problem was still capable of surfacing and causing anxiety. In the early part of 1949, for example, concern was voiced by the Chancellor of the Exchequer — now, of course, the austere Cripps rather than the ebullient Dalton — about the potential dangers arising from a marked increase that had been reported in absenteeism among miners.[40] The energy problem never quite completely disappeared from sight. But its importance and immediacy after the 1947–48 winter were surpassed by other matters, such as the Russian blockade of West Berlin from June 1948 and the consequent airlift, or the financial crisis of 1949 that forced a devaluation of the pound, or for that matter the election campaign of 1950. But for anyone among Attlee's Ministers who harboured the notion that, just because it was no longer headline news, the fuel crisis had gone away for ever, a rude awakening was in store during the government's brief second term of office.

An official review of coal production at the start of the 1949–50 'coal winter' seemed in almost every respect to present a reasonably cheerful picture.[41] Deep-mined and open-cast production in aggregate was higher than at the corresponding part of 1948, though marginally less than the target the government had set for the industry. Distributed stocks, at more than 16 million tons, looked healthy enough. And output per man shift, at 1·20 tons, had not only come a long way since 1947 but was actually in excess of pre-war levels. The only fly in the ointment, perhaps, was the decline in manpower, from 727,000 wage-earners on colliery books in March 1949 to 709,500 in October. Ministers no doubt took note of the situation, but the statement does not seem to have set any alarm bells ringing. Nor did a further review in March 1950, which noted the loss of a further 5,000 men to the industry since October.[42] Production of coal at all costs was evidently no longer an absolute priority: the NCB had begun to embark on a programme to close down the heaviest loss-makers among the mines under its control. Under this, thirty-one pits had been closed in 1949 and a further eleven in the first half of 1950.[43] Meanwhile, however, the drift of labour away from the coal industry continued. By October 1950 the number of men on colliery books had sunk to 688,000, and the loss was continuing at a rate of 2,000 per month.[44] At the start of the 'coal winter' in November the government came alive to the fact that once again it had a fuel crisis on its hands. The Minister of Fuel and Power, Philip Noel-Baker, reported to the Cabinet that because of the decline in manpower and a fall in productivity coal output had fallen well below what had been expected. At the same time, he said, internal consumption of coal had risen considerably, and if things went on as they were there would be an excess of demand over supply of the order of 800,000 or 900,000 tons. To avoid 'a grave fuel crisis', he advocated a cut in the still small export trade in coal – amounting to about 12 million tons so far in 1950 – that had been painfully built up since 1947. The Cabinet responded by setting up an Official Coal Committee on the 1947 model, under the chairmanship of the Chief Planning Officer of the Ministry of Fuel and Power, to assess the gravity of the situation and to propose remedies.[45] The committee rapidly reported that things were worse than Noel-Baker had thought: the gap between supply and demand was nearer $2 \cdot 5$ million tons than 900,000. To retrieve the situation they proposed the immediate purchase of a million tons of American coal, a cut-back in coal supplied for ships' bunkers 'to the greatest extent possible without causing dislocation of shipping', and the reduction of the use of electricity for commercial display lighting. They also recommended the immediate publication of an official statement on the gravity of the situation, enjoining on the public the need for strict economy.[46]

Reading the official papers relating to the fuel crisis of 1950–51 brings inevitably to anyone who has perused the files on 1947 a powerful sense of *déja vu*. Many of the same elements were present in both crises, not least where their causes were concerned. Inadequate labour supply in the coal industry and low productivity among the labour force were prime factors in each case. All the efforts to improve recruitment by enhancing the attractions of mining as a career that had been going on since 1947 had failed to avert the repetition of these labour problems. There was to be found in 1950–51 also a trace of that unwillingness on the part of

Ministers to face up to the full seriousness of the situation that had been manifest in, for example, January 1947. At the Cabinet meeting of 16th November 1950, when the Official Committee's report had been heard, it was recorded that:

> Some ministers felt that the weekly figures of output might show a substantial improvement very shortly ... For this reason, might it not be wise to defer acting for a further week, or even two weeks?

The spirit of Mr Micawber lived on. This time, fortunately, it was given short shrift by the Minister of Fuel and Power. Noel-Baker told his colleagues that the seasonal increase in output they were expecting to restore the situation was already under way, but 'on a greatly reduced scale', and that it had in any case already been taken into account in calculating the prospective gap between production and consumption. *Immediate* action was necessary because American coal prices and ocean freight rates were rising fast.[47] In 1951, as in 1947, official disapproval was voiced of mid-week sport as a distraction from work, especially where coal miners were concerned. The Yorkshire miners' favourite, the St Leger meeting at Doncaster racecourse, was specifically frowned upon.[48] Fresh attempts were made by the government to secure the acceptance of foreign workers into the mines, this time Italians rather than Poles. The NUM was no more enamoured of the idea in 1951 than it had been in 1946, and no more disposed to be co-operative.[49] Once again a publicity campaign was to be launched to enhance the public image of coal mining and so improve recruitment as well as generating 'a better spirit among the miners'.[50]

The whole affair, in sum, had a dreadfully familiar ring about it. There was even the suggestion that, as in 1947, power stations should be given their full allocation of coal at the expense of manufacturing industry if the coal shortage should become really severe.[51] Inevitably, there was much criticism in the press of the government in general and the Minister of Fuel and Power in particular.[52] Noel-Baker was castigated for his optimistic statements on the coal supply position in the weeks before the crisis broke. There was much harking back to 1947, and much was made of the theme that, after four years of nationalisation and all the claims that had been made for it as the way to solve the fuel shortage, the country was no better off. The NUM was attacked for not delivering its part of the nationalisation bargain: the miners had got what they had wanted, but where was the coal? The NCB was criticised for failing to get the best out of the industry through its management and policies — criticisms that were to be given solid substance by the Ridley Committee on national policy for the use of fuel and power resources, set up in 1951.[53] Coal supplies became a live and significant issue in the 1951 general election, and one that was unlikely to favour the government. Indeed the evidence of opinion polls shows that the government's standing dropped sharply at the end of 1950, when the fuel crisis emerged again, and that it never recovered from the fall.[54]

There were, however, significant differences between the situation of 1950–51 and that of 1946–47. One of the most obvious, perhaps, was that the world coal supply position was rather better in 1950. It proved much easier to find substantial sources of imported coal to make up for domestic deficiencies. And the dollar resources to make the purchase of such imports possible were also much healthier than in 1947, thanks to Marshall Aid. Not only that, but the acute aggravation of the coal problem in 1947 caused by the weather was not a factor in 1950: that winter was relatively mild. Nevertheless, the fuel and power problems of 1950–51 were very serious, and there were real fears of severe disruption of industrial activity leading to large-scale, if not necessarily long-term, unemployment. Nor was the 1950–51 crisis a short-term affair capable of rapid resolution. Noel-Baker warned the Cabinet in February 1951, three months after the existence of the crisis was first recognised, of the continued likelihood of 'a severe fuel crisis' in the three months ahead.[55] Nor did he hold out much hope for relief beyond that, as the statement from which the title of this chapter is taken indicates. Right from the start he had recognised the long-term character of the problem and of the measures that would be required to deal with it. At the beginning of November he had drawn the attention of his colleagues to the necessity for increased coal production and reduced internal consumption over a period of years rather than months.[56] His prognosis was confirmed by a detailed assessment of the situation made for his Conservative successor at the beginning of 1952 by the Economic Section of the Cabinet Office.[57] This predicted that in the calendar year 1952 coal consumption would outstrip production by about 8·5 million tons, and that on current trends 'coal supplies would be even more difficult' over the next two to five years.

The events of 1950 and 1951 demonstrated beyond doubt how illusory had been the apparent security of fuel and power supplies since the end of 1947. They also gave fresh impetus to the exploitation of alternatives to home-produced coal as the almost exclusive energy base for the real-isation of Britain's post-war industrial potential and her economic and social aspirations. It had been quite clear that, when the coal-to-oil conversion programme for industrial plant had been instituted in 1946 and 1947, the government had regarded it as no more than a stop-gap measure, intended to hold the line until the National Coal Board should have revitalised the coal industry to 'produce all the coal required in this country'.[58] This highly desirable state of affairs, the Cabinet Fuel Committee was informed, would be achieved by 1949. Equally clearly, however, the oil companies which − acting through the Petroleum Board until its abolition in June 1948 − had been responsible for promoting coal-to-oil conversion within industry did not see the programme as a temporary expedient. To them it represented a long-term opportunity to expand the demand base of their industry. Under government control of the oil business until 1948 they had been forced to accept − albeit with a struggle[59] − the official view, together with the limits imposed on conversion by the government. Under the much less strict State controls of 1951 they were better able to promote the substitution of their product for coal, not only in industry but in the home. Retained imports of crude and refined petroleum, which had been fluctuating between 17 million and 18 million tons per year from 1948 to 1950, leapt to over 23 million tons in 1951, then continued to rise to over 30 million in 1955.[60] A very large part of this growth represented the substitution of oil for coal in industry, both as a fuel and as a replacement for coal tar as a feedstock for the rapidly developing organic chemical industry.[61] The first tentative steps towards greater dependence on oil that had been taken in 1946−47 became a headlong rush as a result of the crisis of 1950−51.

But perhaps future generations will see as the most important outcome of the fuel crises of 1947 and 1951, in terms of the development of Britain's energy policy and resources and in other respects too, the advent of nuclear power generation. The construction of Britain's first nuclear power station at Calder Hall, Cumberland, was put in hand in 1953, and in 1955 the government promulgated its programme for the construction of twelve such power stations over the next decade as an explicit response to the seemingly intractable shortage of coal.[62] It cannot have been without significance that the development programme for the nuclear power technology on which Calder Hall and the other stations in the initial plan were based had been authorised by the Attlee administration in May 1947.

Appendices

Table 1 Coal production, consumption and stocks ('000 tons): production and consumption, weekly averages; distributed stocks at end of period

Period		Total output (deep-mined + open-cast)	Total consumption (inc. exports and ships' bunkers)	Distributed stocks
1935		4,262	4,262	–
1936		4,369	4,369	–
1937		4,610	4,610	–
1938		4,353	4,353	–
1943		3,815	3,815	17,576
1944		3,688	3,720	16,033
1945		3,506	3,597	12,442
1946		3,646	3,758	8,466
1947		3,787	3,629	16,149
1946	April	3,440	3,616	6,849
	May	3,921	3,727	7,335
	June*	3,586	3,437	8,275
	July	3,492	3,283	9,438
	August	3,065	3,144	9,343
	September*	3,759	3,492	10,320
	October	3,891	3,690	10,878
	November	3,896	3,984	10,397
	December*	3,629	4,069	8,466
1947	January	3,714	4,159	6,700
	February	3,784	4,053	5,519
	March*	3,852	3,905	5,477
	April	3,677	3,553	6,056
	May*	3,800	3,446	8,007
	June*	3,856	3,324	10,638
	July	3,333	3,095	12,122
	August	3,346	3,052	12,842
	September*	3,781	3,354	14,905
	October	4,021	3,607	16,419
	November	4,256	3,964	16,991
	December*	3,792	4,048	16,149
1948	January	4,111	4,276	15,179
	February	4,101	4,370	14,053
	March*	3,908	4,074	13,099
	April	4,247	4,038	13,101
	May	3,927	3,757	13,290
	June*	4,195	3,772	14,609

* Average of five weeks.

Source: CSO, *Monthly Digest of Statistics*.

Table 2 Manpower and productivity in the coal industry (weekly averages)

Period		Wage-earners on colliery books ('000)	Absenteeism (% overall)	Overall output per man shift (tons)
1935		759	6·05	1·17
1936		756	6·29	1·18
1937		778	7·08	1·17
1938		782	6·44	1·14
1943		708	12·42	1·03
1944		710	13·62	1·00
1945		709	16·31	1·00
1946		697	15·95	1·03
1947		712	12·51	1·07
1946	April	698	16·17	1·01
	May	699	14·34	1·03
	June*	699	14·54	1·02
	July	699	15·26	1·00
	August	699	15·64	0·99
	September*	697	16·39	1·03
	October	693	15·19	1·05
	November	692	14·82	1·06
	December*	692	14·51	1·04
1947	January	694	16·69	1·06
	February	697	17·76	1·06
	March*	703	16·13	1·05
	April	710	14·46	1·03
	May*	715	9·77	1·08
	June*	717	9·78	1·09
	July	719	10·53	1·06
	August	719	11·51	1·05
	September*	715	10·89	1·07
	October	714	9·96	1·10
	November	714	10·32	1·13
	December*	718	11·52	1·10
1948	January	720	11·31	1·11
	February	722	11·71	1·11
	March*	723	11·17	1·09
	April	724	10·80	1·10
	May	724	10·57	1·09
	June*	725	10·20	1·11

* Average of five weeks.

Source: CSO, *Monthly Digest of Statistics.*

Notes and references

Chapter 1. The very dead of winter

1 H. Dalton, *Memoirs 1945–1960: High Tide and After* (1962), pp. 74–5.
2 *House of Commons Debates*, 13th December 1945, col. 652–3. The government's case was also vigorously put in the House of Lords by John Maynard Keynes, who had been the chief British negotiator with the Americans on matters economic since 1943.
3 B. R. Mitchell and H. G. Jones, *Second Abstract of British Historical Statistics* (Cambridge, 1971), tables XI/8 (trade and payments), X/7 (industrial output). For the situation elsewhere in Europe see M. M. Postan, *An Economic History of Western Europe, 1945–64* (1967) pp. 11–13.
4 Mitchell and Jones, *Abstract*, table XVI/4.
5 J. Wheeler-Bennett, *King George VI: his Life and Reign* (1958), pp. 652, 654.
6 *Daily Mirror*, Thursday 3rd January 1946.
7 *Daily Mirror*, Friday 4th January 1946.
8 CAB 129/17: *Report by Dr. Magnus Pyke on the Nutrition of the People of Britain in March 1947* (21 March 1947).
9 London and Cambridge Economic Service, *Bulletin*, vol. 24 (July 1946), p. 72.
10 *Daily Mirror*, Thursday 3rd January 1946.
11 Crime figures: A. H. Halsey (ed.), *Trends in British Society since 1900* (1972), chp. 15. The 'spivs' are the subject of an entertaining essay by David Hughes in M. Sissons and P. French (eds.), *The Age of Austerity, 1945–51* (1963).
12 The descriptions of weather conditions in late 1946 and early 1947 which follow owe much to the monthly summaries published in the *Meteorological Magazine*, vol. 76 (1947), pp. 24, 48, 72, 120, and to C. K. M. Douglas, 'The severe winter of 1946–47', *Meteorological Magazine*, vol. 76 (1947), pp. 51–6.
13 *Times*, Thursday 23rd January 1947: during the whole period of severe weather, from late January to mid-March 1947, *The Times* published long and detailed accounts daily – usually on p. 4 – of the state of the weather and its impact on the life of the nation. These reports form the basis of this section, together with C. K. M. Douglas, *Meteorological Magazine* (1947).
14 *Times*, Thursday 6th February 1947.
15 The Huddersfield–Bradford incident is recounted in Sissons and French, *Age of Austerity*, p. 49; the saga of the Penzance–Paddington sleeper was reported in the *Railway Gazette*, 7th February 1947.
16 Quoted in *Times*, Thursday 6th February 1947.
17 *Times*, Friday 14th February 1947.
18 In 1945 93% of Britain's energy needs, in terms of thermal output, were supplied by the combustion of coal: Political and Economic Planning (PEP), *The British Fuel and Power Industries* (1947), table 100, p. 328.
19 CAB 129/17: *Coal and Electricity*, memorandum by the President of the Board of Trade (6th January 1947) gave industrial requirements as 950,000 tons. Deliveries to industry and household consumers are given in PREM 8/443 Pt. 2: *Coal, Deliveries and Stocks*, note by the Minister of Fuel and Power (2nd March 1947). For pre-war household coal consumption see PEP, *Fuel and Power Industries*, p. 337.
20 These were, of course, reported in *The Times*: see especially Monday 10th February 1947, p. 2, for an account of the Minister of Fuel and Power's explanatory press conference. An admirably cogent and succinct account of the measures was given by the *Ministry of Labour Gazette* (March 1947), p. 82. See also CAB 128/9 Cabinet Conclusions, 6th February 1947, min. 3.
21 *Times*, 3rd February 1947, from which the following Ministry of Labour figures also come.
22 Sessional Papers 1943–44, Cmnd 6527.

23 *Ministry of Labour Gazette* (January 1947), p. 21, gives a figure for the UK of 391,148 'wholly unemployed', with 4,804 'temporarily stopped'.
24 *Economic Survey for 1947* (S.P. 1946–47, Cmd 7046), p. 27.
25 *Ministry of Labour Gazette* (February 1947), p. 92.
26 *House of Commons Debates*, 7th February 1947, col. 2161.
27 Particularly from the Labour MPs for Stoke (Ellis Smith) and Kings Norton (R. A. Blackburn): see *House of Commons Debates*, 7th February 1947, cols. 2130–3.
28 Dalton, *High Tide*, pp. 203–5.
29 *Economist*, 10 May 1947, p. 727: 'Fuel crisis post-mortem'.

Chapter 2. A product of history

1 Quoted in *Times*, Tuesday 11th February 1947.
2 Quoted in *Times*, Monday 10th February 1947.
3 *Herbert Morrison: an autobiography by Lord Morrison of Lambeth* (1960), p. 257.
4 *Granada Historical Records Interview: Clem Attlee* (1967), p. 52.
5 E. Shinwell, *Conflict without Malice* (1955), p. 180.
6 *Economist*, 15th February 1947: leading article, 'Mr. Micawber's crisis'.
7 *Times*, Friday 14th February 1947.
8 *Times*, Tuesday 18th February 1947.
9 Douglas Jay, *Change and Fortune: a political record* (1980), p. 143.
10 The account of Britain's coal supply and coal production between 1913 and 1945 which follows is based chiefly on PEP, *British Fuel and Power Industries*; W. H. B. Court, *Coal* (*History of the Second World War*, U.K. Civil Series, HMSO, 1951); M. W. Kirby, *The British Coal Mining Industry, 1870–1946: a political and economic history* (1977); N. K. Buxton and D. H. Aldcroft (eds.), *British Industry between the Wars* (1979).
11 Court, *Coal*, pp. 6–8, gives a brief summary of the 1913 situation.
12 N. K. Buxton, 'Coal mining', in Buxton and Aldcroft (eds.), *British Industry between the Wars*, provides a detailed summary of industrial developments. Valuable insights into the plight of mining communities may be gained from Hilda Jennings, *Brynmawr: a study of a distressed area* (1934) and Pilgrim Trust, *Men without Work* (1938).
13 B. R. Mitchell and P. Deane, *Abstract of British Historical Statistics* (1971), pp. 115–23.
14 The coal supply problems of 1914–18 seem to have been ascribed by contemporaries to labour unrest: Kirby, *Coal Mining Industry*, ch. 2.
15 Central Statistical Office, *Statistical Digest of the War* (*History of the Second World War*: UK Civil series, HMSO, 1950), table 73.
16 CSO, *Statistical Digest*, tables 117, 126, 132.
17 Coal consumption figures from CSO, *Statistical Digest*, table 73; quotation from Kirby, *Coal Mining Industry*, p. 169.
18 Open-cast production: PEP, *Fuel and Power Industries*, pp. 68–71. Stock position: CSO, *Statistical Digest*, table 73.
19 Mitchell and Jones, *Second Abstract*, table IV/2.
20 Kirby, *Coal Mining Industry*, table 8, p. 172.
21 Life as a Bevin Boy is described autobiographically in David Day, *The Bevin Boy* (1975).
22 Court, *Coal*, p. 389.
23 The pattern of distribution is revealed in CSO, *Statistical Digest*, table 74: see also Court, *Coal*, pp. 387–8.
24 Mitchell and Jones, *Second Abstract*, tables IV/7, IV/8, IV/10.
25 Electricity generating: L. Hannah, *Electricity before Nationalisation* (1979), ch. 9; also *Times Survey of Export Industries*, 1st January 1947, p. 14. For the gas industry, PREM 8/443/III, *Gas Industry: Requirements for Plant, etc.* (8 March 1947) and *Times Survey of Export Industries*, p. 20. Coal supplies to gasworks and power stations were increased by 27%, 1939–45: CSO, *Statistical Digest of the War*, table 74.
26 Court, *Coal*, pp. 387, 389.
27 PREM 8/18: Memorandum by the Minister of Fuel and Power, *Budget for the Coal Year 1945–46* (9 March 1945).

28 CAB 71/19: Minutes of the 16th Meeting of the Lord President's Committee, 21 March 1945.
29 Promulgated as the Foot Plan in January 1945: see Kirby, *Coal Mining Industry*, pp. 193–5; R. Eatwell, *The 1945–51 Labour Governments* (1978), p. 56.
30 Letter to *The Times*, quoted in Kirby, *Coal Mining Industry*, p. 191.
31 POWE 20/122: 28 August 1945.
32 PREM 8/18: Prime Minister's personal minute to Minister of Fuel and Power, 7th August 1945.
33 PREM 8/18: Minister of Fuel and Power minute to Prime Minister, 8th August 1945: a copy of Gwilym Lloyd George's memorandum of 9th March was appended.
34 CAB 71/19: Minutes of the 27th Meeting of the Lord President's Committee, 17th August 1945.
35 Shinwell, *Conflict without Malice*, p. 174.
36 PEP, *Fuel and Power Industries*, p. 72: he rapidly changed his mind.
37 CAB 71/19: Minutes of the 32nd Meeting of the Lord President's Committee, 13th September 1945.
38 C. I. Savage, *Inland Transport* (*History of the Second World War*: UK Civil series, HMSO, 1957), p. 634.
39 CAB 78/38: Report by Minister of Fuel and Power to Ministerial Coal Committee, November 1945.
40 CAB 71/19: 35th Meeting of Lord President's Committee; 2nd October 1945, min. 4.
41 CAB 78/38: Ministerial Coal Committee, First Meeting, 4th October 1945.
42 CAB 78/38: Ministerial Coal Committee, Progress Report by Minister of Fuel and Power, November 1945.
43 POWE 18/33: Internal correspondence on house-coal supplies, Ministry of Fuel and Power, 18th January – 29th March 1946.
44 George H. Gallup (Gen. Ed.), *The Gallup International Public Opinion Polls; Great Britain, 1937–75* (New York, 1976), vol. I (1937–64), January – February 1946.
45 CAB 78/38: Ministerial Coal Committee, Third Meeting, 25 March 1946.
46 *House of Commons Debates*, 13th October 1943, cols. 921–2.
47 *House of Commons Debates*, 29th January 1946, col. 751.

Chapter 3. O come, O come, Emanuel!

1 CAB 78/38: Minister of Fuel and Power, Report to the Ministerial Coal Committee, March 1946; also Chancellor (Dalton) to Lord President (Morrison), 30th March 1946.
2 CAB 78/38: Dalton to Morrison, 30 March 1946.
3 Jay, *Change and Fortune*, p. 143.
4 *Monthly Digest of Statistics*, No. 13 (January 1947), table 32.
5 PREM 8/440: Jay to Attlee, 2nd April 1946.
6 *Monthly Digest of Statistics*, No. 24 (December 1947), table 31.
7 *Loc. cit.*
8 CAB 129/10; Cabinet Memorandum CP(46)232, 17th June 1946, appendix.
9 CAB 78/38: Minister of Fuel and Power, Report to the Ministerial Coal Committee, March 1946, para. 3; Proceedings of the Ministerial Coal Committee, 25 March 1946, p. 2.
10 PREM 8/440: Report of the Working Party on Coal Industry Recruitment, 10 July 1946.
11 PREM 8/440: Memorandum from Shinwell to Attlee, 19th September 1946.
12 PREM 8/440: Memorandum from G. Isaacs (Minister of Labour) to Attlee, 27th June 1946.
13 RG 23/85: Social Survey, *Recruitment of Boys to the Mining Industry* (survey conducted August – October 1946). There was particular concern in government and in the coal industry about an acute decline in the recruitment of young men and boys who would be the backbone of the industry's future labour force.
14 PREM 8/440: Jay to Attlee, 30th January 1946; Jay repeated the suggestion in a further minute on 16th February 1946.

15 PREM 8/440: Shinwell to Attlee, 4th March 1946; Sir Ben Smith (Minister of Food) to Attlee, 1st March 1946.
16 CAB 124/716: Proceedings of the Official Coal Committee, 2nd September 1946.
17 See CAB 129/17, Cabinet Memorandum CP(47)6, 16th February 1947; also CAB 128/9, Cabinet Conclusions, 18th February 1947.
18 The definitive version of the Miners' Charter is probably that contained in CAB 129/8, Cabinet Memorandum CP(46)116, March 1946.
19 See, e.g., CAB 128/5, Cabinet Conclusions, 24th June 1946, item 7.
20 CAB 129/8, Cabinet Memorandum CP(46)237 by Minister of Labour, 22nd June 1946.
21 PREM 8/440: Lord President's Committee, Working Party on Foreign Labour, 10th July 1946.
22 PREM 8/440: Jay to Attlee, 16th May 1946: also POWE 20/116, Interdept. Supplementary Labour Comm., papers and correspondence January – May 1946.
23 On the Polish experience of Soviet captivity see, for example, *The Dark Side of the Moon* (London, 1946), B. Mlynarski, *The Seventy-ninth Survivor* (London, 1978). On postwar employment of Poles in coal mining and other British industries see CAB 128/5, Cabinet Conclusions CM(46) 15th meeting, 14th February 1946, item 7; POWE 20/116, Interdept. Supplementary Labour Comm., papers, May – July 1946; POWE 20/117, Official Committee on the Employment of Poles, November 1946 – December 1947.
24 Bertrand de Jouvenel, *Problems of Socialist England* (London, 1948), p. 93.
25 PREM 8/729: Ministerial Coal Committee, 22nd October 1946, item 3.
26 CAB 128/5, Cabinet Conclusions, 14th February 1946, item 7. Compare, e.g., with PREM 8/729, Coal Committee Proceedings, 22nd October 1946, item 3.
27 Jay, *Change and Fortune*, pp. 150–1.
28 On progress in employment of Poles see the reports of the Official Committee on Employment of Poles (POWE 20/117), February – December 1947.
29 PREM 8/440: Jay to Attlee, 6 June 1946: CAB 129/10, Cabinet Memorandum CP(46) 232 by Minister of Fuel and Power, 17th June 1946.
30 CAB 128/5: Cabinet Minutes, 24th June 1946, min. 7. See also CAB 129/10: Cabinet Memoranda, for papers by Isaacs (CP(46)237) and Morrison (CP(46)242).
31 PREM 8/440: Jay to Attlee, 19th June 1946: Jay's final memorandum on the subject as Attlee's private secretary.
32 British Library of Political and Economic Science, Archive Section (BLPES), Meade Diary, vol. 1/6, 27th July 1946, pp. 140–1.
33 PREM 8/440: Attlee to Dalton, 24th July 1946.
34 CAB 129/10, Cabinet Memorandum CP(46)242, 21st June 1946: compare with PREM 8/440, Jay to Attlee, 19th June 1946.
35 Shinwell, *Conflict without Malice*, pp. 180–2.
36 *House of Commons Debates*, 24th July 1946, cols. 68–70.
37 See, for example, his speech in the Coal Situation debate in October: *House of Commons Debates*, 16th October 1946, cols. 921–30.
38 Both *The Times* and *Daily Mirror*, for instance, carried brief reports more or less without comment on 25th October 1946.
39 Shinwell, *Conflict without Malice*, p. 182.
40 CAB 129/10, Cabinet Memorandum CP(46)232, 17th June 1946.
41 PREM 8/440: Lord President's Committee, 19th July 1946.
42 CAB 78/38: *Revised Coal Budget for the Coal Year 1946–47*, 31st July 1946. PREM 8/440: Ministerial Coal Committee minutes, 1st August 1946.
43 PREM 8/729: Ministerial Coal Committee, Memorandum by the Minister of Fuel and Power, *Coal Situation during the Coming Winter*, 17th October 1946.
44 PREM 8/440: Lord President's Committee, 19th July 1946.
45 PREM 8/440: Ministerial Coal Committee, 16th September 1946.
46 PREM 8/440: Jay to Attlee, 2nd April 1946. *Monthly Digest of Statistics*, No. 24 (December 1947), tables 27–31.
47 PREM 8/440: Ministerial Coal Committee, 1st August and 19th September 1946.
48 PREM 8/440: Ministerial Coal Committee, 16th September 1946. *Monthly Digest of Statistics*, No. 24 (December 1947), table 30.
49 *Monthly Digest* (December 1947), tables 27, 32.

50 PREM 8/440, Dalton to Attlee, 17th September 1946. The Coal Committee had met the previous day.
51 *Economist*, 21st September 1946, p. 447.
52 Quoted by *Economist*, 21st September 1946, p. 447.
53 *Economist*, 12th October 1946, p. 594.
54 PREM 8/440: Ministerial Coal Committee, 22nd October 1946.
55 PREM 8/440: Ministerial Coal Committee, 22nd October 1946. PREM 8/729, Shinwell to Attlee, 22nd October 1946.
56 PREM 8/729: Attlee to Shinwell, 29th October 1946.
57 The officials' proposals are given in CAB 129/14, Cabinet Memorandum CP(46)419, *Winter Fuel Supplies to Industry*, 11th November 1946.
58 See Shinwell's covering letter to CP(46)419, together with his own prescription in CAB 129/14, Cabinet Memo. CP(46)423, 19th November 1946.
59 CAB 129/14, Cabinet Memo CP(46)423, 19th November 1946.
60 *News Chronicle*, 4th November 1946.
61 *Economist*, 9th November 1946, p. 739.
62 *House of Commons Debates*, 5th November 1946, col. 1342.
63 *Economist*, 7th December 1946, pp. 903, 919.
64 *Times Survey of Export Industries*, 1st January 1947, pp. 14 (electricity), 20 (gas): this is the source of the quotations about the two industries' capacities in relation to demand. See also CSO, *Monthly Digest*, No. 24 (December 1947) table 32: BT 171/185, Statement by CEB on electricity cuts, November 1946: PREM 8/443/III, *Gas Industry Requirements for Plant, etc.*, 8th March 1947.
65 BT 171/185: Correspondence to Board of Trade, London, From Regional Officers, November 1946: quoted is a letter from the Eastern Regional Board for Industry, 6th November 1946.
66 *Daily Mirror*, 20th December 1946: see also *Economist*, 28th December 1946.
67 The accusation was made by the columnist 'Cassandra', *Daily Mirror*, 24th December 1946: see also Shinwell's view reported in the *Economist*, 28th December 1946, p. 1040.
68 *Economist*, 4th January 1946, p. 32.
69 BT 171/185: Correspondence to Board of Trade, London, from Regional Officers, 31st December 1946 – 1st January 1947: also Summary of Regional Officers' Reports for week ending 4th January 1947.
70 BT 171/185: Teleprinter message, Miss Belson to Board of Trade, London; 1st January 1947.
71 This description of events is based upon *The Times*, 31st December 1946 – 5th January 1947; *Manchester Guardian*, 1st–4th January 1947; *Economist*, 4th January 1947; BT 171/185, correspondence from Regional Board officers to Board of Trade, London, 31st December 1946 – 2nd January 1947.
72 These developments are described in *The Times* and *Manchester Guardian*, 7th–8th January 1947.
73 CAB 129/16: *Coal and Electricity*, memo. by Minister of Fuel and Power, 3rd January 1947. PREM 8/729: Gorell Barnes to Attlee, 6th January 1947, commenting on Shinwell's memorandum.
74 CAB 129/16: CP(47)6, *Coal and Electricity*, Memorandum by the Minister of Fuel and Power, 3rd January 1947.
75 Hercules Cycles Ltd, one of the largest firms in the then substantial midland cycle industry: *Times*, 31st December 1946.
76 BLPES Archive: Dalton Diary, vol. 34, 20th December 1946.
77 *Economist*, 15th February 1947, pp. 265–6; Jay, *Change and Fortune*, pp. 142–51.
78 PREM 8/440: Dalton to Attlee, 28th June 1946: Attlee to Shinwell, 30th June 1946.
79 The peat alternative had first been considered by the Churchill government in 1945: the whole story is documented in POWE 22/197 and 201. See also *Aberdeen Press and Journal*, 18th December 1946.
80 *House of Commons Debates*, 8th April 1946 (Oral Questions).
81 POWE 33/1623: Ministry of Fuel and Power internal memorandum, 7th July 1946.
82 POWE 33/1623: Ministry of Fuel and Power internal memorandum, 27th September 1946.

83 POWE 33/1623: Summary of conversions at end 1946.
84 *House of Commons Debates*, 16th October 1946, col. 928.
85 POWE 33/1623: Joint meeting of officials of Board of Trade, Ministry of Fuel and Power, Ministry of Supply and Petroleum Board, 14th June 1946.
86 POWE 33/1624: letter from Sir A. Agnew (Petroleum Board) to Sir D. Fergusson (Minister of Fuel and Power) on progressing problems, 18th April 1947.
87 CAB 129/14: CP(46)427, *Coal Requirements of the Steel Industry*, Memorandum by Minister of Supply, 15th November 1946.
88 BT 171/185: Teleprint to Board of Trade, London, 1st January 1947.
89 Jay, *Change and Fortune*, p. 149.
90 See Shinwell, *Lead with the Left*, pp. 132–6.
91 *Daily Mirror*, 29th July 1946.
92 *Daily Herald*, 23rd October 1946.

Chapter 4. The times that try men's souls

1 CAB 128/9; Cabinet Minutes, 7th January 1947. The papers tabled were: CAB 129/16: CP(47)6, memorandum by Minister of Fuel and Power, 3rd January 1947; CP(47)15, memorandum by Minister of Transport, 5th January 1947; CP(47)17, memorandum by Lord President; CP(47)18, memorandum by President of the Board of Trade, 6th January 1947. All four were headed *Coal and Electricity*. The Cabinet also considered the proceedings of the Ministerial Coal Committee on 6th January, outlined by Dalton.
2 I.e. Shinwell's December measures, which had come into effect on 1st January 1947. Cripps dismissed their continuation as 'quite impracticable'.
3 CAB 128/9; Cabinet Minutes, 7th January 1947.
4 In Shinwell's preamble he reported an estimated excess of demand over generating capacity for January 1947 of 1·2 million kW. The rated capacity of generating plant available on 30th January was just over 9 million kW (BT 171/186: Analysis of operating conditions in the National Grid system, 6th February 1947). The *actual* excess of peak demand over load delivered on 30th January was 1·8 million kW, or 20%.
5 PREM 8/729: Williams to Attlee, 8th January 1947; an example of the kind of newspaper article that caused Williams such concern may be seen in *Daily Telegraph*, 8th January 1947, which Williams specifically drew to Attlee's attention.
6 *Economist*, 18th January 1947, pp. 114–5; *Times* and *Manchester Guardian*, 14th–15th January 1947.
7 *Times*, 21st January 1947.
8 *Times*, 23rd January 1947.
9 *Economist*, 15th February 1947, p. 265.
10 BT 171/185: Board of Trade Summaries of Regional Reports, 4th and 18th January 1947.
11 BT 171/185: Regional Summary, 4th January 1947.
12 BT 171/185: teleprint, Belson to Pankhurst, 30th January 1947.
13 *Times*, 3rd February 1947.
14 BT 171/185: teleprint, Grassick to Pankhurst, 1st February 1947.
15 CAB 128/9: Cabinet Minutes, 4th February 1947, item 1.
16 CAB 128/9: Cabinet Minutes 7th January – 4th February (exclusive), 1947.
17 CAB 124/1079: *Some Thoughts on the Present Economic Position*, memorandum for President of Board of Trade by Parliamentary Secretary for Overseas Trade (Hilary Marquand), 16th February 1947.
18 Dalton Diary, vol. 35, 5th February 1947; Ellen Wilkinson died the following day.
19 *Ibid.*, 17th January 1947.
20 The new arrangements are discussed in a following section of this chapter.
21 *Times*, 31st January 1947.
22 *Times*, 3rd February 1947.
23 *Times*, 4th February 1947.
24 CAB 128/9: Cabinet Minutes, 4th February 1947.
25 CAB 129/16: CP(47)50, *Dislocation of Coal Supplies through Transport Difficulties*, memorandum by Minister of Fuel and Power, 5th February 1947.

26 *Times*, 6th February 1947.
27 Shinwell seems to have conducted a kind of campaign to embarrass Barnes while improving his own stock in the Cabinet Fuel Committee in Feruary: PREM 8/443/II: A. Johnson to Gorell Barnes, 28th February 1947. For Shinwell's later attitude see especially Shinwell, *I've lived through it all* (1973), p. 194.
28 These matters were examined in CAB 129/16; *Coal and Electricity*, Memorandum by the Minister of Fuel and Power, 3rd January 1947, and *Coal and Electricity*, Memorandum by the Minister of Transport, 5th January 1947.
29 Undistributed coal stocks (i.e. those held at pitheads and an open-cast sites) had fallen from over 5 million tons in 1939 to less than 3 million at the end of 1945 (CSO, *Statistical Digest of the War*, table 73). By December 1946 they stood at less than 1·75 million, officially described for the most pat as being 'of inferior quality' (CSO, *Monthly Digest*, No. 24, December 1947, table 25, which gives average weekly stock levels for October 1946 and succeeding months).
30 *Times*, 6th February 1947; *Railway Gazette*, 7th March 1947, p. 200.
31 PREM 8/729: A. Barnes to Attlee, 24th February 1947: also Graham-Harrison to Attlee, 24th and 26th February 1947.
32 Railway coal supplies: *Railway Gazette*, 7th March 1947, p. 200. PREM 8/443/II: Shinwell to Fuel Committee, 26th February 1947; A. Barnes to Fuel Committee, 28th February 1947.
33 Railway maintenance, etc., problems: *Railway Gazette*, 14th March 1947, p. 231: *Economic Survey for 1947* (1946–47, Cmd 7046), p. 23; PREM 8/443/II; A. Barnes to Fuel Committee, 28th February 1947.
34 CAB 128/9: Cabinet Minutes, 6th February 1947.
35 CAB 128/9: Cabinet Minutes, 7th February 1947.
36 Dalton Diary, vol. 35, 7th February 1947.
37 *House of Commons Debates*, 7th February 1947.
38 *Times*, 10th February 1947.
39 *Times*, 11th February 1947.
40 *Times*, 10th February 1947.
41 *House of Commons Debates*, 7th February 1947, cols. 2130–9.
42 Dalton Diary, vol. 35, 7th–10th February 1947; quotation from entry for 7th February.
43 PREM 8/426: minute, Gorell Barnes to Attlee, 11th February 1947; see also PREM 8/426: Cabinet Fuel Committee, note by the Cabinet Secretary, 12th February 1947.
44 PREM 8/443/I: note to Prime Minister, initialled T.L.R., 11th February 1947. The credit for the idea of the Fuel Committee may be said properly to belong to the writer of this note rather than to Gorell Barnes.
45 The sub-committee consisted of Cripps (chairman), Shinwell, Alfred Barnes (Transport) and George Isaacs (Labour), with others attending by invitation. PREM 8/426: *Cabinet Fuel Committee*, note by Cabinet Secretary, 12th February 1947.
46 For these subsidiary arrangements see PREM 8/443/I: Fuel Committee, first meeting, 12th February 1947, item 1, 'Work of the Committee'. For convenience, future references to the Fuel Committee minutes will be expressed in abbreviated form, e.g. FC(47) 1st mtg., 12th February, item 1.
47 P. M. Williams, *Hugh Gaitskell: a political biography* (1979), p. 137.
48 FC(47) 1st mtg., 12th February.
49 FC(47) 2nd mtg., 14th February, item 1.
50 *Times*, 24th February 1947; FC(47) 8th mtg., 28th February, item 2. The Gas Council thought the government was exaggerating the danger to gas supplies; in its view 'there was no crisis in the stock position of gas coal' (*Times*, 25th February).
51 *Ministry of Labour Gazette*, vol. 55 (1947), p. 92.
52 FC(47) 3rd and 4th mtgs., 18th/21st February.
53 FC(47) 2nd mtg., 14th February, item 2.
54 *Railway Gazette*, 7th March 1947, p. 200.
55 FC(47) 4th and 5th mtgs., 21st/24th February, item 1 in each.
56 FC(47) 1st mtg., 12th February, item 2(i).
57 FC(47) 1st mtg., 12th February, item 2(k).

58 Details of coal stocks at power stations and gasworks from daily situation report produced for the Fuel Committee by the Ministry of Fuel and Power, filed in PREM 8/443/I. Particularly useful are reports numbered 2 (13th February) and 11 (22nd February).
59 FC(47) 3rd mtg., 18th February, item 2; 4th mtg., 21st February, item 1.
60 PREM 8/443/II: *Coal Deliveries and Stocks*, note by Minister of Fuel and Power (n.d., but probably 28th February).
61 FC(47) 3rd mtg., 18th February item 2.
62 PREM 8/443/II: *Coal Deliveries and Stocks*, c. 28th February; FC(47) 8th mtg., 28th February, summary of decisions.
63 CAB/128/9: Cabinet Minutes, 14th February 1947. FC(47) 2nd mtg., 14th February, item 4. PREM 8/516, personal letter from Léon Blum to Attlee, 1 January 1947. T230/23: *Coal*, paper by A.J. Brown (Economic Section), 2nd December 1946, detailing the seriousness of the European coal shortage. Brown calculated the excess of demand over supply in Western Europe in 1946 at 140−50 million tons.
64 CSO, *Monthly Digest of Statistics*, vol. 24 (December 1947), tables 27, 30, 31.
65 FC(47) 6th mtg., 25th February, item 1(c).
66 *Board of Trade Journal*, 29th March 1947, p. 482.
67 FC(47) 1st mtg., 12th February, item 2.
68 FC(47) 2nd mtg., 14th February, item 1.
69 FC(47) 8th mtg., 28th February, item 2.
70 *Railway Gazette*, 7th March 1947, p. 200. FC(47) 3rd mtg., 18th February, item 1(e).
71 FC(47) 8th mtg., 28th February, item 2(c).
72 FC(47) 6th mtg., 25th February, item 1(e).
73 FC(47) 3rd mtg., 18th February, item 2(c); 4th mtg., 21st February, item 1(1); 8th mtg., 28th February, item 2(1).
74 FC(47) 3rd mtg., 18th February, item 2; 4th mtg., 21 February, items 2−3.
75 FC(47) 5th mtg., 24th February, items 2−4; 6th mtg., 25th February, items 2−3.
76 FC(47) 7th mtg., 27th February.
77 *Times*, 25th−6th February, 1 March 1947.
78 FC(47) 3rd mtg., 18th February, item 2.
79 POWE 10/426: Ministry of Fuel and Power internal minute, R.J.G. to D.M., 19th February 1947.
80 POWE 10/426: F. Johnston (Regional Controller, Newcastle) to D. Moffat (Fuel and Power, London), 15th February 1947.
81 POWE 10/426: E. Cadbury (Regional Controller, Bristol) to D. Moffat (London), 19th February, 1947.
82 *Times*, 13th February 1947; FC(47), 1st mtg., 12th February.
83 CAB 128/9: Cabinet Minutes, 10th February 1947.
84 PREM 8/443/I: note from R. Kelf Cohen to Minister of Fuel and Power on technical problems of restricting power supplies, 7th February 1947.
85 FC(47) 1st mtg., 12th February, item 2(g).
86 FC(47) 3rd mtg., 18th February, item 2(b); 8th mtg., 28th February, item 2(b).
87 See, e.g., FC(47) 2nd and 4th mtgs. 14th/21st February.
88 See, e.g., FC(47) 4th mtg., 21st February, item 1.

Chapter 5.   Overdoing the joke

1 *Gallup International Public Opinion Polls: Great Britain, 1937−75*, vol. I, January and June 1946.
2 Ibid., January 1947.
3 POWE 18/33, Innes to Fergusson, 1st March 1946: *Monthly Digest*, No. 24, December 1947, table 28.
4 Mitchell and Jones, *Second Abstract*, p. 71.
5 Data on benefit from K.O. Morgan, *Labour in Power, 1945−51* (1984), p. 171: on earnings from Mitchell and Jones, *op. cit.*, p. 148.
6 FC(47) 1st mtg., 12th February 1947, item 2(j).

7 *Manchester Evening News*, 31st January 1947, reporting the case of J. Dewhurst and Co.

8 *Loc. cit.*

9 *Times*, 8th January 1947.

10 *Manchester Evening News*, 21st–5th January 1947.

11 Mass Observation, file report No. 2483, *Fuel Crisis* (May 1947), p. 13. Hereafter cited as MO 2483.

12 FC(47) 1st mtg., 12th February 1947, item 2(j).

13 Mass Observation, file report No. 2468, *Fuel Crisis: Gains and Losses* (1947). Hereafter cited as MO 2468.

14 POWE 10/426: Instruction to Regional Officers, 17th February 1947.

15 MO 2483, 15; see also pp. 10, 14. PREM 8/443/II: Note by Interdepartmental Policy Committee, 27th February 1947.

16 All examples drawn from MO 2468.

17 *Manchester Evening News*, 29th January 1947.

18 MO 2483, p. 16.

19 *Ibid.*, p. 17. I am indebted to Mrs Anne Whittaker of Sale, Cheshire, for the story of the shoes. For the briquettes and the quotation, see MO 2483, p. 15.

20 *Manchester Evening News*, 31st January 1947.

21 Registrar General, *Statistical Review of England and Wales for the Years 1946, 1947: Tables* (HMSO, annually, 1948, 1949), tables 4 and 23 in each annual volume. Also Registrar General, *Statistical Review of England and Wales for the two Years 1946 and 1947: Text, vol. I, Medical* (1951), pp. 13–14.

22 MO 2483, p. 15.

23 *Ibid.*, pp. 11, 13.

24 Emigration was a regular subject of written and oral parliamentary questions from March 1947 onwards: see especially *Commons Debates*, 3rd March 1947, cols. 22–3; 30th October 1947, col. 1082; 22nd January 1948, cols. 361–2; 3rd February 1948, cols. 264–6 (written answer). *Times*, 2nd July 1947, reported Arthur Calwell's press conference: he was in London to try to persuade the British government to release more shipping.

25 *Picture Post*, 19th April 1947 (special issue: 'Britain in Crisis'), pp. 10–11.

26 *Manchester Evening News*, 31st January–1st February 1947.

27 Mass Observation, file report No. 2461B, *Who are the Fuel Wasters?* (February 1947), p. 8. Hereafter cited as MO 2461B.

28 *Times*, 11 February 1947.

29 MO 2483, pp. 21–4.

30 MO 2461B, p. 9.

31 POWE 10/426: teleprints to Ministry of Fuel and Power, London, 20th January 1947.

32 PREM 8/443/III: Fuel Committee, *Report on the Fuel Situation*, 10th March 1947.

33 PREM 8/443/III: Fuel Committee, *Fortnightly Report on the Fuel Situation*, 1st April 1947.

34 *Ministry of Labour Gazette*, vol. 55, March 1947, p. 82.

35 FC(47) 4th mtg., 21st February 1947, item 1: see also POWE 10/426, teleprint Scottish Region (Edinburgh) to Ministry of Fuel and Power, London, 20th February 1947.

36 FC(47) 6th mtg., 25th February 1947, item 1.

37 FC(47) 8th mtg., 28th February 1947, item 6.

38 PREM 8/443/II: Gorell Barnes to Attlee, 27th February 1947.

39 PREM 8/443/IV: *Economies in Domestic Consumption of Gas and Electricity*, Memo. by Minister of Fuel and Power, 15th July 1947: *Times*, 23rd April 1947.

40 FC(47) 9th mtg., 3rd March 1947, item 1.

41 PREM 8/443/III: *Fortnightly Report on the Fuel Situation*, 1st April 1947, table 5.

42 *Times Educational Supplement*, 22nd February 1947, p. 6.

43 MO 2468.

44 POWE 26/451: National Greyhound Racing Association to Minister of Fuel and Power, 18th February 1947.

45 CAB 128/9: Cabinet Minutes, 13th March 1947, item 6.
46 CAB 132/1: Lord President's Committee Minutes, 27th September 1946: see also FC(47) 10th mtg., 4th March 1947, item 4.
47 FC(47) 10th mtg., 4th March 1947, item 4; CAB 128/9, Cabinet Minutes, 13th March 1947, item 6.
48 *Times*, 17th February 1947.

Chapter 6   Come were but the spring

1 *Times*, 7th March 1947.
2 *Meteorological Magazine*, vol. 76 (1947), p. 54.
3 *Times*, 17th March 1947.
4 *Meteorological Magazine* (1947), pp. 120, 144.
5 Both quotations from MAF 222/136: Ministry of Agriculture and Fisheries press statement (undated, but probably 15th June 1947).
6 MAF 222/101: Thames Conservancy Report, May 1947; *Times* 13th–19th March 1947.
7 *Times*, 17th, 26th March 1947.
8 *Times*, 17th, 19th, 20th, 24th, 25th, 26th, 31st March 1947.
9 *Times*, 24th, 31st March; 5th, 14th April 1947.
10 *Times*, 25th March 1947.
11 MAF 222/136: Ministry of Agriculture and Fisheries press statement: *Times*, 18th March 1947.
12 Gasworks and power-station coal consumption: PREM 8/443/III; Fuel Committee fortnightly situation reports, 1st April and 29th April 1947, table 5 in each. Summer Time: FC(47) 4th mtg., 21st February 1947, item 2.
13 FC(47) 14th mtg., 20th March 1947, item 2; 17th mtg., 21st April 1947, item 1.
14 FC(47) 15th mtg., 2nd April 1947, item 6.
15 PREM 8/489/I: *Food Import Programme*, Memo. by Minister of Food, 31st May 1947.
16 CAB 129/17: CP(47) 99, Report to Cabinet by Dr M. Pyke, 21st March 1947.
17 CAB 128/6: Cabinet Minutes, 31st October 1946, item 6.
18 *Times*, 3rd March 1947.
19 Details from MAF 82/197: Ministry of Agriculture, *Monthly Reports on Agricultural Conditions in England and Wales*, October 1946 to February 1947.
20 MAF 82/197: Ministry of Agriculture, *Monthly Report*, 10th March 1947.
21 Around Gainsborough, Lincs.; *Times*, 31st March 1947.
22 *Times*, 25th March 1947.
23 Details from CAB 129/18: CP(47) 128: *Home Production of Food*, Memorandum by Minister of Agriculture, 18th April 1947.
24 MAF 222/136: Text of Ministerial Broadcast, 2nd April 1947.
25 PREM 8/509: Report from Central Statistical Office to Lord President's Committee, annexed to L.P. Committee Minutes, 7th March 1947. Personal Minutes, P.M. to Dalton, 10th March 1947; Dalton to P.M., 14th March 1947.
26 CAB 128/6: Cabinet Minutes, 4th November 1946, item 5. CAB 129/17: *Exhaustion of the Dollar Credit*, Memo. by Chancellor of the Exchequer, 21st March 1947.
27 Compensation arrangements: CAB 128/9: Cabinet Minutes, 25th March 1947, item 9; 1st April 1947, item 9. *Times*, 26th and 31st March, 5th April 1947.
28 Lord Mayor's Fund: *Times*, 29th March and 30th April 1947. Criticism of royal tour: Mass Observation file report No. 2483, pp. 13–14; PREM 8/454, Appendix to telegram from Sir A. Lascelles to Attlee, 6th March 1947. It appears that the King had suggested cutting short his tour and returning to face the vicissitudes of the weather and fuel shortage with his subjects. But Attlee advised against it (PREM 8/454: telegram, Attlee to Lascelles, 4th March 1947).
29 CAB 129/18: *Home Food Production*, Memo. by Minister of Agriculture, 18th April 1947.
30 FC(47) 11th and 12th mtgs., 7th March 1947.
31 BT 171/186: *Fuel Position of Board of Trade Industries*, 8th March 1947.

32 BT 171/186: *Interim arrangements for deliveries of coal to industry*, teleprint to Regional Board Chairman, 7th March 1947.

33 BT 171/186: Teleprint from B.T. London, to Regional Board chairmen, 10th March 1947.

34 BT 171/186: *Fuel Position of Board of Trade Industries*, 8th March 1947.

35 BT 171/186: Teleprints to B.T., London, from B.T., Manchester (14th March 1947), and B.T., Bristol (13th March 1947).

36 BT 171/186: *Fuel Position of Board of Trade Industries*, 15th March 1947. *Times*, 11th March 1947.

37 FC(47) 15th mtg., 2nd April 1947, item 3.

38 *Times*, 11th April 1947.

39 *Loc. cit.*

40 BT 171/186: *Fuel Position of Board of Trade Industries*, 12th April 1947.

41 FC(47) 1st mtg., 12th February 1947, item 1.

42 PREM 8/443/I: *Plans for avoiding a Fuel Crisis in the Winter of 1947–48*, Memorandum for Fuel Committee by Prime Minister, 17th February 1947.

43 PREM 8/443/I: Fuel Committee Memoranda by Fergusson (FC(47)10) and Shinwell (FC(47)14), 21st February 1947.

44 PREM 8/443/II: Gorell Barnes to Attlee on Fergusson's FC(47)10, 27th February 1947.

45 PREM 8/443/II: *Generating plant in relation to anticipated demand*, Memo. for Fuel Committees by CEB Chairman, 26th February 1947. PREM 8/443/III: *Gas industry plant requirements*, Memo. for Fuel Committee by Minister of Fuel and Power, 8th March 1947.

46 FC(47) 6th mtg., 25th February 1947, item 3(c).

47 PREM 8/443/I: *Scheme for domestic and non-industrial fuel rationing*, 22nd February 1947.

48 On attitudes to the Watkinson scheme see PREM 8/443/II: Gorell Barnes to Attlee, 25th February and 6th March 1947: Fuel Committee paper by Minister of Fuel and Power (FC(47)36), 5th March 1947: Prime Minister's paper on 1947–48 Coal Budget (FC(47) 37), 6th March 1947.

49 FC(47) 17th mtg., 21st April 1947, item 1; announced in *Times*, 25th April 1947.

50 *Times*, 25th April 1947.

51 INF 2/135: Domestic Fuel Saving Campaign Report, 1947.

52 FC(47) 17th mtg., 21st April 1947, item 1.

53 *Times*, Budget Report, 16th April 1947.

54 FC(47) 4th, 6th, 10th, 12th and 15th mtgs., 21st February–2nd April 1947.

55 CAB 129/18: *Coal for industry during the summer*, Memorandum for Fuel Committee by President of Board of Trade, 17th April 1947, appended to *Coal Allocations to Industry*, Memo. for Cabinet by Cabinet Secretary (Sir N. Brook), 28th April 1947.

56 CAB 128/9: Cabinet Minutes, 28th April 1947, item 1; 1st May 1947, item 4.

57 *Times*, 29th April 1947.

58 FC(47) 11th mtg., 7th March 1947; *Times*, 28th March 1947.

59 PREM 8/443/I: *Plans for avoiding a fuel crisis in the winter of 1947–48*, 17th February 1947.

60 POWE 33/1624: Report on Coal/Oil Conversion for Minister of Fuel and Power by B. J. Ellis (MFP Petroleum Division), 5th March 1947. Also internal Petroleum Division correspondence, 4th–10th March 1947, between Ellis, F. Hemming and V. Butler.

61 POWE 33/1624: Ellis to Hemming and Butler, 10th March 1947.

62 POWE 33/1624: Ministry of Fuel and Power internal correspondence between Ellis, Burgoyne and Butler, 10th April 1947.

63 POWE 33/1624: *Coal/Oil Conversion Programme*, Memo. for Fuel Committee by Minister of Fuel and Power, 14th April 1947.

64 FC(47) 17th mtg., 21st April 1947, item 4.

65 FC(47) 13th, 16th, 17th mtgs., 14th March–21st April 1947.

66 PREM 8/443/I: *Plans for avoiding ...*, 17th February 1947. CSO, *Monthly Digest*, 24 (December 1947) table 29.

67 PREM 8/443/I: Gorell Barnes to Attlee, 21st February 1947.

68 CAB 129/17: *Inducements to Coal Miners*: Memo. by Minister of Food, 16th February 1947.

69 INF 12/65: Central Office of Information Home Production Conferences, January–June 1947.
70 CSO, *Monthly Digest*, 24 (December 1947), table 29.
71 *Ibid.*, table 28.
72 CAB 128/9: Cabinet Minutes, 18th April 1947, item 2; 25th April 1947, item 8.

Chapter 7   The end of it all

1 T 229/9: *Report of the Export Target Committee*, 31st July 1947, para. 2.
2 CAB 129/18: *Coal for Industry during the Summer*, Memo. by President of the Board of Trade, 17th April 1947, para. 4.
3 *Economist*, 10th May 1947, p. 727; CSO, *Monthly Digest*, 30 (June 1948), table 23.
4 CSO, *Monthly Digest*, 30 (June 1948), table 23.
5 PREM 8/443/III: FC(47) 17th mtg., 21st April 1947, item 3.
6 1946–47, Cmd 7046, para. 81.
7 CAB 124/1044: BPWP (47) 1, *Import Programme, 1947–48*, 18th April 1947.
8 For an authoritative account see A. K. Cairncross, *Years of Recovery: British economic policy, 1945–51* (1985), Ch. VI.
9 *House of Commons Debates*, 8th July 1947, col. 2150.
10 CAB 129/19: *Balance of Payments*, Memo. by Chancellor 28th May 1947. See also CAB 124/1044: *Import Programme, 1947–48* prepared by Treasury Economic Section, 3rd May 1947.
11 For Attlee's view see *House of Commons Debates*, 6th August 1947, col. 1506. Also T 267/3: Sir Hugh Ellis-Rees, *The Convertibility Crisis of 1947* (Treasury Historical Memo., No. 4, 1962).
12 Cairncross, *op. cit.*, p. 366, note 38.
13 T 229/9: Central Economic Planning Staff, internal correspondence and memoranda, April–July 1947: see especially Cairncross to Plowden, 3rd June 1947; Andrew to Weeks, 25th June 1947.
14 T 229/9: Cairncross to Plowden, 3rd June 1947.
15 *Annual Statement of Trade of the United Kingdom for the Year 1947* (HMSO 1949), abstract tables 2 and 3.
16 Cairncross, *op. cit.*, p. 366, note 38.
17 *Ibid.*, p. 375.
18 PREM 8/443/II: Daily Fuel Situation Report, 1st March 1947.
19 CAB 129/16: *Coal and Electricity*, Memo. by Minister of Fuel and Power, 3rd January 1947. See also P. Williams, *Hugh Gaitskell*, p. 136.
20 For details see Fuel Committee daily fuel situation reports (PREM 8/443/I–II), 12th February to 1st March 1947.
21 FC(47) 1st mtg., 12th February 1947, item 1(k).
22 *Loc. cit.*
23 Fuel savings at power stations achieved in areas where *only* domestic and non-industrial restrictions applied ('White Areas'), 10th–28th February 1947; and in 'Black Areas' after industrial restrictions had been lifted, 28th February to 9th March 1947. The base against which savings were calculated was that of week ending 9th February 1947. See Fuel Committee daily situation reports.
24 PREM 8/516: Blum to Attlee, 1st January 1947. T 230/25: *Coal*, Cabinet Secretariat discussion paper by A. J. Brown, 10th June 1947 (first draft 2nd December 1946).
25 Even before the second world war, household electricity consumption had been much more severely restricted in most Continental countries than in Britain, by the use of very expensive tariffs and technical devices for limiting domestic loads. In particular, the use of electricity for domestic space-heating was almost unknown in Western Europe. See I. M. D. Little, *The Price of Fuel* (1953), ch. VI.
26 PREM 8/440: Jay to Attlee, 2nd April, 16th May, 19th June 1946.
27 *Gallup International Polls, 1937–75*, August 1946–May 1947.
28 MO 2483, pp. 4–8, 34.

29 F.W.S. Craig, *British Electoral Facts, 1885–1975* (1976).
30 *Picture Post*, 19th April 1947, p.11.
31 MO 2483, p.28.
32 F.W.S. Craig, *British Parliamentary Election Results, 1918–49* (1969) and *1950–70* (1971), pp.346 and 374 respectively. Boundary changes after the 1945 election left Shinwell with a slightly smaller constituency. He continued to hold the revised seat with huge majorities (25,000–27,000) until his retirement in 1970.
33 Harris, *Attlee*, p.336.
34 Comment on nationalisation: MO 2483, p.35, and MO 2997, pp.1–2. Nature of reactions: MO 2483, p.40.
35 *Ibid.*, pp.39–40.
36 Dalton, *High Tide and After*, p.205.

Chapter 8   The more distant prospects

1 PREM 8/443/I: *Coal Position, 1947–48*, memorandum for Fuel Committee by Minister of Fuel and Power, 21st February 1947.
2 PREM 8/443/III: Fuel Committee Fortnightly Situation Report, 29th April 1947. Gorell Barnes to Attlee, 2nd May 1947.
3 PREM 8/443/IV: Gorell Barnes to Attlee, 11–12 August 1947.
4 PREM 8/443/IV: *Revised Coal Budget, Winter 1947–48*, 27th September 1947.
5 PREM 8/443/IV: Gorell Barnes to Attlee, 1st October 1947. For inflow and outflow of labour see CSO, *Monthly Digest*, No.24 (December 1947), table 28.
6 CSO, *Monthly Digest*, No.36 (December 1948), table 25.
7 *Ibid.*, table 25.
8 Polish recruitment – POWE 20/117: Official Committee on Employment of Poles, *Placings in Employment*, 13th December 1947. Polish complaints: OCEP 19th mtg., 14th October 1947. On Irish defections: CAB 128/10: Cabinet Minutes, 17th August 1947, min.3.
9 RG 23/129A: *Men and Mining* by G. Thomas, based on fieldwork in February 1948.
10 Mass Observation Survey Report No.2585 (MO 2585), *Survey of Opinion in London on Miners*, published April 1948.
11 PREM 8/443/IV: Fuel Committee, 1st October 1947, item 1. CSO, *Monthly Digest*, 36 (December 1948), table 29.
12 *Ibid.*, table 28.
13 The record of these discussions is to be found in CAB 124/741: *Coal Productivity Campaign*, correspondence and papers, July–September 1947.
14 Mass Observation Survey Report No.2997 (MO 2997), *The Miner on the Hearth*, April 1948, pp.8–9.
15 CAB 128/10: Cabinet Minutes, 17th August 1947, min. 2.
16 CAB 128/10: Cabinet Minutes, 25th September 1947, min. 6.
17 CSO, *Monthly Digest*, No.36 (December 1948) table 28.
18 Problems of coal industry mechanisation, see PREM 8/443/III: *Coal Production*, memorandum by Minister of Fuel and Power, 12th March 1947. Also POWE 33/1624: Lord Hyndley (NCB) to Attlee, 4th March 1947.
19 PREM 8/443/III: Preliminary Report on the Effect of the Five Day Week, 4th June 1947.
20 Absenteeism and shift-work figures from CSO, *Monthly Digest*, No.36, table 28.
21 CAB 128/12: Cabinet Minutes, 6th May 1948, min. 6. POWE 33/1625: Llewellyn to Burgoyne, 15th December 1947.
22 POWE 33/1625: Meeting on Fuel Oil Transport Requirements, 21st July 1947.
23 CAB 128/10: Cabinet Minutes, 18th December 1947. POWE 33/1625: B. White (Federation of British Industry) to G.L. Watkinson (Min. Fuel), 7th October 1947; Press Statement by Parlt. Secy. Min. Fuel and Power (A. Robens), 18th December 1947.
24 INF 2/135: Domestic Fuel Saving Campaign Report prepared for Central Office of Information by F.C. Pritchard, Wood and Partners. This file includes the Social Survey investigation report by D. Ginsburg.

25 All figures from CSO, *Monthly Digest*, No. 36, table 25. Consumption includes the small amounts of coal allocated to exports and ships' bunkers.
26 *Meteorological Magazine*, vol. 76 (1947), p. 214.
27 *Ibid.*, p. 238.
28 PREM 8/443/III: Fuel Committee, 6th June 1947, item 1.
29 PREM 8/443/IV: Fuel Committee Fortnightly Situation Reports, 11 June to 1st October 1947.
30 Stock figures: CSO, *Monthly Digest*, No. 36, table 27.
31 *Meteorological Magazine*, vol. 77 (1948), p. 141.
32 PREM 8/443/IV: Fuel Committee, 1st October 1947, item 1.
33 PREM 8/443/II: *Generating Plant relative to Anticipated Demand*, Note for Fuel Committee by Chairman of CEB, 26th February 1947.
34 L. Hannah, *Electricity before Nationalisation* (1979), pp. 322–3.
35 *Loc. cit.*
36 CAB 128/13: Cabinet Minutes, 15th July 1948, min. 4.
37 Hannah, *op. cit.*, p. 322.
38 POWE 37/54: *State of the Nation: Gas and Coke Ovens*, 3rd January 1952. T. I. Williams, *A History of the British Gas Industry* (1981), pp. 118–9.
39 Morgan, *Labour in Power*, p. 480.
40 CAB 128/15: Cabinet Minutes, 20th January 1949, min. 5; 28th March 1949, min. 2.
41 CAB 129/37/I: Chancellor's Economic Report, 4th November 1949.
42 CAB 129/38: Chancellor's Economic Report, 24th March 1950.
43 POWE 37/256: Cleaver (Min. Fuel Coal Division) to Parlt. Secy., Min. Fuel and Power, 26th August 1950.
44 CAB 129/42: Chancellor's Economic Report, 27th October 1950.
45 CAB 128/18: Cabinet Minutes, 6th November 1950.
46 CAB 128/18: Cabinet Minutes, 16th November 1950, min. 5, discussion of Official Committee report (CP(50)271).
47 CAB 128/18: Cabinet Minutes, 16th November 1950 and 17th November 1950. Discussion of the point spanned two consecutive meetings.
48 CAB 128/19: Cabinet Minutes, 15th January 1951. The St Leger was moved to a Saturday; mid-week soccer was also discouraged.
49 CAB 128/18: Cabinet Minutes, 4th December 1950, min. 5. Also POWE 37/54: *Coal Production: Report to Cabinet*, 15th January 1952.
50 CAB 128/18: Cabinet Minutes, 17th November 1950.
51 CAB 128/18: Cabinet Minutes, 4th December 1950. The suggestion came from the Minister of Fuel and Power.
52 A selection of press reactions to the whole affair is to be found in POWE 37/256: Daily Press Digest No. 720.
53 The crisis of 1950–51 set in train a number of critiques of coal and fuel policy and management. The Committee on National Policy for the Use of Fuel and Power Resources (the Ridley Committee) reported in 1952 (*Report*, 1952, Cmd 8647). See also Little, *Price of Fuel*.
54 *Gallup Polls, Great Britain*, vol. I (1937–64): polls on the government's record, August and December 1950, February, April, September 1951. On the coal issue in the 1951 general election see D. E. Butler, *The British General Election of 1951* (1952), pp. 54–56, 67.
55 CAB 128/19: Cabinet Minutes, 1st February 1951, min. 3.
56 CAB 128/18: Cabinet Minutes, 6th November 1950.
57 POWE 37/54: *Coal Production*, 15th January 1952.
58 PREM 8/443/III: Fuel Committee, 6th June 1947, item 4.
59 It seems, for example, that, after the Ministry of Fuel and Power suspended consideration of new applications for conversion, the Petroleum Board went on canvassing for new projects: POWE 33/1624 J. Burgoyne to B. J. Ellis, 19th May 1947.
60 Mitchell and Jones, *Second Abstract*, p. 75.
61 G. C. Allen, *British Industries and their Organisation* (5th edn 1970), p. 210.
62 M. Gowing, *Independence and Deterrence: Britain and atomic energy, 1945–1952*, vol. I (1974), pp. 189–93.

Bibliography

1. Archive material

(a) Public Record Office, Kew (PRO)

Board of Trade
BT 171 (Regional Division)

Cabinet
CAB 71 (Lord President's Committee, 1945)
CAB 78 (Ministerial Coal Committee, 1945–46)
CAB 124 (Official Coal Committee, 1946; Ministerial Committee, 1946–47)
CAB 128 (Cabinet Minutes, 1945–51)
CAB 129 (Cabinet Memoranda, 1945–51)
CAB 132 (Lord President's Committee, 1946)
CAB 134 (Home Information Services)

Central Office of Information
INF 2 (Publicity campaigns)
INF 8 (Monthly Divisional Reports)
INF 12 (Home Production Conference)
RG 23 (The Social Survey)

Ministry of Agriculture
MAF 82 (Monthly Agricultural Reports)
MAF 222 (Press Statements)

Ministry of Fuel and Power
POWE 10 (Internal correspondence)
POWE 16 (Open-cast coal)
POWE 18 ⎫
POWE 20 ⎬ Coal Division papers ⎧ Distribution
POWE 22 ⎭ ⎨ Labour
⎩ Production
POWE 26 (Miscellaneous papers)
POWE 33 (Petroleum Division)
POWE 37 (General files)

Prime Minister's Office
PREM 8 (Correspondence and papers, 1945–51)

Treasury
T 172 (Treasury discussion papers)
T 229 (Central Economic Planning)
T 230 (Economic Section)
T 267 (Historical Memoranda)

(b) Britsh Library of Political and Economic Science

Diary of Lord Dalton of Forest and Frith (Hugh Dalton, Chancellor of the Exchequer, 1945–47): vol. 33 (July–December 1945)–vol. 36 (January–December 1948)

Meade Papers (Professor J. E. Meade, Director, Treasury Economic Section): Files 1/6–1/7 (1946–47).

(c) Tom Harrisson Mass Observation Archive, University of Sussex: File Reports

2461B *Who are the Fuel Wasters?* (February 1947)
2468   *Fuel Crisis: Gains and Losses* (April 1947)
2483   *Fuel Crisis* (May 1947)
2585   *Survey of London Opinion* (April 1948)
2997   *The Miner on the Hearth* (May 1948)

2. Parliamentary and official publications

Annual Statement of Trade of the United Kingdom for the Year 1947 (1949).
Board of Trade Journal.
Brazell, J. H., *London Weather* (Meteorological Office, 1968).
Central Statistical Office, *Monthly Digest of Statistics.*
Economic Survey for 1947 (1946−47, Cmd 7046).
History of the Second World War: UK Civil Series
    Central Statistical Office, *Statistical Digest of the War* (1951).
    Court, W. H. B., *Coal* (1951).
    Payton-Smith, D. J., *Oil: a Study of Wartime Policy and Administration* (1971).
    Savage, C. I., *Inland Transport* (1957).
House of Commons Debates (Hansard, fifth series).
Ministry of Labour Gazette.
Registrar General, *Statistical Review of England and Wales for the Years 1946 and 1947: Text*, vol.I, *Medical* (1951); *Tables* (1948−49).
Report of the Coal Mining Technical Advisory Committee (Reid Committee: 1944−45, Cmd 6610).
Report of the Committee on National Policy for the Use of Fuel and Power Resources (Ridley Committee: 1952−53, Cmd 8647).

3. Contemporary newspapers and periodicals

(a) **Newspapers**

Aberdeen Press and Journal, Daily Herald, Daily Mirror, Daily Telegraph, Glasgow Herald, Manchester Evening News, Manchester Guardian, News Chronicle, Sunday Times, The Times.

(b) **Periodicals**:

Bulletin of the Oxford University Institute of Statistics (vol. 9, 1947), *Economist, Farmer and Stockbreeder*, London and Cambridge Economic Service *Bulletin* (vols.24−6, 1946−48), *Meteorological Magazine* (vols. 76−7, 1947−48), *Midland Bank Review* (May 1947), *Picture Post, Punch, Railway Gazette, Vogue.*

4. Books

Allen, G. C., *British Industries and their Organisation* (5th edn, 1970)
Butler, D. E., *The British General Election of 1951* (1952)
Buxton, N. K., and Aldcroft, D. H. (eds.), *British Industry between the Wars* (1979)
Cairncross, A. K., *Years of Recovery: British Economic Policy, 1945−51* (1985)
Craig, F. W. S., *British Parliamentary Election Results, 1918−49* (1969)
— *British Parliamentary Election Results, 1950−1970* (1971)
— *British Electoral Facts, 1885−1975* (1976)
Dalton, H., *Memoirs 1945−60: High Tide and After* (1962)
Day, D., *The Bevin Boy* (1975)
Dow, J. C. R., *The Management of the British Economy, 1945−1960* (1970)
Eatwell, R., *The 1945−51 Labour Governments* (1978)
Gallup, G. H. (ed.), *The Gallup International Public Opinion Polls: Great Britain, 1937−75* (2 vols. 1976)
Gowing, M., *Independence and Deterrence: Britain and Atomic Energy, 1945−52* (2 vols. 1974)
Granada Historical Records Interview: Clem Attlee (1967)
Halsey, A. H., *Trends in British Society since 1900* (1972)
Hannah, L., *Electricity before Nationalisation* (1979)
Harris, K., *Attlee*, (1982)

BIBLIOGRAPHY

Horner, A., *Incorrigible Rebel* (1960)
Jay, D., *Change and Fortune: a political record* (1980)
Jouvenel, B. de, *Problems of Socialist England* (1949)
Kirby, M.W., *The British Coal Mining Industry, 1870–1946* (1977)
Little, I.M.D., *The Price of Fuel* (1953)
Mitchell, B.R., and Jones, G., *Second Abstract of British Historical Statistics* (1971)
Morgan, K.O., *Labour in Power, 1945–1951* (1984)
Morrison, H., *Herbert Morrison: an autobiography* (1960)
Pimlott, B., *Hugh Dalton* (1985)
Political and Economic Planning, *The British Fuel and Power Industries* (1947)
Postan, M.M., *An Economic History of Western Europe 1945–64* (1967)
Shinwell, E., *Conflict without Malice* (1955)
— *The Labour Story* (1963)
— *I've lived through it all* (1973)
— *Lead with the left* (1981)
Sissons, M., and French, P. (eds.), *The Age of Austerity, 1945–51* (1963)
Wheeler-Bennett, J., *King George VI: his Life and Reign* (1958)
Williams, F., *A Prime Minister Remembers: the Memoirs of the Rt. Hon. Earl Attlee* (1961)
Williams, P.M., *Hugh Gaitskell: a political biography* (1979)
Williams, T.I., *A History of the British Gas Industry* (1981)

Index